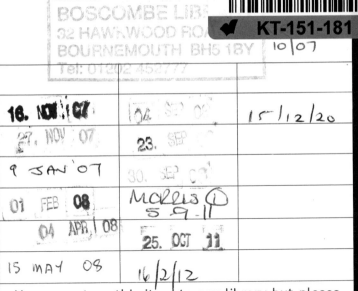
You can return this item to any library but please
note that not all libraries are open every day.
Items must be returned on or before the due date.
Failure to do so will result in overdue charges.
Items may be renewed unless requested by
another customer, in person or by telephone, on
two occasions only. Your membership card number
will be required.
Please look after this item – you may be charged
for any damage.

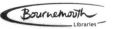

THE TERRACOTTA ARMY

www.rbooks.co.uk

Also by John Man

Gobi
Atlas of the Year 1000
Alpha Beta
The Gutenberg Revolution
Genghis Khan
Attila
Kublai Khan

THE TERRACOTTA ARMY

China's First Emperor and the
Birth of a Nation

JOHN MAN

BANTAM PRESS

LONDON · TORONTO · SYDNEY · AUCKLAND · JOHANNESBURG

TRANSWORLD PUBLISHERS
61–63 Uxbridge Road, London W5 5SA
A Random House Group Company
www.rbooks.co.uk

First published in Great Britain
in 2007 by Bantam Press
an imprint of Transworld Publishers

A CIP catalogue record for this book
is available from the British Library.

ISBN 9780593059296 (cased)
9780593059302 (tpb)

Addresses for Random House Group Ltd companies outside the UK
can be found at: www.randomhouse.co.uk
The Random House Group Ltd Reg. No. 954009

The Random House Group Ltd makes every effort to ensure that the papers
used in its books are made from trees that have been legally sourced from
well-managed and credibly certified forests. Our paper procurement policy
can be found at: www.randomhouse.co.uk/paper.htm

Typeset in 11.5/14.5 Sabon by
Falcon Oast Graphic Art Ltd.

Printed and bound in Great Britain by
CPI Mackays, Chatham, Kent ME5 8TD

2 4 6 8 10 9 7 5 3 1

CONTENTS

MAPS

A NOTE ON SPELLING

Most Chinese words in this book are names, and all except for the occasional very well-established one are transliterated using the modern system, pinyin (as opposed to the old one, known as Wade–Giles). In pinyin, most letters and diphthongs are roughly as in English, but some have their own pronunciation. These are the main ones:

Consonants:
c as in rats
q as in church
x is between s and sh
z as in suds
zh as in fudge

Vowels:
e as in the US pronunciation of nurse
ie as in yeah
ue as in a contracted form of 'you were' – y'were
eng as in sung
ei as in gay

Commonly, pinyin omits the tones, which helps define the Chinese character. In Mandarin, there are four tones, indicated with accents on the vowel (the first, in diphthongs):

First (high, level) tone: ā ē ī ō ū

Second (rising) tone: á é í ó ú
Third (falling-rising): ǎ ě ǐ ǒ ǔ
Fourth (falling) tone: à è ì ò ù

Even so, pinyin cannot always specify the exact sign, so in cases of doubt or particular significance I add the Chinese signs; not, however, for proper names, which are generally well known to specialists and need neither tones nor signs to identify them.

ACKNOWLEDGEMENTS

Catharina Blänsdorf, Chair of Conservation, Technische Universität, Munich; Pat Cox, former senior tutor, Fire Service College, Moreton-in-Marsh; Anne Cullen, London; Prof. Duan Qingbo, Director of Archaeology, Shaanxi Province; Vince Dunn, fire expert; Hu (Howard) Xiaojun, Intrepid Travel, Xian; Tom Jenen, Pharm; Miu Yee (Polly) Kwong; Joe Lally, fire expert, US Dept of Interior, Bureau of Land Management, Albuquerque, NM; Ningrui (Aileen) Ren; Helen Tang, SOAS; Jin Kai, Terracotta Army Museum; Li Bin, Cultural Affairs Bureau, Xian; Li Junyi, Jerry Wong and Cha Hai Bo (Charlie), Xian Ceramics and Lacquer Factory; Li Naifu, Xian Architecture and Technology University; Stephanie Lin Feng (Manager) and Anthony Lee (my terrific guide), Xian Everbright International Travel Service, Xian; Maggie, Huaqing Aegean International Hot Springs Resort, Lintong; Ma Yu, Restoration Dept, Terracotta Army Museum; Nin Shodo, Grandmother Temple, Mount Li; Niu Xinlong, Stone Armour Archaeology Team, Terracotta Army Museum, Lintong; Jane Portal, British Museum, London; James Quintière, fire expert and author of *Principles of Fire Behaviour*; Wang Tao, SOAS; Wang Lianyuan, Qin-Style Eighth Wonder Reproduction Factory, Beitian; Wang Zhan, monumental sculptor, Xian; Wang Qinren and Yi Xiaoqiang, China Youth Press, Beijing; Wang Zhigao, the best of drivers; Pablo Wendel, performance artist, Stuttgart; Bob Wyllie, Fire Service College, Moreton-in-Marsh; Yang Shuanshuan, Xi Yang village; Yang Zhefa, Terracotta Army Museum; Yuan Zhongyi, former President, Terracotta Army Museum, Lintong; Zhang Hui (Roy), Xian; Zhao Kangmin, Lintong; Zhong Tangyan, Xian Centre, China Geological Survey. And on the production of this book: Doug Young, Simon Thorogood and Sheila Lee at Transworld; Gillian Somerscales, for superb editing; Malcolm Swanston and Jonathan Young, Red Lion Mapping; and, as always, Felicity Bryan and her wonderful staff.

PICTURE ACKNOWLEDGEMENTS

All the photographs were taken by the author except for the following:

Endpapers – Terracotta Army Museum.

FIRST SECTION

Pages 2–3 Present-day view of the tomb-mound: Terracotta Army Museum; photograph taken by Victor Ségolen, 16 February 1914, now in the Musée Guimet, Paris: © Photo RMN-© Richard Lambert.

Pages 4–5 Still from *The Curse of the Golden Flower*: Rex Features/© Sony Pics/Everett.

Pages 6–7 Kneeling figure: Terracotta Army Museum; excavations 31 October 1975: AP/PA Photos.

Pages 8–9 Pit No. 1, general view: Terracotta Army Museum.

Pages 10–11 All photos except for restoration shot: Terracotta Army Museum.

Pages 12–13 Pit No. 2, general view, archer and polychrome head: Terracotta Army Museum; Pit No. 3: Zeng Nian/Gamma/Camera Press London.

Pages 14–15 Pit No. 2, archers and restoration *in situ*: Terracotta Army Museum.

Page 16 General from Pit No. 2: Terracotta Army Museum; reconstruction: Hardlines.

SECTION TWO

Page 17 Official and detail: Terracotta Army Museum.

Pages 18–19 Various figures, top left, centre bottom, Terracotta Army Museum; bottom left, top right, centre right and bottom right: akg-images/Laurent Lecat.

Pages 20–1 All photos: Terracotta Army Museum.

Pages 22–3 Chariot: www.araldodeluca.com.

Pages 26–7 Entertainer: Terracotta Army Museum.

Pages 30–1 Tomb reconstruction: Duan Qingbo.

Page 32 Performance by Pablo Wendel: Brouwer-Editions.

PREFACE: AN ARMY OF THE PAST AND PRESENT

The Terracotta Army attracts clichés as light attracts moths, and none of them do it justice. Part of the impact made by those ranked figures comes from the gut feeling that they are the guardians of hidden universes – of artistry, organization, religious and historical significance, and raw power.

All these lead back to one man, the First Emperor, the man who turned a China of warring states into the core of today's single nation. It was an astonishing achievement by one of history's towering personalities, a man who combined vision, leadership and utter ruthlessness to force unwilling rivals together. Even more astonishing, it was all done in under ten years (230–221 BC), a decade which many believe to be the most significant in China's 5,000 years of history. The First Emperor took a vague sense that unity was a good idea, and thrashed it into an ideal that has anchored China to this day.

Unity, character, the Army, the vast tomb-mound and the body it contains: these elements are inseparable. Without the First Emperor's skills, there would be no unity; without unity, no organization, no industrial-scale artistry, no tomb-mound, no need for a spirit army at all.

There are many surprising things about the Army. For one thing, the warriors were never intended to be seen, or at least not by human eyes. For another, it is strange that these clay figures – terracotta means nothing more than 'baked earth' – with their shades of greys and blue-greys and browns and oranges were not like this when they were buried, but lurid with bright colours. Our view of them is skewed by events: by the fire that destroyed them, by the passage of time that stripped them of their colours, by the desire to see them arrayed in parade-ground magnificence – a prospect that no one ever had until the opening of Pit No. 1 in 1979.

Perhaps the most surprising thing about the Army is its contemporary significance. It emerged into the light of day only because the First Emperor's character and achievements suited the times, as defined by the inspirational, authoritarian, ruthless, nation-building Mao Zedong. As a result, the Army has escaped its original purpose as defence against malign spirits, and has come to stand for the nation, past and present. Like the Great Wall, it states two grand themes of China's history: geographical unity and continuity.

I

ORIGINS

1

DISCOVERY

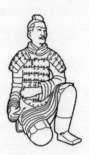

APPROACHING THE TERRACOTTA ARMY FROM XIAN, CHINA'S one-time capital, feels like a movement towards something of immense significance: the throne room in a palace, perhaps, or the altar of a great cathedral. First, the expressway eastwards. You will be grateful for it, because you are free at last from Xian's glutinous traffic. Then, if the day is clear of haze, the mountains welcome you, a ridge of greenery swinging in from the right. That's Mount Li in the distance, the Army's backdrop. You can follow the expressway to the warriors' gates if you like the fast, bland approach, but I prefer the other way, through Lintong, where emperors came to bathe in mineral-rich hot springs, and where tourists now do the same. Lintong, once a little place of mud-walled farmers' houses, is today all new building, with its own university and a growing number of plush hotels, proof of the wealth brought by the Army over the last 30 years.

At the town's centre the road divides, and in the split between the two stands a formidable monument to the Army's creator. From several thousand tonnes of granite explode horses and a chariot, driven by the man himself, the First Emperor, who made the armies that unified China and the Army that still guards him in the spirit world. At his shoulder stands his greatest general, Meng Tian, builder of the Great Wall designed to hold back the northern barbarians. The Qin Unification Statue is energy petrified, a modern (1993) declaration of what this man and his achievements mean.

Keep right, past the old Winter Palace and its hot springs, past the cable car which would carry you up Mount Li if you had the time, until you come to a line of factory outlets offering reproductions of the warriors, harbingers of the real things.

On your right rears the tomb itself, a vast, shallow-sided green mound against the mountains, a presence that has brooded over the surrounding orchards and fields for 2,200 years. It is veiled in firs now, but they are new. Historically, it had no veil but its earth, which is deep enough to keep its secrets hidden: the emperor's coffin, his underground palace, and who knows what treasures.

And who or what was there to protect it all? A kilometre more, and you're almost there. A low wall edges the huge estate that surrounds the Terracotta Army Museum. There's a car park, dominated by a towering white statue: the First Emperor, of course, ruling over a parade-ground of concrete, cars and tourists. On the gentle uphill walk, with your destination concealed by the rise and the newly built gauntlet-run of stalls, you sense again that you are approaching something grand.

Once through the turnstiles, standing on the immense concourse, you will feel the urge to enter Pit No. 1, and gaze down at last on the ranks of the clay warriors. Don't rush it. The warriors will wait, and you have a chance to imagine what this place was like before the coming of the tourist-trap shops, the seven halls, the vast plaza, the camera-clicking crowds. Stand in front of the great railway-station arch of Pit No. 1 and look to your left. You will see a white-tiled building, rectangular, 1980s utilitarian. It contains a circular film-screen, which shows a docu-drama about the warriors. The film is on a loop, so there's no hurry. Pause in the entrance lobby, where stalls sell books and reproductions of warriors, from full-size down to chessmen.

Over on the left, if you press through the throng, you come to a book counter, behind which sits an old man wearing heavy round glasses. He scribbles his name hastily in books thrust at him by tourists, but he meets no one's eye. He's not happy. Much of the time he covers his head with a paper fan. He is hiding, from attention, and, because his eyesight is poor, from the occasional camera-flash. 'No photo!' pleads a notice on the table in front of him, in English as well as Chinese, but not everyone obeys. His name is Yang Zhefa, and he is one of four surviving brothers (two others have died), all in their eighties, all of whom earn a living signing books here, and at other stalls outside, and at the hot springs resort nearby, because they were the ones who, as your guide will tell you, were the 'discoverers' of the warriors. They are too old, too deaf, too weary of media interest, too battered by attention, to retell their story yet again, and anyway you would be unlikely to hear the details, because there are aspects that do not quite fit the image of discoverers. Look at Mr Yang, present your book for his signature, do not take his picture, and bear in mind that this was a discovery he and his brothers emphatically did not wish to make.

*

5

In the spring of 1974, the middle of Shaanxi province was stricken by drought. Normally, the steep flanks of Mount Li, rearing up to the south, kept the rocky ravines flowing with enough water to fill the wells and nourish the orchards of persimmon and pomegranate. Not that year.[1]

One evening in mid-March, the six Yang brothers gathered among the persimmon trees edging the village that bore their family name, Xiyang (West Yang). Squatting on their haunches and smoking, they worried out loud about the lack of water. All in their forties and fifties, they had spent their whole lives here, in the simple mud-brick houses of their village, venturing down to the road a few hundred metres below to lay out their fruit in late summer, but seldom taking the bus to the ancient capital of Xian, 40 kilometres away. If this kept up, there would not be enough of the fat red fruit to see their families through the following winter. They all agreed that someone had to do something. They needed water, fast. That meant a new well. They should have had help from the boss of their commune; but they and their forefathers had been used to relying on themselves since long before Mao's 1949 revolution.

'OK, let's make a start,' said one.

But where? The most senior of the brothers, Yang Peiyan, looked up at Mount Li, and pointed out a cleft. If there was any water to be had, it would follow that course and feed into the orchards that lay a couple of hundred metres uphill to the south. Nods and grunts of assent: that would be the best spot.

So next morning the brothers carried their spades up through the little trees, some already showing spring shoots, and started to dig, taking turn and turn about to make the

---

[1] This section is based on Yue Nan, *Xi Bu Mai Fu* / 西部埋伏 (*Hidden Underground in the West*), with additions and modifications from my interview with Zhao Kangmin and Wang Lianyuan.

beginnings of a hole, a big one, some 4 metres across, because they knew they would be digging deep. Everything went well. By noon they were a metre down when they hit an unexpected layer of red earth, hard as iron it seemed – so hard some of them said they could see sparks fly when they struck it.

'What's this – the top of an old kiln?' one of them wondered. Perhaps, because it was common knowledge that there used to be a lot of kilns for firing pottery here in times past. If it was a kiln, it should be possible to cut through its roof. It was either that or start again somewhere else. So they agreed they had to press on. Taking turns, they began to hack their way into the hard red earth.

It took them the next two days to chip through 30 hard-packed centimetres, at which point they found the going easy once again. As they dug deeper, about half a metre a day, they propped a ladder against the side and tossed the soft earth into a basket, which was hauled to the surface and emptied. They began to turn up small bits of pottery, which was not too surprising if they had just chopped through the top of a kiln. They hadn't, of course. It was earth baked by fire, and they were now inside the burial pit of the Terracotta Army, digging down through the ashes of collapsed roof-timbers and earth that had built up over the intervening 2,000 years. At the end of a week, they had a hole as deep as it was wide.

On 29 March 1974, one of them – Yang Zhefa says it was him, others dispute it – unearthed the first large piece of pottery. Not that anyone paid much attention. What they wanted was water, not useless bits of pottery. On they went, throwing up unidentifiable little pieces, until someone sighed, 'How come there's so much rubbish?'

'Well, it's a kiln. So obviously there's rubbish,' said another. 'Get on with it. We need water.'

A few minutes later, Yang Zhefa, who happened to be digging down in the hole at the time, suddenly stopped and shouted up: 'I've found a jar, a big one!' All his brothers crowded round above him and peered down at what looked like the top of an earthen jar still buried in the soil. This could be useful. If it was intact, they could take it back home and store persimmons and pomegranates in it for the winter.

The find lifted their spirits. With two or three working together in the pit, and the others above hauling dirt up in the basket, they slowly scratched away the soil, until Yang Zhefa gave a sigh of disappointment. It wasn't a jar at all, but part of a torso made of pottery. Completely useless, like all their other finds – and also bad luck, because it came from underneath the ground, where the dead dwelled. He hauled it into the basket and called out, 'Pull it up and throw it away. It's nothing.'

But as he started to dig again, earth fell from the side of the dip made by the torso, and he saw something that made him shout out.

'An earth-god!'

Again everyone crowded round, and there was a collective gasp of horror. Sticking out of the earth was a head: two eyes staring up at them, long hair tied into a bun, and a moustache. Someone touched the head with a spade, and they all heard the dull clunk which told them it was intact, and very solid.

'Yes, an earth-god,' someone said.

'If this is a kiln,' said another, 'how come there's an earth-god here? I think this is a temple.'

'Kiln or temple, what does it matter?' said Yang Zhefa, keen to suppress his fears. 'Stop imagining things. Let's keep digging.'

So they all dusted themselves down, muttered re-assurances to each other and told themselves not to mention anything about an earth-god because it would bring bad luck and stop them reaching water.

The head came up, followed by the rest of the torso, arms, legs and other bits, all hauled up in the basket and thrown aside on the field.

Now some local kids who had been playing nearby saw what was happening, and ran across to examine these odd objects. Enemies, said one, let's get them. Some started throwing stones at them. Others took a few bits back to their own orchards and fields. One group put a long pole in the hand of an almost intact torso, wound a cloth round a head and put the two together to make a scarecrow. A few adults came to stare. A 70-year-old lady picked up a head, took it home, washed it, put it on her table, lit incense and prayed to it.

Meanwhile, there were other discoveries back at the well, now down to 5 metres – brickwork, three pieces of bronze which turned out to be crossbow triggers, and many bronze arrowheads. Obviously, these had nothing to do with kilns or temples, and the Yang brothers were delighted. They may not have found water, but what they had was something almost as good. Back in the 1920s, around the tomb of the First Emperor, their fathers had found bricks like these, so they knew they came from Qin times. This had been considered wonderful luck, because wealthy people liked to buy them, and because, if they were used as pillows, they cooled the blood, improved eyesight, brought good luck and lengthened life.

Among those eager to profit from the finds were several who saw possibilities in the bronze arrowheads. Bronze was good scrap metal. One young farmer started the rush, collecting several kilos of arrowheads and taking them through the orchards to Dai Wang village 2.5 kilometres away, where a recycling centre gave cash for scrap.

One who almost followed his example was a six-year-old boy named Wang Lianyuan, now a man of some consequence in the area, because he controls a business making copies of the terracotta warriors. In a sense, that day in early April was the start of his interest. 'I recall one thing clearly,' he told me in the reception room that now stands a few paces from the site of the well. 'One of my friends, he was a few years older, took me to the place and we gathered up some arrowheads that had been thrown down in a pile. He took them off to the recycling centre and got some pocket money for them. I couldn't go, because I was too small.'

In under two weeks, events seemed to have run their course. The bricks had gone, the arrowheads had been sold, the bits and pieces scattered. The Yang brothers were not eager to talk about how they had found strange and possibly evil things in their field, and went on with their digging.

They had no idea, of course, that their well with its strange contents lay right at the south-east corner of the pit that contains the Terracotta Army. A few paces south or east and they would have missed it entirely. Even so, their find might still have escaped wider notice if their boss, the head of the agricultural cadre, had not decided to check on all the work his team had been doing. He saw the bits and pieces of what looked like the pottery equivalent of a massacre, and decided someone had better be told. The Yang brothers, who had been so determined to ignore the apparitions from the world of the dead, were about to have their lives changed willy-nilly.

The man who engineered that change was working in the small county museum in nearby Lintong, which was then a small place of low brick houses and unpaved backstreets and fields that came right into town. Zhao Kangmin had been running the museum since 1961, when no other county in the province had its own museum. He regarded himself as a lucky man. His job had been farming, but he loved history, and read what he could in his spare time. When the provincial government decided to set up a museum, they needed someone to run it. There was no archaeologist to hand, but they heard of Zhao's interest and offered him the job. Not bad for a 24-year-old. From then on archaeology became his life. He taught himself, delighting in the work because it provided the evidence to support written sources. When the warriors brought fame and fortune to Lintong in the 1980s, he was given another opportunity: to design a new museum. He made it charming, and traditional – three halls of painted columns and criss-cross beams and upturned eaves. He's still there today, retired but living in a basic little grace-and-favour apartment in the museum, a gaunt and frail 71-year-old who put on a trilby hat and brown weatherproof jacket to show me round.

It's not really true to say the warriors were discovered in 1974, he explained. People had always known there were figures hidden underground. When they dug up the warriors, they found five Han graves dating from the first or second century, and 20 Ming tombs from the fifteenth century. The graves were right in among the warriors, some of which were missing, so of course people had known, in one sense. But they didn't *want* to know, because such things were bad luck, as was everything to do with the land of the dead; so the news never spread beyond those who made the burials.

Nor did it spread last century, when other finds emerged. In 1948, farmers (it was always farmers who made these finds) working just outside the outer wall of the First Emperor's tomb unearthed a complete figure: not a warrior, but a demure 'kneeling servant'. They didn't know what it was, so they put it in a temple and prayed to it as if it were a Buddhist deity, an immortal. In 1956 another was found, and soon after that both figures were moved to the museum. No one showed much interest in them, because no one knew what they were or when they had been made. In 1962 Zhao himself dug out three kneeling crossbowmen, in excellent condition, which were later dispersed, one each to the provincial museum in Xian, the Terracotta Army Museum and Beijing's History Museum.

'So it wasn't a huge surprise when the Yangs made their finds?'

'Oh, it was, because one of the kneeling servants had been destroyed in the Cultural Revolution' – that crazy time when teenage Red Guards became Mao's hooligans and set about assaulting anything old – 'and not many people knew about the other one. Anyway, we could not know for sure they were Qin.'

Zhao, the guardian of old things, had found himself embroiled in this madness. Soon after Mao launched the Cultural Revolution in the summer of 1966, Zhao was summoned to one of those meetings at which crowds of callow revolutionaries threw insults at the victims, forcing them to 'purify' themselves by self-criticism.

'They knew I was involved with old things which had something to do with an emperor,' Zhao said, 'so they accused me of encouraging feudalism. Everyone sat, except for me. I was made to stand. They read out a long article list-ing my mistakes, and told me to admit them. I refused, because I knew everything I had done had been correct. Later I was told to write a letter of apology. Again, I refused. But just to avoid trouble I joined the revolutionary guards until the fuss died down.'

He was lucky. These were early days. Later the same year, Mao chided the Red Guards for being 'too civilized', and they turned extremely nasty: officials were brutalized and murdered, books burned, historical monuments desecrated (almost 5,000 in Beijing alone) – but only one terracotta statue smashed, thanks to Zhao's zeal.

Not much of this affected the villages scattered around the First Emperor's tomb, but those terrible years burned into Zhao's memory, and were with him still when he heard of the farmers' finds.

'The first I knew was on April the twenty-eighth, a month after the find, when my bureau chief called me: "The cadre chief says some farmers have found pottery heads the size of human ones."

'I thought: This could be an important discovery. "Anything else?" I asked.

' "Bronze arrowheads. You'd better go and check."

'So I got on my bicycle and rode to the field. The Yangs were still at work there, digging their well. I saw seven or eight pieces – bits of legs, arms and two heads – lying near the well, along with some bricks. All the bronze arrowheads had gone.'

He knew at once that these were finds of immense, perhaps national, significance. They had to be bits of Qin figures, because the bricks were Qin – he knew that because he had seen others found near the First Emperor's tomb. They were all alike: hard and smooth, with a particular pattern and the name of the kiln in old-style characters.

So he also knew at once the historical events that had preceded and followed the burial of these objects. His two passions, archaeology and history, made past and present one. The seven Warring States that had kept China bitterly divided for 200 years from the fifth to the third century BC; the rise of Qin; the dictatorship of the man who defeated all six of his rivals, united China in 221 BC and called himself the First Emperor; his ruthlessness, his paranoia, his obsessive desire to rule as effectively in the life to come as in this; the building of the tomb that he, Zhao, had known from childhood; the sudden fall of the dynasty to its successors, the Han. All this was familiar because Zhao had read Sima Qian, the great Han historian whose account, written a century after the First Emperor's death, had brought these events to life for generation after generation for the last 2,000 years.

So Zhao didn't hesitate. He ordered all work on the well to stop, and had the pieces collected – no small matter, because the legs were solid clay – and taken down to the museum. Then he went to the recycling station and bought back as many bronze arrowheads as he could. Finally, that same evening, he started work on restoring the figures – two of them, as it turned out, both of which still stand in his museum, along with the kneeling servant that survived the Cultural Revolution.

It's an odd figure, this kneeling servant. In a simple wrap-around costume, he is humble, his hands resting lightly on his thighs, fingers slightly bent, his head slightly cocked, as if listening for instructions. The coat is wrinkled but below the waist there are no mouldings, as if he is on a plinth. But the odd thing is his head: shaved, no beard, no moustache. It is a face that looks almost feminine. There are no women among the terracotta figures, but I wondered if perhaps this very unmilitary figure was a eunuch.

So here we are at the end of April 1974. The finds that will transform the area from poor villages and orchards to China's second most important tourist site after the Great Wall are in the hands of an expert who recognizes them for what they are – life-size clay figures, almost certainly created for the tomb of the First Emperor, a find unmentioned in any source, and totally without precedent. No doubt about it: as his card states in English, 'He is the very first man who dis- covered, determined, restored and unearthed' the warriors.

'Do you wonder what would have happened if you had not gone to the field that day?' I asked. 'Perhaps the war- riors would never have been found?'

'It would have been a disaster. The farmers would have destroyed the figures, because they thought they were unlucky things. They would have abandoned the well, and no one would have told the authorities.'

Yet Zhao hesitated. What if he made his report, and because of it he was summoned again for anti-revolutionary activities? The Red Guards were gone, but Mao was old and who knew what madness might erupt? Better to wait until he was sure of his ground.

So, despite Zhao's awareness and expertise, the warriors still might have remained a secret. How they were revealed is another story. In China, the present echoes the past more intensely than in most other cultures; politics and history are intertwined. To tell the story involves looking at the power struggle gripping the upper reaches of the Communist Party in 1974 – but to understand that, you first have to know about the First Emperor, his empire and the circumstances leading up to his death.

2

THE GRAND HISTORIAN'S
HIDDEN AGENDA

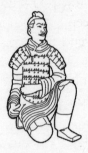

WHY DO THOSE CLAY FIGURES SO FASCINATE CHINA AND THE world? One reason is because they are ghosts from history's subconscious, capturing in outward and visible form the crucial two decades – the years from 230 to 210 BC – when the First Emperor forced seven states to become one and then imposed on his new nation a series of giant projects. It's not simply that the upright military figures seem to symbolize their times; it's that their faces seem to reflect the character of the man himself: stern, expressionless, implacable.

Power made the First Emperor a terrifying figure. He seems to have been physically unattractive – high pointed nose, slit eyes, pigeon breast, stingy, cringing, graceless. Traditional portraits of him don't conform to this lean and hungry image, showing him as bearded, bulky, and always wearing headgear like a mortarboard with tassels dangling down the front to hide his semi-divine features from mortal gaze. It's all totally inauthentic, of course, since there were no contemporary portraits; but as with Christ, Genghis Khan and alien abductors, there arose an accepted, iconic version of what he was supposed to look like. Certainly he was moody, easily angered, unpredictable: traits that he shared with other dictators (Hitler and Stalin come to mind). Almost from his own day, the First Emperor was seen as a 'brutal tyrant, inhumanely impressing hundreds of thousands of people into forced labour to fulfil his grandiose ambitions'.[1] It has been part of accepted history that he burned books, destroyed the records of his predecessors and buried scholars alive because they opposed him. His ruthlessness has been a fact of life for the past two millennia. National unity was bought with extreme suffering, was it not?

Perhaps. Probably. But before we get to the details, it is worth asking: How do we know what we think we know? For it almost all comes from one man, the historian Sima Qian (Ssu-ma Ch'ien in Wade–Giles) and his monumental *Shi Ji* (*Historical Records*), the usual English title of which is *Records of the Grand Historian*. The book covers the whole history of China down to Sima Qian's own day in 130 chapters. A brilliant synthesis of oral and written sources, it is to China what the histories of Herodotus or Thucydides are to western culture: original in structure, fundamental, judicious – and therefore, given its virtues, traditionally considered to be totally reliable.

Is it, though? Sima Qian's experiences suggest that his reputation needs revision. He was writing 100 years after the events we are interested in (and centuries after many

[1] Li Yuning in his Introduction to *The First Emperor of China*.

17

others he records), using sources that he does not quote. He was active during the Han dynasty,[2] which succeeded the Qin in 202 BC, after four years of civil war, and it was always the habit of new dynasties to rubbish the old. He was writing during the reign of an emperor every bit as ambitious and every bit as ruthless as the First Emperor. Throughout history, politicians and writers wishing to criticize their own bosses have directed their venom at substitute targets whose character and actions resemble those of the real objects of their remarks. And in addition to his historian's perspective, Sima Qian had deeply personal reasons for such criticism: he was the victim of a gross miscarriage of justice that left him with a powerful motive to criticize his own emperor by exaggerating the truth about the First.

Actually, Sima Qian, born around 145 BC, owed his inspiration to his father, who had planned and perhaps started the *Records*. When his father died in 110 BC, his 35-year-old son took over the labour. He was appointed Taishi (Grand Historian) at court, and all went well, until disaster struck. To understand how he came to suffer as he did, you need some background.

One of his themes was the threat posed by a tribe known as the Xiongnu, the 'barbarians' who dominated what is now Mongolia and other lands north of the Great Wall. Once, 50 years before, they had almost seized Xian, the Han capital. Now they were kept in check by hand-outs of cash and silk. It's hard to say who was more to blame for the

[2] Confusingly, Han (*Hàn* 汉) the dynasty, which also gives its name to China's dominant ethnic group, is not the same as the state of Han (*Hán* 韓), one of those defeated by Qin, which is sometimes transliterated Hann.

antipathy – the Xiongnu, who wanted to trade their furs and horses for Chinese goods, or the Han, who refused to have anything to do with a people they considered utterly inferior. Whoever was to blame, the result was confrontation. In effect, the Xiongnu did what they could to help themselves by turning to extortion, with the price rising and raids continuing.

It couldn't go on. No emperor of a unified China could claim the Mandate of Heaven and at the same time tolerate as neighbour a 'barbarian' ruler who saw himself as an equal, and who was liable to launch raids whenever he felt like it. The man who grasped this nettle was Sima Qian's emperor, Wu (140–87 BC). Wu was a monarch of genius – autocrat, statesman, strategist, artist – with a court to match his own brilliance, and a reign long enough to allow both to flourish: 53 years, a tenure unmatched for 1,800 years thereafter. His despotic ways mirrored those of the First Emperor, and his achievements – his laws, institutions and conquests – would mark China from then on. His answer to the Xiongnu menace was to set the boundaries of China wider, and to do that he decided to escalate the rumbling rivalry into a full-scale war.

From this decision flowed many consequences – for the Xiongnu, who were eventually broken and scattered; for China, which spread westward, defended by the newly extended Great Wall; and for poor Sima Qian, who incurred the emperor's displeasure and paid a terrible price.

Wu's was a high-risk strategy, with two aims. The first was to control the grasslands of Mongolia, which started just north of the Yellow River and ran eastward. The other was to seize the 26 independent tribal areas which lay westward, along the Gansu Corridor leading to the Central Asian deserts of the Western Regions. The difference between them was this: the steppe, which was in effect infinite and open, could not be conquered and held; the oasis kingdoms of the Western Regions could, because they were small and enclosed. The war aim that Wu adopted, therefore, was to 'cut off the right arm' of the nomads (the west, since the dominant direction for nomads was south-ward) – i.e. to pick off the tribal kingdoms one by one and garrison them in order to deny them to the Xiongnu. With the Western Regions in Chinese hands, it would be possible to isolate, invade and destroy – if not to hold – Xiongnu lands.

The war was catastrophic for both sides. Repeatedly, the opposing armies thrust into each other's territory. A dozen times – almost every year – the Xiongnu went on the offensive. Sources speak of 20,000 horsemen here, 30,000 there (though as usual the figures are suspiciously round and suspiciously large). Almost every year, too, the Han launched an offensive, with anything from 40,000 horsemen (129 BC) to 100,000 (124 BC). The 124 BC attack probed 350 kilometres northward, snaring 15,000 Xiongnu captives and 'several million' animals; another 19,000 Xiongnu casualties were notched up the following year, 30,000 more in 121 BC. Han, too, suffered appalling losses: tens of thousands of dead, 100,000 horses lost in 124–123 BC alone. But eventually, for the Han Chinese, the risk and the effort paid off, because the great campaign of 121 BC snatched from the Xiongnu most of the strategic Gansu Corridor and com-pelled the surrender of 40,000 Xiongnu, who were forcibly resettled south of the Great Wall.

Military victory itself, though, was not enough. Something had to fix the frontier, define what was China and what wasn't. That something was, of course, the Wall. So Wu picked up where the First Emperor had left off. In the centre and east, old walls were repaired and sections linked. In the west, new bits of the Wall arose, running over the border of what is now Xinjiang. Soldier–farmers began to arrive by the hundred thousand, supplementing volunteers, conscripts and convicts. Families followed, bringing the total number of settlers to an estimated 1.5–2 million – roughly equal to the whole Xiongnu population – and all were provided with land, animals and seeds. Where there was water, villages and farms arose. Roads would lead to the Wall, canals would be built. Silk began to flow westward in prodigious amounts.

But the results of this immense effort, which drained the Han economy, took some time to emerge. Meanwhile, war continued. In 103 BC a Han force of 20,000, which had advanced 1,000 kilometres across the Gobi, was surrounded and massacred. In 99 BC another campaign ended in total catastrophe. One army, attacking westward, killed 10,000 Xiongnu yet lost 60–70 per cent of its men. A second army, 5,000 men with wagonloads of food and arrows, struck northward under a general named Li Ling, an acquaintance of Sima Qian. 'We never so much as drank a cup of wine together,' wrote the historian. 'But I observed that he was clearly a man of superior ability. He was filial to his parents and trustworthy with his associates, honest in money matters and just in all his giving and taking . . . I believed him to be truly one of the finest men of the nation.' This was the man who was soon to become the focus of his attention, and the unwitting cause of his tragedy.

Li Ling led his troops for a month across the Gobi and the Mongolian heartland, aiming for northern Mongolia, where the Xiongnu had built at least one large city and established a royal necropolis.[3] It was not a big force for so ambitious a

---

[3] Noyan Uul, 50 km north of the present-day capital, Ulaanbaatar. I give an account of the Xiongnu and Noyan Uul in *Attila: A Barbarian King and the Fall of Rome* (Bantam Press, 2005).

project. Perhaps Li Ling was confident that his repeating crossbows, with arrows carried by the hundred thousand in his wagons, would sweep him to victory. But even these terrifyingly effective weapons, the ancient equivalent of machine guns, were no match for 30,000 Xiongnu horsemen, reinforced by another 80,000 from neighbouring tribes.

Li Ling staged a fighting retreat over grasslands and the Gobi's gravel plains to the Gurvan Saikhan (Three Beauties) range. Perhaps he fled into these dark, rocky hills and valleys because he needed water – there is at least one river that flows year-round through a ravine, now known as Vulture's Gorge, so shadowy that its winter ice never melts. Anyway, he and his wagons were trapped. 'The enemy was lodged in the hills, surrounding him on all sides and shooting arrows like drops of rain,' according to the first-century historian Ban Gu, who speaks of half a million arrows being shot in one day. In Sima Qian's words: 'Li Ling with one cry gave courage to his army, so that every man raised himself up and wept. Washed in blood and choked with tears, they stretched out their empty bows and warded off the bare blades of the foe.'

The surviving Chinese – only half of the number that had set out – fled through a narrow valley, while the Xiongnu tossed rocks down on them, blocking escape until night fell. That night, Li Ling took ten men and galloped clear, only to be hunted down and forced to surrender. Just 400 of his men, armed with clubs made from the spokes of their wagons, made it back home.

Emperor Wu was enraged, first by the defeat and second by the humiliation: he expected his military leaders to die in battle rather than surrender. Naturally, all his officials backed him up – all except Sima Qian.

A subject who will go forth to face ten thousand deaths,

giving not the slightest thought for his own life, but hurrying only to the rescue of his lord – such a man is rare indeed! Now he has committed one act that was not right, and the officials who think only of saving themselves . . . vie with each other in magnifying his shortcomings. Truly it makes me sick at heart!

Unfortunately for Sima Qian, Li Ling's superior was the eldest brother of the emperor's favourite concubine. To exculpate the No. 2 would be to blame the No. 1, which was inconceivable, since he was still in office at the behest of the emperor himself. Sima Qian was summoned to explain himself, and spoke again in Li Ling's defence. The general, he pointed out, had always shared hardships with his officers and men, always commanded loyalty, always served his emperor to the best of his abilities. 'But I could not make myself fully understood,' Sima Qian wrote, with outward humility that (I suspect) was bitterly ironic. 'Our enlightened ruler did not wholly perceive my meaning.' He was charged with attempting to deceive the emperor, and was arrested. There was no money to buy his freedom; no one spoke up for him. He was condemned to the ultimate humiliation: castration.

He wrote of his experience to an old friend who was at the time accused of some unspecified offence and was under threat of execution. In his memorial,[4] widely seen as one of the finest and most deeply personal pieces of writing in Chinese literature, he equates himself with the lowest of the low. The least a man can achieve is to bring no shame on his ancestors, or himself. Below such a person, he writes, is one who is bound with ropes, and below him, in a descending

[4] Included as an appendix in Burton Watson's fine translation, *Records of the Grand Historian: Qin Dynasty.*

sequence of degradation, are the prisoner, the fettered, the beaten, the shaven-headed, the manacled and the mutilated. Finally, lowest of all, is the eunuch. 'Alas! Alas! A man like myself – what can he say? What can he say?'

The customary way out of such humiliation would be to commit suicide. As he says, a gentleman would surely settle the affair in accordance with what is right. 'Even if the lowest slave and scullion maid can bear to commit suicide, why shouldn't one like myself be able to do what has to be done?' he asks, and then answers his own question. 'The reason I have . . . continued to live, dwelling in vileness and disgrace without taking leave, is that I grieve that I have things in my heart that I have not been able to express fully, and I am ashamed to think that after I am gone my writings will not be known to posterity.'

In brief, he had a higher purpose: to finish his history, to bear witness to his times. To do this demanded that he tell the truth about his emperor and the imperial excesses – not simply the military campaigns, but the ruthless commandeering of men to build and guard the Great Wall, the burdens of taxation, the overspending on vast palaces, and the obsession with death that led to a lunatic hunt for the 'elixir of immortality' and to decades-long labour to build a tomb that would outdo the First Emperor's.

But, having received his punishment, Sima Qian still held his position as a court official. He could not be direct in his criticism. So he was indirect, attacking the First Emperor instead of Wu. The result was an overblown portrait which, in Burton Watson's words, skilfully juxtaposes 'examples of the grandiose rhetoric employed by the monarch to celebrate his achievements with grim accounts of the cruelty, folly and oppression of the populace for which he has been remembered in later ages'. Sima Qian also had a go at the First Emperor's officials for 'bowing too readily to the will of the ruler, for accommodating themselves too readily to the trend of the times, instead of endeavouring to reform it'.

So, in what follows, bear in mind Burton Watson's caveat: 'No one, it seems to me, would have greater reason than Sima Qian himself to paint a grim picture of the reigns of the First and Second Emperors, and almost no one in succeeding centuries to my knowledge ever accused Sima Qian of being unfair in his treatment of the Qin or attempted to correct the record.'

Until recently: for the First Emperor has acquired even greater significance, and some nuances. In part this was due to Mao, who dismissed his ruthlessness as necessary egg-breaking to complete the omelette of unification (as we shall see in more detail in chapter 12). This, however, was not a revision of the First Emperor's character, but of the way his ruthlessness was to be judged. Bad became good. What Burton Watson is suggesting is that he was not as bad as Sima Qian painted him, and others make the same point.

One of the people I spoke to when researching this book was the man in charge of archaeology for all Shaanxi province, Duan Qingbo. Before he would see me, he sent a message to say I would have to get permission from the local government, so I assumed he would be a bureaucratic type, backing traditional views of the First Emperor. Not a bit of it. He turned out to be a youthful forty-something brimming with enthusiasm, and very much his own man. 'Remember,' he said, 'that some of Sima Qian is a literary fiction. Here was his own emperor spending money on grand projects, building palaces, the Great Wall, a tomb that he started in the second year of his reign, which would last another fifty-three years, wasting money [in a way] that threatened his realm with collapse. Sima Qian could not criticize his emperor directly. So he criticized the First Emperor instead.'

Where does that leave us?

Re-evaluating, that's where. Not taking things at face value. Using archaeology to reassess tradition. Ready to ask whether the First Emperor was less of a tyrant and more of a brilliant and original leader, as befits the man who unified China and left a spirit army that is the admiration of the world.

3

WARRING STATES, CONFLICTING IDEAS

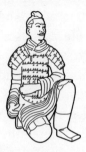

FROM HIS REPUTATION, YOU WOULD THINK THAT THE FIRST Emperor, who 'unified China', invented the very idea of unity. Not so: it was an idea rooted much further back, in a dreamtime of scanty records where figures and themes and events drift like ghosts.

It is surprising that such a vast and varied region should have yearned for unity. Geographically, it seems to have none. It is the same size as the United States, but with no shining seas to hem it in. Yet its fertile heartland, as defined by its two great rivers, the Yellow River and the Yangtze,[1] is turned in upon itself by the deserts of Central Asia, the

---

[1] Yangzi in pinyin, but the old spelling is a fixture in English. The name, from an ancient ferry crossing on the lower part of the river, was adopted in English and many other languages for the whole. The modern Chinese name, Chang Jiang ('Long River') is increasingly used internationally.

highlands of Tibet and the forests of the south. By about 1800 BC the lower Yellow River, with its deep and fertile soils, was home to a kingdom named after its people, the Shang. You would hardly equate this with China – it was only the size of England – but it was the core from which China would eventually spring. The Shang confronted a host of rivals and enemies, of whom little is known, but who shared the main elements of Shang culture. On this basis, later rulers came to believe that political unity was an ideal towards which they should strive.

For many centuries, however, unity in China was an ideal in abeyance. In about 1050 BC Shang fell to one of its rivals, Zhou. Over centuries, cultural practices and spiritual beliefs became more complex, more sophisticated. Divination remained popular, becoming dependent on that wonder of simplicity and complexity, the *Book of Changes, Yi Jing* (*I Ching*, in its Wade–Giles transliteration). Kings looked to heaven as the source of their authority and morality. They believed they ruled with the Mandate of Heaven, which could be withdrawn should they not come up to scratch. But as Zhou's cultural influence spread – supposedly destroying 50 statelets in the process – so political unity receded. Zhou rulers appointed family members and local chiefs as lords of estates of all sizes, from provinces down to single cities – 1,763 of them, according to one source. Though bound to the king by feudal ties and providing troops for the king's army, all these princelings had their own courts, armies, administrations and rituals, and asserted their differences from one another with intense pride. All were obsessed with war, and all fought according to arcane rules of chivalry: no attacking a state if it was in mourning; charioteers to take turns shooting at each other in battle. Over five centuries, in what is known as the Spring and Autumn Period (*c.*700–475 BC) and the Warring States Period (*c.*475–221 BC), these states, mini-states and city-states struggling for survival absorbed each other and whittled themselves down to seven.

Under the pressure of constant warfare, social evolution went into overdrive. As bronze gave way to iron, tools improved, agriculture became more productive, trade increased. Qin, for instance, imported white silk from Qi, jade from the Kunlung mountains to the west, dyes from Sichuan, horses from the northern grasslands, drums made of bronze, tin and iguana skins from Jiangxi and Anhui provinces in the south-east, pearls and rhinoceros horn and ivory from even further away.

A principal effect of this mix of rivalry and trade was on warfare itself. Little, temporary armies of upper-class charioteers gave way to large peasant forces. For any ruler, success in war was the prime consideration, marking 'the road either to survival or to ruin'. The words are those of Sun Zi (Sun Tzu in Wade–Giles) in the opening to his classic of war theory, *The Art of War*, which sprang from the heart of his turbulent times, probably in the fourth century BC. It sprang also from the mind of a supreme professional who had studied every aspect of war, beginning with the 'five fundamentals' – politics, weather, terrain, command and management – and continuing down to details like the cost of entertaining envoys and the price of glue. It contains lessons that are valid for most times, if not all: avoid battle except when victory is assured; don't take risks; overawe an enemy with psychological means; plan well; strike hard and fast. 'While we have heard of stupid haste in war . . . there has never been a protracted war which benefited a country.' He was studied by Norman Schwarzkopf, commander of US forces in the first Gulf War of 1991; not studied by President Bush, who in 2002 was warned of trouble ahead in Iraq by Missouri's Democratic representative Ike Skelton, quoting

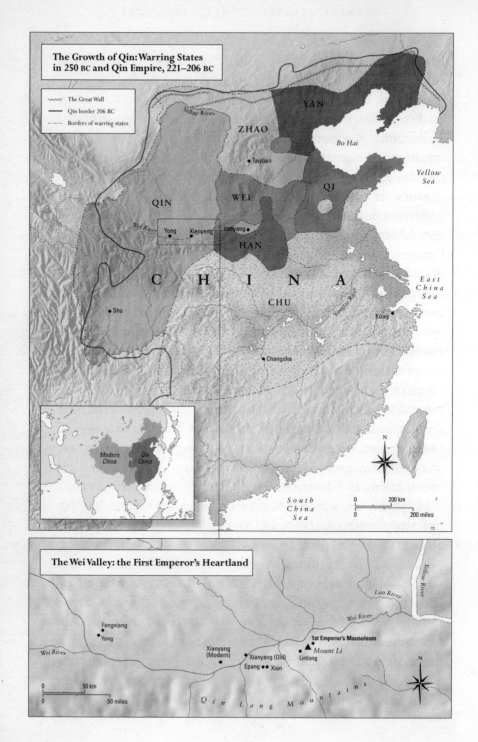

The Growth of Qin: Warring States in 250 BC and Qin Empire, 221–206 BC

- 〰〰〰 The Great Wall
- ——— Qin border 206 BC
- ‐ ‐ ‐ Borders of warring states

Yellow River

YAN

ZHAO

Bo Hai

Taiyuan

Yellow Sea

QI

QIN

WEI

Wei River

Yong   Xianyang   Luoyang

HAN

C H I N A

East China Sea

CHU

Shu

Yangtze River

Kuaiji

Changsha

Modern China   Qin China

South China Sea

0   200 km
0   200 miles

The Wei Valley: the First Emperor's Heartland

Yellow River

Luo River

Wei River

Fengxiang
Yong

Wei River

Xianyang (Modern)   Xianyang (Old)   1st Emperor's Mausoleum
Epang   Xian   Lintong   Mount Li

Qin Liang Mountains

0   50 km
0   50 miles

Sun Zi: 'To win victory is easy; to preserve its fruits, difficult.'

But this obsession with war was accompanied by equal and opposite obsessions: with peace, diplomacy, art, philosophy and poetry. Great thinkers struggled with great questions, the greatest being Kong Fuzi, or Confucius to give him his Latinized name. Dismayed by the evils of his sixth-century BC world, he devised a system of ethics and government that promoted the good. He taught that people should see clearly their place in a hierarchical universe, from king to commoner, and fulfil their responsibilities to those above and below, exercising loyalty, piety, filial respect and benevolence. This was the way to divine approval, the way for rulers to deserve and preserve the Mandate of Heaven. At bottom, human beings are part of one big family, governed by family virtues. That is the core of his teaching, as revealed by his Conversations (or Discourses, or Analects), gathered by his followers and revered as a fundamental guide to good behaviour and good government ever since. Some of it is surprisingly close to Christianity as promulgated by medieval reformers such as St Francis and St Benedict, who sought to regenerate the established church by returning to Christ-like basics.

How do we know what the virtues are? How do we practise them? Guidance lay in the hands of scholars and advisers, those learned men who understood rituals, calendars, divinations and record-keeping – men like Confucius's greatest follower Meng Zi, Master Meng or Mencius, who travelled around from state to state in the fourth century BC offering advice to rulers. He had no time for power and profit; the only virtues he recognized were those of goodness. When the king of Liang (c.100 kilometres north-east of Xian) asked about ways to profit his state, Mencius replied, 'Why must Your Majesty use the word

"profit"? All I am concerned with are the good and the right.'
Those virtues come naturally to us, and will emerge if encouraged. 'Goodness is to human nature what flowing downward
is to water.' In brief, the advice to rulers from Confucius and
Mencius was: Rule virtuously and peace will follow.

Peace, though, was not a condition achieved for long amid
the incessant squabbling of the Warring States. A school of
cynics arose, asking each other and their rulers a tough
question: what was the point of cultivating the arts of peace
if they did not lead to peace? Their answer was brutally
pragmatic: none at all. The only thing that mattered was
effectiveness, in war and in peace. In peace, the wise ruler
prepared for war; in war, he ensured victory; in victory, he
preserved peace by preparing for yet more war. Stability was
all, and stability could be guaranteed only under strong
leadership. Out went the notion that virtue and wisdom
would spread by example. There was no room now for the
old families, the old feudal estates, the old rules of chivalry,
the old individualism, the old Confucian virtues.

This line of thought, known as Legalism, was given force-
ful expression by an ambitious young scholar named Shang,
Lord Shang (Shang Yang) as he became known. Shang was
born in the state of Wei, which dominated the middle Yellow
River, probably around 400 BC. As the protégé of the prime
minister, he presented his ideas to the king, Hui, who didn't
approve of them. The prime minister, Gongshu Cuo, was so
awed by Shang's abilities that he feared what might happen
if the young man took his ideas to a rival king. Visited on his
deathbed by the king, Gongshu advised Hui to keep Shang's
loyalty by making him the next prime minister. If not, he
said, 'be sure to have him killed. Don't allow him to leave
the state!' King Hui, lacking both insight and ruthlessness,

dismissed both ideas (Gongshu was very sick, he confided to attendants, 'Quite out of his mind') – and did nothing, thus ensuring that Gongshu's fears were realized.

For Shang turned to the neighbouring state of Qin. Originally Qin had been nothing more than one of Zhou's little fiefdoms. From its capital, Yong (100 kilometres west of Xian), it had carved itself into an independent kingdom dominating the broad and fertile valley of the river Wei, which ran eastward into the Yellow River valley. Now, in the long struggle among the seven Warring States, Qin was emerging supreme. Its base, present-day Shaanxi, now considered the cradle of Chinese civilization, was then a backwater on the southern edge of the semi-desert known today by its Mongol name, Ordos (an old plural of *ordon*, a palace-tent, after the many Mongol chiefs who used to live there). Qin, the most westerly of the seven contending states, was considered by the others almost as barbaric as the nomad tribes who lived to the north and west. As a prince of neighbouring Wei put it to his king over a century later: 'Qin has the same customs as the Rong and Di [barbarians]. It has the heart of a tiger or wolf. It is avaricious, perverse, eager for profit, and without sincerity. It knows nothing about etiquette, proper relationships and virtuous conduct.' By the early fourth century BC, it had 400 self-assertive years of history behind it, and was ambitious for more of the same. It advertised for expert help. Not a place for gentle Confucians, but perfect for an ambitious, ruthless Legalist.

Shang responded to Qin's expressions of interest, moved to its capital Yong, and put his ideas to Qin's ruler, Duke Xiao. The duke liked what he heard, and Shang was given a free hand, so much so that he was able to shift the capital 100 kilometres eastward from Yong to Xianyang, with its better strategic position on the river Wei. Here he 'carried out the construction of the Memorial Gate and of palaces and gardens', the Memorial Gate possibly becoming the core of the palace that would later be the home of the First Emperor.

We know Shang's thinking, for he (or – more likely, in the view of most scholars – one or more of his followers) recorded it in a book that became one of the classics of ancient China. *The Book of Lord Shang* has special significance for our story because it is the programme adopted not just by Duke Xiao, but also 140 years later by his heir, the First Emperor.

Shang's teaching was the mirror image of Confucius's. Intended solely for the ruler, it was the essence of institutionalized ruthlessness. Might is right, power the only virtue. Human beings are idle, greedy, cowardly, treacherous, foolish, shifty; so Confucius's idea that they respond well to good treatment is simply naïve. The only way to rule is to entice, terrify, reward and punish. This treatment is not arbitrary (as has often been the case with dictators), but is to be based on the stern rule of law, applied to everyone without distinction. 'Law', wrote Shang, 'is the basis of government. It is what shapes the people.' The ruler's task is first to devise the law, then to record it, then to ensure that it is applied impartially through officials utterly subservient to the state's institutions.

His programme might be a manual for totalitarian rulers down the ages, with astonishingly strong echoes in organizations and states attempting centralized control in the twentieth century. The Gestapo, East Germany's Stasi, the KGB and the Romanian Securitate were his modern offspring, born of the same urge. In the words of his follower Han Fei: 'Lord Shang taught Duke Xiao of Qin how to organize the people into groups of five or ten families that would spy on each other,' and 'anyone who failed to report criminal activity would be chopped in two at the waist'.

Moreover, 'he advised him to burn the *Book of Odes* [i.e. poetry] and *Book of Documents* [i.e. historical records] . . . and to glorify the lot of those who devote themselves to agriculture and warfare.'

Note the book-burning reference, which will return to haunt us later. These books were not the same as our books, because paper would not be invented for another 400 years, and China never used papyrus; instead, 'books' were scrolls of silk or bamboo-strips bound together. Reading and writing were for the very few and the very wealthy. That made the imposition of controls relatively easy. Shang's advice was intended to impose the ultimate control – on records of the past, on memory itself, an aim famously pin-pointed by George Orwell in *Nineteen Eighty-Four*: 'Who controls the past controls the future: who controls the present controls the past.'

These grim policies are justified by the tyrant's defence of tyranny down the ages: if you do no wrong (as defined by the state), you have nothing to fear. As Orwell observed, the perfect totalitarian society is one whose citizens are so drilled to conformity that there is no need to kill or torture anyone. Lord Shang foreshadows *Nineteen Eighty-Four*: the aim of Legalism is to create a world in which laws are never broken, and so there is no need for punishment. If light offences are punished heavily, then heavy offences are not committed. 'This is said to be abolishing penalties by means of penalties, and if penalties are abolished, affairs [of state] will succeed.' In such a system, in which officials prove themselves by the rigidity with which they administer the law, the ruler's court will not be a prey to flattery and slander. Intelligence, thoughtfulness, judgement: these qualities are undesirable in an official, for they inspire criti-cism and opposition.

All of this had one principal end: to ensure the strongest

possible army. As Mark Lewis, Professor of Chinese Culture at Stanford University, writes, all social rank and status reflected military performance.[2] Advancement up a hierarchy of 20 ranks depended entirely on the killing of enemies. The whole country was divided into units of military service, administered by the imposition of a grid of paths and roads that ran north–south and east–west, dividing all agricultural land into blocks that could be worked by a single adult male. 'In this way the state could obtain the maximum amount of land in cultivation and the highest possible number of adult males liable for military service and taxes.'

History has no laws, but it does throw up the occasional generalization. Here's one: similar conditions are likely to produce similar reactions. Take Italy in the early sixteenth century, with its proud city-states, its bitter rivalries, its intrigues, its unreliable mercenaries, its brutal little wars, its brilliant artists and its writers. Among them was Niccolò Machiavelli, whose book *The Prince* offers advice remarkably similar in its cold realism and cynicism to Lord Shang's. He too was a keen observer of his world, and what he saw drove him to equally grim conclusions. The state is all, and power the only currency. Theology, metaphysics, idealism – all should be set aside, unless they serve the state. The bottom line is self-interest. If the Prince wishes to display idealism, it must only be for show. 'A prudent ruler', he said, 'ought not to keep faith when by doing so it would be against his interest.' Machiavelli's best-known portrait shows a man with a mean and hungry look, just the type, you might think, to propose such cold and uncompromising views. Not at all. He was an astute diplomat, conventionally Catholic, a good poet and the author of a first-rate comedy.

[2] Lewis, *Sanctioned Violence in Early China*.

He simply believed that his advice sprang inevitably from a world that would self-destruct unless taken firmly in hand.

Machiavelli drew on precedents to argue his case. Shang, several shades more authoritarian, refused to acknowledge any. Ancient customs and other schools of thought were all anathema, for nothing must rival his prince's laws, not even the cries of the people: 'A weak people means a strong state,' he wrote; 'a strong state means a weak people.' Out went Confucianism, with its subtle arguments for private virtue. Out went the old feudal system, with its local lords, their self-serving intrigues and their destructive little wars. In came a triumvirate of powers: a professional army; farm labourers who supplied food; and the Law, applied uniformly and without exception to everyone, high and low, except of course the king himself, for he personified the Law and administered it by whatever means he could, moral or immoral, and was above such distinctions. Shang even persuaded the Qin ruler to punish the crown prince. As you might imagine, he was not popular, nor did he go out of his way to cultivate allies. As his follower Han Fei recorded, 'when he came and went at court, he was guarded by iron spears and heavy shields to prevent sudden attack'. When Duke Xiao died, being succeeded by the very prince whom Shang had punished, Shang didn't last long. He was caught, 'tied to two chariots and torn apart by the men of Qin'.[3]

But his policies worked. Qin grew strong, and expanded. Protected by the Yellow River and mountains to the east, hardened by dealing with even more uncouth barbarians to the north and west, Qin spread southward into Sichuan, then eastward into neighbouring Zhou. War followed war, and death piled on death. The main source (Sima Qian, as

---

[3] Both quotes from Han Feizi, *Basic Writings*, in Burton Watson's translation.

always) claims 1.5 million dead in 134 years, probably a wild exaggeration, but one that reflects the emotional impact of extended warfare. Applying Legalism in its most extreme form, Qin toughened itself, turning itself into a Chinese Sparta, the most centralized, the most authoritarian, the hardest of the hard. Its ideologues would have approved of Fascism: virtue and tradition were out, power the only virtue. Every official act had to go towards making the state rich, the bureaucracy efficient, the army strong, agriculture productive and expansion rapid.

Yes, totalitarianism can work, for a while at least. It makes trains run on time, it builds armies, it is good for grand projects. In Qin's case, for example, it provided the cash and manpower to confront the problem of meltwaters that every spring devastated the valley of the river Min in Sichuan. One official, Li Bing, came up with a solution. He cut away a mountain to create a spillway and then divided the river with an artificial island. The result: no more floods, and controlled irrigation for the surrounding countryside, turning the Chengdu plain from an annual catastrophe into China's most productive farmland. It still works today. Li Bing is a local hero and his creation, Du Jiang Yan, is a major tourist attraction, a UNESCO World Heritage Site and a national treasure.

Some good works, then; but they are incidental. Shang's advice was not for rulers who wished to be remembered for their good works, but for those interested in power. In addition, it was advice for a leader who was already in power, having inherited his position. There was nothing here about how to win power in the first place, nothing about the wider aspects of leadership: the need for an inspiring vision, the business of winning friends, the need for virtues like loyalty and generosity – all the positive traits that we associate with charismatic leadership, as exemplified by (among others) Alexander, or Napoleon, or Genghis Khan, or Mohammed.

Shang's spirit lived on in Han Fei, a prince of a neighbouring state from which he took his family name. Han the state was smaller and weaker than Qin, and therefore often an unwilling ally, acting like a weakling cowed by a bully. Han Fei's destiny was fixed by three apparently unrelated facts. The first was that he became a student of a famous Confucian philosopher named Xun Zi (Master Xun), under whom he 'learned the methods appropriate to an emperor or king', that is, political science, except that he steadily turned against the teachings of his master as they applied to rulers, and developed instead a deep attachment to Legalist theory. The second was that he had a terrible stutter, with the result that he could never master the eloquence demanded of a court adviser; so he wrote a book to publicize his ideas, setting out the Legalist agenda with brilliant clarity and readability. The third was that one of his fellow students was an ambitious but not quite so brilliant young man named Li Si, who 'considered himself not equal to Han Fei', according to Sima Qian. Despairing of getting a job in his home state – and perhaps eager to escape from Han Fei's shadow – Li Si moved to Qin, saying 'The king of Qin wants to swallow up the world . . . this is the moment for commoners like myself.'

It was Han Fei's book that was the making of him, and his undoing. It took Shang's teaching to its logical conclusion, proposing an agenda of a cynicism far more Machiavellian than Machiavelli, more Shangian than Shang. Since Han Fei was a great essayist and stylist, with a flair for historical anecdote, he has been admired ever since. You can see aspects of his thinking reflected in many of China's more extreme rulers, down to the present day. Take four pieces of his polished, sharp and extremely scary advice on how rulers should behave:

- 'It is said: "So still he seems to dwell nowhere at all; so empty no one can seek him out." The enlightened ruler reposes in non-action above, and below his ministers tremble with fear.'
- 'This is the way of the enlightened ruler: he causes the wise to bring forth their schemes, and he decides his affairs accordingly; hence his wisdom is never exhausted. He causes the worthy to display their talents, and he employs them accordingly; hence his own worth never comes to an end. Where there are accomplishments, the ruler takes credit for their worth; where there are errors, the ministers are held responsible for the blame; hence the ruler's name never suffers.'
- 'Be empty, still, and idle, and from your place of darkness observe the defects of others. See but do not appear to see; listen but do not seem to listen; know but do not let it be known that you know.'
- And finally: 'This is the way to listen to the words of others: be silent as though in a drunken stupor. Say to yourself: Lips! teeth! Do not be the first to move; lips! teeth! Be thicker, be clumsier than ever! Let others say their piece – I will gain knowledge thereby.'

Other writers have independently come to similar conclusions about the nature of kingship. Take the analysis of the role of the British monarchy by the great Victorian editor and political analyst Walter Bagehot: A monarch 'should not be brought too closely to real measurement. He should be aloof and solitary . . . [Royalty] seems to order, but it never seems to struggle. It is commonly hidden like a mystery, and sometimes paraded like a pageant, but in neither case is it contentious.'

Unfortunately for Han Fei, there is a logical flaw in his advice. If the god-ruler must remain forever on guard, distrusting everyone, he must also distrust the man who offers this advice. This was the catch-22 that, with the malign intervention of his former fellow student Li Si, would lead to Han Fei's sad end.

First, however, he had to meet the man who would welcome his ideas, apply them in this life, and then take them even further, into the next.

4

FROM PRINCE TO KING

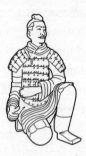

THE SCENE IS SET FOR THE ARRIVAL OF THE FIRST EMPEROR: THE man who forged a new unified China, sealed it with a Great Wall to protect himself in this life, and made a clay army to fight for him in the next one.

It started, as it always seems to with dictators, in a deep sense of insecurity rooted in his origins.

As Sima Qian tells it, the story opens in the next-door state, Zhou, with a rich and ambitious merchant named Lü Buwei meeting a down-at-heel Qin prince, Zichu, the son of a junior concubine of the heir to the Qin throne.[1] Zichu, it seems, is never going to amount to much. He is not in line for succession – indeed, there is no line, because the crown

[1] These anecdotes are from Bodde's translation of Sima Qian, *Statesman, Patriot and General in Ancient China*.

prince's official wife, of whom he is very fond, is barren. One of 20 sons by various concubines, Zichu has been sent off to the Zhou court as a hostage, a common diplomatic ploy to provide a guarantee of Qin's good behaviour. But being low in the pecking order, Zichu lives frugally, without a retinue or carriages, or indeed a future, until Lü spots in him a chance of advancement.

Lü is a novelty in the changing society of the time. Merchants had previously been despised by Confucians as non-productive, undereducated parasites, their low status preserved by legal restrictions. But in these Legalistic times, Confucianism is at a low ebb. Smart, self-serving, unscrupulous, Lü invites the prince into a back room and proposes a scheme to lever him on to the Qin throne. The prince has nothing to lose. If it works, he promises, he will share the state of Qin with his benefactor.

Lü begins to put his plan into action. He gives the prince some cash to hire himself a band of followers, and with a similar sum he buys some 'rare objects, trinkets and toys', which he takes to the Qin capital, Xianyang. He strikes up an acquaintance with an intermediary and has his purchases delivered to the queen, along with a message about how Zichu is distraught at being separated from the queen, whom he adores. Since she has no son, he says, she will have no one to look after her interests when the emperor dies. She had better find a stepson. Then 'as long as your husband lives, you will enjoy honour; and when his hundred years of life are ended, and the one whom you call son becomes king, you need never fear any loss of position'. The one she should choose is, of course, Zichu, whose own mother is out of favour and who is therefore devoted to the queen. So it happens. The emperor agrees, Zichu becomes the crown prince's heir – second in line to the throne – money is sent to Zichu and Lü becomes his tutor.

Now comes an incident which adds to the drama but which seems highly suspicious. Lü has a very beautiful girlfriend. She becomes pregnant. Zichu sees her, falls in love, and asks for her. Lü, whose whole future is now tied to Zichu, swallows his outrage and hands her over. Then, in Bodde's translation, 'The concubine kept to herself the fact that she was pregnant and [in 259 BC] at the expiration of a great period [or 'when her time was up' in Burton Watson] she bore a son,' whose name is Zheng.[2] This is the future First Emperor, unifier of China and maker of the Terracotta Army.

Why be suspicious of this? Because it is a little too convenient, a little too glib. It is just the sort of smear you would expect from a later dynasty, but not from Sima Qian. It's not his style. He would have supported it with something more convincing, not tossed it away in half a dozen lines. In a detailed analysis of this matter in 1940, Derk Bodde pointed out that the story does not appear in Sima Qian's major source,[3] that his text is corrupted by obvious interpolations – unnecessary repetitions that he would not have made – and that a very similar story from another state appears in another source. He concludes: 'The story of the First Emperor's birth, therefore, is probably the clever invention of some Han Confucian, who has used it to defame the First Emperor by representing him as the bastard son of a shrewd, unscrupulous, uneducated merchant, and a mother who was little better than a prostitute.' Interpolation or not, the slur stuck. For the last 2,000 years Chinese have believed that the First Emperor was a bastard, literally as well as figuratively.

[2] Two characters are used in the sources for his name, 政 ('government') and 正 ('upright'), both of which are pronounced *zhèng*.

[3] *Zhanguo Ce / Stratagems of the Warring States* (third century BC).

Eventually, after a couple of royal deaths, Zichu becomes king and Lü his prime minister, having been made a marquis controlling 100,000 households around present-day Luoyang, 350 kilometres east of the capital. Four years later [in 247 BC] Zichu dies, leaving twelve-year-old Zheng to succeed, under the control of his mother and his all-powerful patron. Lü sets about increasing Qin's power and influence still further, recruiting 3,000 well-educated retainers. Among them is the ambitious young social scientist Li Si, who has come to Qin because he has heard that its king 'wants to swallow up the world'. Since the old king has just died and the new one is so young, he will have to wait.

Eager for the status that comes with literary fame, Lü commissions from his entourage a book to record what his retainers know of philosophy and metaphysics, and has the results published under his own name as *Lü's Spring and Autumn* [*Annals*]. This is to help realize his ambition to achieve total domination of the state and government before the prince comes of age and can act alone. It is also a piece of supreme vanity, for it was a title of several other regional histories, including one attributed to Confucius himself. Lü is so proud of 'his' work that he has a copy attached to one of the capital's gates, with 1,000 pieces of gold hanging above it, together with a notice that if anyone could improve it by so much as a single character, the cash was theirs. No one dares try. Bodde adds a succinct comment: 'At the present day we are still not unfamiliar with the activities of the crude, uncultivated, self-made man, who becomes a patron of the arts chiefly in order that he may gain the plaudits of the *élite*.'

Meanwhile, Lü and the beautiful queen restart their affair, but Lü, afraid of discovery, hatches another plot so complicated it sounds unworkable, and so lurid it sounds incredible. Some of it probably is. Yet no one has suggested

the following paragraph was forged by some Han inter-
polator. It seems we should accept the story, with its startling
details, as Sima Qian's own words. Here it is:

> The queen dowager did not cease her wanton behaviour. Lü
> Buwei began to fear that, if her conduct were ever brought
> to light, he himself would become involved with the scandal.
> He therefore searched about in secret until he found a man
> named Lao Ai who had an unusually large penis, and made
> him a servant in his household. Then, when an occasion
> arose, he had suggestive music performed and, instructing
> Lao Ai to stick his penis through the centre of a wheel made
> of paulownia wood, had him walk about with it, making
> certain that the report of this reached the ears of the queen
> dowager so as to excite her interest.

Never mind the queen: this extraordinary image would
surely excite anyone's interest. It contains just the sort of
detail lacking in passages that are possible forgeries. Why
paulownia wood, for heaven's sake? I had never heard of it,
but Google throws up websites by the score. Paulownias,
with their huge dark-green leaves and decorative mauve
flowers, have been cultivated in China for over 2,300 years.
Also now known as the 'princess' or 'royal' tree, the most
popular species (*Paulownia tomentosa*) is fast-growing
(almost 3 metres a year, good for reforestation); is easily
worked; resists rot well; has a very high ignition point; is
good for making the soundboards of stringed musical instruments; and much more. Why a 'wheel' of it should be
suitable for showing off the attributes of a stud-in-waiting is
not clear; but I believe the scene.

So did the queen, with more astonishing revelations to
come. She wanted to see Lao Ai in the flesh. But there was a
problem. The palace system did not allow 'real' men into the

dowager empress's quarters. So Lü's complicated plot gets its next twist. He arranges for Lao Ai to be falsely accused of a crime for which the punishment is castration. The official in charge of castration is then bribed to pretend to carry out the procedure, plucking out Lao Ai's beard and eyebrows to make him look like a eunuch. 'In this way he eventually came to wait on the queen, who carried on clandestine relations with him and grew to love him greatly.'

I don't think we should take all this at face value. What 'crime' exactly might Lao Ai have been accused of? How would anyone have known? But the outlines carry conviction. Bear in mind this is deceit on a huge scale. The queen has her own palace, staffed by hundreds. Lao Ai himself, now in a position to exert great influence, acquires a retinue of 1,000 retainers, all hoping for advancement.

The affair continues for many years, with the queen bearing Lao Ai two sons, who thus became half-brothers and possible heirs of the teenaged King Zheng, the future First Emperor; and Zheng is still being advised by his mentor, Lü Buwei, his mother's ex-lover and – according to word on the street – his father. This was a time-bomb ticking towards an explosion.

It would be good to place these dramatic events in their setting, to see something of the Qin capital, Xianyang, and its array of palaces. I'm sorry to say you can't. Qin architecture, like almost all building of its day, was all rammed-earth walls and wooden rafters, which rotted away or were burned. But if you go to the site, not far from today's Xianyang, you can get a feel for what King Zheng faced in his struggle to make Qin China's dominant power.

His ancestors had moved from the west two centuries before on the advice of Lord Shang, who saw that an ambitious, centralized state needed a capital better placed for assault. Both new and old Xianyang lie on the north bank of the river Wei, which flows eastward to the Yellow River, 130 kilometres away. What a contrast it makes to drive between the two Xianyangs. If you start with new Xianyang, half an hour by expressway from the later capital, Xian, there is nothing in the surge of new building to suggest an ancient past. For that you have to visit the charming old museum, with its brightly painted beams and upturned tiles and its Qin and Han artefacts, all the broken bits and pieces picked up from sites like the one we were on our way to visit.

The name 'Qin' lives on, but it takes fine-tuning to pick up the faint echoes of Qin culture, and its swaggering machismo. A ten-times-life-size three-legged cauldron in the middle of a roundabout is a modern reminder that power once depended on the ability to cast bronze. Other cultures were proud of their swords; in Qin times, they loved their cooking-pots. Still do, actually, because of what comes from them. It was the first day of spring, and lunchtime, and on sunny sidewalks people addressed themselves to Qin noodles. Unlike the thin, effete, girly, machine-made noodles eaten everywhere else, Qin noodles are rough-cut, hand-made symbols of manliness, solid as leather armour. And the pancakes: none of your wimpy sheets that fall apart at a touch, but bars of dough solid as telephone directories. 'There were no chopsticks then,' said my guide 'Tony' Lee, 'No knives and forks. So we tore our food apart with our hands.'

So, strengthened by Qin cuisine, driver Wang powered his 4×4 eastward out of new Xianyang, heading for the old one, King Zheng's capital. It was a fine day; one of those charming-if-puzzling roadside signs in English reminded us how lucky we were to be alive, if we acted correctly: 'Life does not come twice, so don't run inversely.' Then we were away from Xianyang's dual carriageways, away from any risk of running inversely. As we rolled along back roads, through fields of winter wheat and budding apple orchards that dusted the grey earth with green, Tony – a lanky thirty-something with hair fizzed as if by electric shock – spoke of the traits that define Qin culture.

'They like yodelling.'

'What?'

'I mean yowling. No, yelling. They talk very loud. Listen to Qin opera. Maybe it will scare you because it is so loud and piercing.' He experimented with the radio-tuner, and to my astonishment found a station that broadcast nothing but Qin opera. 'You see? It sounds like shouting or crying. We think this must have been King Zheng's entertainment too.' This struck me as very likely, because it was clearly based on the battle cries of berserk warriors and the screams of tortured criminals. (Later, in a Xian club that specialized in Qin opera, I heard the real thing. It starred both professionals and amateurs, who stepped out of the small audience to belt out the songs through a microphone at a gut-wrenching volume. I felt shaken by sound, like a rat by a terrier; shaken also by my ignorance, for this was a serious sub-culture, with aficionados as dedicated and expert as Wagner freaks.)

My attention swung outwards again, away from the fortissimo howl of Qin opera. The road was now running past hillock after hillock, the royal tumuli left by the Han dynasty, the Qin's successors. There was not a house in sight.

'Where on earth are we?'

'Today we are in the middle of nowhere,' said Tony, who was rightly proud of his idiomatic English. 'We are in the back of beyond. But two thousand years ago, it was different. There were Zhou tombs here before the Qin came, and Han afterwards. This was a historic place for centuries.'

We turned between two Han burial mounds, along a lane, past a little museum that was closed for repairs, and up a path towards higher ground. A little gnarled old lady working in a field of vines happily and effusively told us we were on the right track. 'How friendly she is,' remarked Tony. 'You ask her one question, she answers ten. And listen.' A tinny noise came faintly through the vines. 'You hear her radio? Qin opera!' She noticed our interest and carried the radio over, so I could appreciate the clashing cymbals and high shrieks. I wonder how many farm workers anywhere in the world listen to opera while they work.

An overgrown brick path led between fir saplings and plantations of palm bushes. Then we were on a plateau, its undulating surface covered with coarse grasses and thorny bushes that grabbed at trouser-legs and shoelaces. A sign said that this had been declared 'a national cultural relics protection spot' in 1988, which must have been when the gardens were made. But in almost 20 years nothing else had been done: there was no sign of any building. The archaeologists had done their work, taking roof-tiles and floor-tiles and drains off to museums, tracing post-holes, sketching ground plans, leaving nothing but rolling earth and coarse vegetation. Once, there had been the remains of the base of a terrace; if there's anything left now, I missed it. There was no one else around except the little old lady and her radio – not surprisingly, because the place was hard to get to, with no public transport and nothing to see.

Suddenly, though, the attractions of the site for Qin rulers were revealed. We waded clear of bushes, towards a . . .

At this point my attention was snatched away by a very odd sound, a vibrato twanging that rose and fell in volume, but always on the same note. I looked around for some electrical source, a wire vibrating in the wind, perhaps, or some machine. A second later, I saw where the sound came from: a flight of birds swooping and swerving overhead. Obviously they were some local species with a peculiar cry, or a weird evolutionary adaptation of their wing-feathers. I stood spellbound. Such is the idiocy brought on by ignorance. They were pigeons, explained Tony, to whom the sound was so routine he had hardly heard it. Domestic pigeons. Their owners tied whistles to their feet to keep track of them.

A cliff. That was what lay beyond the bushes. A cliff of clay and earth, about 10 metres high, at the base of which was a village of earth-brick houses, and beyond an immense plain leading to the Wei river, invisible in the distance. Perhaps 2,200 years ago, when King Zheng ruled from here, it had been a marshy flood plain. Serenaded by the flying choir, we made our way along the cliff-top. A bluff jutting out a few metres gave a view along the whole site, a 5-kilometre platform of scrub and little mounds, which at last provided a framework for a mind's-eye view of what had once been here.

The centrepiece had been King Zheng's palace. Actually, according to the reconstruction based on archaeological surveys,[4] it was a graceful, low-rise building, more a villa than a palace. In King Zheng's day, as the many repairs and reconstructions revealed, this villa had been there for some time, perhaps ever since Lord Shang created Xianyang as the new Qin capital 200 years earlier. If you get a chance, look at the model in the Xianyang museum; otherwise imagine a gallery of 40 arches stretching for 120 metres, topped by a terrace along which courtiers could stroll. Above, and set back, was a third storey, each wing having three low towers:

[4] The best single account in any language is in Ledderose and Schlombs, *Jenseits der Grossen Mauer*, which contains many Chinese sources.

in effect, three separate houses, the central one of which – the emperor's quarters, perhaps – had another terrace, giving a fine view southward over the plain. Surprisingly for a man dedicated to war, there were no defences. Surprisingly also, considering King Zheng's massive expenditures, it was quite modest. What turned it from a villa into a palace was its depth – 40 metres – and its decorations: ceramic tiles, bronze hinges, wall-paintings. One round tile-end was embossed with a text: 'Only with the approval of Heaven can our dynasty last for over 10,000 years and everything under Heaven thrive and live in peace.'[5] Inside was a warren of rooms and corridors floored by embossed red tiles, all supplied with water and drained through four systems of terracotta pipes, and all decorated with scenes of men, horses and mythological beasts, the oldest Chinese wall-paintings yet discovered.

And that was only the crown jewel of Xianyang's buildings. It was set in a palace complex almost a kilometre long and 500 metres wide, among many more buildings, some probably linked by roofed corridors and bridges. All along the earthen platform were scattered other grand houses, some 270 of them, either side of a gorge, now called the Ox and Goat Creek, that sliced southward through the platform of earth to the Wei. In all, the city was 7.2 kilometres (east–west) by 6.7 kilometres (north–south), though a good deal of the southern section seems to have been washed away when the river Wei changed course. The capital was supplied by seven bronze and iron foundries, proof that Qin was the centre of a rich, self-confident little kingdom long before Zheng took it over. As the ex-president of the Terracotta Army Museum, Yuan Zhongyi, has written,

[5] The dating of this piece is uncertain. It may be Han. But the manufacturing technique and the sentiment could just as well be Qin.

Formerly, as a result of the lack of documentation and archaeological finds, it was assumed that Qin had been backward. Now, following a wealth of new discoveries, this judgment has to be thoroughly revised . . . The Qin dynasty reigned over a glorious, flourishing period in the cultural history of old China . . . a treasure worthy of scrupulous research and compilation.[6]

This was the base where King Zheng planned the unification of China and his own elevation to its first emperor. But these ambitions presented him with a new insight, and inspired new ambitions. Xianyang might be a lot better placed than the previous capital, Yong, 100 kilometres further west, but for campaigns to the south and east it was not ideal. The Wei and Yellow rivers were in the way. Armies could be based the other side of both, but to lead them, he himself, and his entourage of officials, needed to cross the Wei. Back then, the Wei spread much more widely at certain times of the year. Was there a bridge? Certainly not a stone one, because China did not as yet have a tradition of building in stone. Possibly a wooden one; probably, for such a broad and variable river, a pontoon bridge. But pontoon bridges were rickety structures, vulnerable to floods. He needed a permanent base south of the Wei. That was where he would plan conquest with his army commanders and his officials. And that was where he would build the tomb from which he would rule his kingdom in the afterlife.

In the ninth year of his reign (238 BC), 'someone reported' to King Zheng the truth about his mother's affair with Lao Ai. Moreover, ran the report, 'He and the queen dowager

---

[6] Quoted in Ledderose and Schlombs, *Jenseits der Grossen Mauer*.

have agreed that, when the present king passes on, one of
[their two] sons shall succeed him.' The king ordered an
investigation; then, before hearing the results, he had to
travel 100 kilometres westward to the old capital of Yong to
perform some essential ritual sacrifices. Lao Ai, afraid his
deception was about to be revealed, turned to revolution.
'Using the queen dowager's seal of authority without her
permission, [he] called out troops and initiated a revolt.'
Action focused on a palace close to where the king was performing his rituals, presumably with the idea of capturing
him. Once the news reached Zheng, however, the uprising
was quickly crushed. Lao Ai fled, with a reward of one
million strings of coins offered for his capture alive, and half
that if dead. He was soon taken, though Sima Qian does not
record any pay-out.

The investigation was completed, and all the sordid facts
revealed. Imagine the young king's reaction. Zheng knows
something of his origins – son (perhaps) of a minor prince
who had no real right to the throne, which he came to by
luck and scheming, and an ex-dancer of ill-repute. His
paternity is already in doubt. Now his mother turns out to
be not only obsessed by a well-endowed – and treacherous –
gigolo, but also conspiring to control the succession, probably with the connivance of the man to whom he owes his
throne.

The 22-year-old king, having just 'donned the cap and
sword' that symbolized his coming of age, faced his first
hard choices as fully fledged ruler. The stakes could hardly
be higher. Either he would remain a puppet, or he had to
assert himself, crushing his mentor, his mother, her lover and
all their armies of retainers. Action would risk civil war; but
inaction spelled annihilation. He had Lao Ai killed by the
long-established method of being tied to four chariots,
which were then driven off in different directions. His

associates and relatives were executed. So were the two boys, Zheng's half-brothers and possible future rivals. Lao Ai's 1,000 hangers-on and 4,000 other noble families had their estates confiscated and were sent off to Shu, Qin's southern borderland (today part of Sichuan). His mother he exiled to Yong; 100 kilometres away was not too dire – and anyway she was soon brought back to Xianyang, where she remained until her death ten years later.

What to do with Lü Buwei was not so easily determined. He deserved death, but his past distinctions spoke for him, as did many of his followers. So the king fired him and exiled him to his estates around Luoyang – and, to make extra certain that no similar conspiracy could ever happen again, he announced that he would expel all foreigners from the state of Qin. This was an ill-considered edict, for it would have removed his other chief adviser, Li Si, a native of Chu (before he moved to Han). As Li Si quickly pointed out in a memo, a rejection of foreign things would mean the loss of a good deal of what adorned the palace, including the 'lovely and enchanting women of Zhou, such as blend in with our custom and lend elegance to the scene'. In these matters, His Majesty selected carefully, yet now, when men and talents are at stake, he says: 'He is not a native of Qin, so away with him! Because he is an alien expel him!' Did His Majesty really want to cast away aliens so that they might become an asset to enemy countries? 'This is what is called lending arms to bandits and supplying rations to thieves.' That did it. The king rescinded his order, and Li Si remained in position, to serve his king for another 20 years.

As for Lü Buwei, 350 kilometres turned out not to be far enough. He remained influential with the feudal lords, whose followers and envoys flocked to his palace, so much so that 'carriages were never out of sight of each other on the road'. To remove the threat still further, the king sent a note of steely politeness: 'Be so good as to take your family and retinue and move your residence to Shu!'

To be sent off to the Qin equivalent of Siberia was one humiliation too many. To refuse to move would be to risk the death penalty, not only for himself but for his family and followers. So Lü committed suicide by drinking poison.

That leaves King Zheng, aged 24, alone, betrayed by his father-figure and his mother, without his closest adviser, surrounded by thousands of clamorous courtiers, any one of whom may turn traitor. What should he do?

Well, he already has the answer, from Li Si, who had been advising him throughout his teenage years: Look at Lord Shang, and the stern Legalist advice that served your forefathers so well. Prince Zheng had listened, and was ahead of his teacher. He had come across chapters by a Legalist author who seemed to wish to remain anonymous, and admired them. The author told charming little stories to state great truths. Take, for instance, his essay entitled 'The Five Vermin':

> There was a farmer of Song who tilled the land, and in his field was a stump. One day a rabbit, racing across the field, bumped into the stump, broke its neck, and died. Thereupon the farmer laid aside his plow and took up watch beside the stump, hoping he would get another rabbit in the same way. But he got no more rabbits, and instead became the laughing stock of Song. Those who think they can take the ways of ancient kings and use them to govern the people of today all belong in the category of stump-watchers!

The Confucian past was no guide for the present, let alone the future. 'Benevolence and righteousness served for ancient times,' Zheng read in the same essay, 'but no longer serve today . . . Men of today vie to be known for strength and spirit.' In the past, rulers were compared to fathers, people to children, and the rule was one of love. But love cannot prevent children from becoming unruly, so how can it bring the people to order? People will bow only to authority, 'and he who wields authority may easily command men to submit'.

Should a ruler admire Confucius? Of course. He was a great sage, a truly righteous man. Once, rulers aimed to achieve the benevolence and righteousness he advocated. But that was then, and states were destroyed. Should a ruler today follow Confucius, when preserving the state is all-important? Certainly not, because that would be 'to demand that the ruler rise to the level of Confucius', not that of a ruler. The love of parents is not enough to make children learn what is right, 'for people by nature grow proud on love, but they listen to authority'. Even lame sheep may graze up and down a mountain, even the humble abuse easy laws; 'therefore the enlightened ruler makes his laws precipitous and his punishments severe'.

Here, too, King Zheng found advice on how to behave as ruler. If the ruler was the maker of the Law, and above it, how should he act? Obviously, he, as the Son of Heaven, could not be guided by the same principles as his earth-bound officials. Like a Daoist sage, he is above right and wrong, and must withdraw into a world of mystery and transcendence, shunning all contacts that might breed familiarity, concealing his thoughts and motives. He must guard against all impulses towards mercy and affection. Since all – officials, family, even his wife – stand to gain personal freedom by his death, he must trust no one. He must be beyond emotion, doing only that which increases his power, whatever it takes. Self-interest should be his only concern.

The ways to power are these: make the Law; make it simple; never look for men of integrity, because you will not find them; keep your officials on the straight and narrow with rewards and punishments. If people can get rich and eminent without hard work on the land and risking death in battle, they will do so, and the state is weakened; therefore discourage the pursuit of wisdom. 'In the state of the enlightened ruler there are no books . . . there are no sermons . . . there are no fierce feuds of private swordsmen; cutting off the heads of the enemy is the only deed of valour.' Don't think that you can build security by playing at foreign affairs, for no alliance is reliable. 'Neither power nor order can be sought abroad – they are wholly a matter of internal government.'

Remember this: in the past, when Confucians were honoured, states fell; what people praise and the ruler honours are actually policies that lead to the ruin of the state.

These, then, are your enemies, the 'five vermin' of the essay's title: scholars who praise the ways of former kings and speak in elegant phrases; speech-makers who propound false schemes and borrow influence from abroad; swordsmen who gather bands of followers; draft-dodgers who bribe their way out of military service; and merchants and artisans who make articles of no practical use, accrue wealth and exploit farmers. 'These groups are the vermin of the state. If the rulers do not wipe out such vermin . . . Then they should not be surprised . . . to see states perish and ruling houses wane and die.'

On reading this, King Zheng could have felt the contemporary equivalent of an air-punched '*Shi!*' ('Yes!'), but came out with something rather more formal. '"Alas!" he said to Li Si,' in Sima Qian's account. '"If I could once catch sight of this man and move with him, I would die without regret."

'Li Si said: "These writings have been made by Han Fei,"'

and would surely have explained that this man had once been his fellow student, and had remained in Han, trying, without much success, to secure a position as royal adviser. King Zheng could only bide his time.

Soon after this, in 234 BC, to meet some unspecified 'critical situation', King Zheng planned an attack on his junior ally, Han, the state where Han Fei had been trying to convince his own king of the merits of his uncompromising Legalism. Unexpectedly under threat, the Han king suddenly decided that Han Fei must know what he was talking about, and sent him off to Xianyang as an ambassador to King Zheng, with a persuasive list of reasons for restraint. Han, he argued, had always been as submissive as a straw mat, had supplied Qin with soldiers, and had paid tribute; but, having endured the attacks of others, it had also taken care to build up its defences. It would not be a pushover. An attack might weaken Qin, and offer others a chance. Best, surely, to conserve one's strength for assaults on Qin's real enemies.

Zheng was delighted to see him, until Li Si, in what seems to have been a fit of jealousy, warned the king that Han Fei was, after all, a Han, and that his home state was where his loyalties would always lie. His memo was nothing more than self-serving deception: Although Han is Qin's vassal, there has never been a time when it has not been a disease to Qin. War on other fronts would simply grant Han a chance to attack. Han Fei 'makes dialectical speeches and well-rounded phrases, and utters falsehoods and invents cunning plots . . . while he spies on Your Majesty for Han's benefit.' 'Such is human nature. If now Your Highness . . . returns him after detaining him for a long time, this will bring disaster upon yourself. The best thing would be to punish him for having transgressed the laws.'

It was a spiteful thing to do, to betray a fellow student, a foreign envoy and a thinker with whom he was in full agreement. Zheng concurred, and Han Fei was arrested. To make sure that there would be no comeback by his former colleague, Li Si made it impossible for Han Fei to see the king; then, with his prisoner reduced to despair, he had poison sent into the prison and induced him to commit suicide.[7]

Li Si was on his own, unrivalled, free to advise his young monarch, guiding him to conquest, unification and an empire of this world and the next.

[7] Another source (*Zhanguo Ce / Stratagems of the Warring States*) implicates a certain Yao Jia, but Bodde dismisses it as unreliable: 'The motives . . . for Li Si's deed are sufficiently strong, and make the reasons for absolving him unconvincing.'

5

THE MAKING OF CHINA

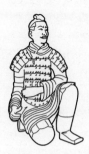

GIVEN THE SPEED WITH WHICH KING ZHENG CONQUERED all his six rivals – in eleven years, 230–221 BC – you might think that the army possessed some secret weapon. Not so. The same repertoire of equipment – bows, arrows, halberds, swords, armour – was used by all the warring states; even the crossbow, a devastatingly effective weapon because it was far more powerful than an ordinary bow, and could be prepared and held ready like a loaded rifle.

The crossbow is worth a small digression because crossbow triggers were found when the Terracotta Army was first unearthed, which may seem to suggest that Qin had a monopoly on this fearsome weapon. In fact, the days of aristocrats with bows and arrows exchanging shots from chariots were long gone, and the crossbow had been in wide use for over a century, as Sima Qian's account of a famous battle near Maling (in western Shandong, almost on the Henan border) shows.

It took place in 341 BC. A Qi army, advised by Sun Bin, a descendant of *The Art of War*'s author, had invaded Wei, and was being pursued to Maling by Wei troops commanded by Pang Juan. One evening, Sun Bin saw that the Wei army was about to enter a certain defile which was ideal for a night-time ambush:

> He cut down a big tree, whittled off the bark and wrote on the exposed white wood: 'Pang Juan will die under this tree!' Then he got together 10,000 of his best crossbow marksmen, hid them along the narrow road, and ordered: 'Shoot together if you see a fire lit!' Pang Juan came across the place where the tree had been felled. He saw there was something white with writing on it, so he lit a torch. Before he had finished reading what was written on it, the 10,000 crossbows fired together and the Wei forces fell about in disorder. Pang Juan realized that his whole force was lost through his own lack of judgement and so he committed suicide, saying 'So much for my reputation now!'

A decade or so later, it was the state of Han, apparently, that had the best crossbowmen. An ambassador to Han commented on them: they 'have a range of more than 600 paces. Your Han troops use their feet to pull their crossbows and when they shoot, not a shot in one hundred fails in its effect: they pierce the chest of an enemy who is far off.' According to one source,[1] crossbowmen used bows

---

[1] Quoted in Selby, *Archery Traditions of China* and *Chinese Archery*, which are my major sources here.

with a draw-weight of up to 12 *shi*, which is just over 350 kilos.[2]

We are not concerned with the most powerful weapons, because they took time to load, and in the heat of battle there was no time. You can see the remains of a crossbow – actually more like a fossil – preserved in the earth in the Terracotta Army Museum, and it is quite simple, loaded probably by standing on the bow and hauling the string back with both hands until it was caught and held by the trigger.

It was the bronze trigger (see illustration on p. 64) that was the key to the military crossbow, because it held the taut bowstring in place until the moment of release. Triggers were wonderful devices. As Joseph Needham puts it in his monumental *Science and Civilisation in China*, they were 'among the greatest triumphs of ancient metallurgical and engineering practice in any civilisation'.[3] In its most sophisticated form, the crossbow trigger consisted of up to six pieces of bronze, which all fitted together on two shafts in the stock of the bow. It would cock automatically, and may even have had a safety catch. It had to have the precision of a bolt-action rifle. As Lü Buwei (or rather, one of his

[2] This is a murky subject. No one could have loaded a 350 kg bow by hand, even lying down. Pulling a bowstring like this is like performing a 'deadlift' in weightlifting, with the severe handicap of pulling on a string rather than a bar. Today's world record deadlift is about 440 kg, almost 1,000 lb, achieved by super-heavyweights. For the world record in 'flight archery', firing an arrow by muscle power alone (1.8 km in 1971), the American Harry Drake lay on his back, placed his feet on the bow and pulled the bowstring with both hands. His bow's draw-weight was 'only' 300 lb (136 kg). To draw a bow over two and a half times that 'weight' needed a lever or winch (as Europe also discovered some 1,600 years later), though no examples have survived. On the other hand, units of weight varied over time by anything up to threefold, so perhaps we are talking of crossbows with draw-weights of only 120 kg.

[3] Needham, *Science and Civilisation in China*, vol. 5, sec. 30.

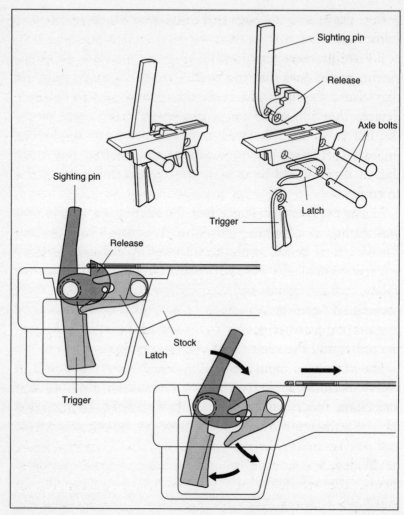

Crossbow trigger

commissioned authors) put it in his *Spring and Autumn Annals*, 'If the mechanism of a crossbow trigger is out of alignment by no more than the size of a rice-grain, it will not work.' This was what made the crossbow the ancient equivalent of the Kalashnikov: sophisticated but simple, easily made, easily dismantled, easily maintained.

But triggers had been around for 400 years before unification (the first known triggers date from about 650 BC). Possibly there was something special about Qin bronze casting techniques that made their triggers better than anyone else's. Possibly also Qin crossbowmen had sighting devices that improved accuracy. But it was not any substantial advantage in weaponry that underpinned Qin's military successes. What was it, then? Something obviously did, or there would have been no conquests, and no reason to commemorate the army full-size in terracotta.

The answer lay in organization, on every level. Qin society was a state-sized fighting machine. At its heart, under King Zheng's iron hand, were three interdependent elements: efficient agriculture, based on the rich farmland of the Wei valley, which provided food and excess manpower; a committed bureaucracy which gathered taxes, made lists of recruits, oversaw irrigation and managed the food supply to the army; and the army itself, a large, professional force.

The army was the nation's spearhead: tough, mobile and highly disciplined, the product of years of training for men and commanders alike. They could march 50 kilometres a day in leather armour, carrying crossbows, pikes, swords, and provisions for three days. The main force, which could be divided, was backed up by separate groups of reinforcements, the whole being coordinated by messengers in four-horse chariots. And of course the commanders all knew the vital importance of quick and accurate commands on the battlefield, as Sun Zi had recognized over a century earlier: 'Gongs and drums, banners and flags are used to unify the action of the troops. When the troops can be thus united, the brave cannot advance alone, nor can the cowardly withdraw. This is the art of directing large masses of troops.'

No doubt discipline underlay the way crossbowmen fought, for the layout of the Terracotta Army shows them in front of the infantry. Possibly they operated as an eleventh-century source described.[4] A crossbow 'needs to be used so that the men within the formation are loading while the men in the front line of the formation are shooting . . . each in their turn draw their crossbows and come up; then as soon as they have shot bolts they return again into the formation. Thus the sound of the crossbows is incessant and the enemy can hardly even flee. Therefore we have the following drill: shooting rank – advancing rank – loading rank.'

We cannot be sure, because there are no contemporary accounts of the way crossbowmen and infantry interacted, but it seems we should imagine a Qin army engaging their crossbowmen rather as early nineteenth-century European armies used their riflemen, advancing rank by rank, each kneeling, firing and reloading in sequence, except that crossbowmen withdrew after firing, allowing the next rank its turn, instead of advancing before firing.

There was nothing new in any one element. It was the whole coordinated package – the food supply, the recruitment, the vision of conquest and unity, centralized control, communication, training, discipline, weaponry – that set the Qin army apart. Thus, for the first time in Chinese history, an army arose dedicated not simply to victory in battle but to the conquest of territory, from which Qin would gain more food, men, weapons and forward bases, all of which would secure progress and provide the foundation for yet more conquest.

Of the conquests themselves, hardly anything is recorded, except their dates. Han fell in 230, Zhou two years later.

[4] Zeng Gongliang, quoted in Needham, *Science and Civilisation in China*, vol. 5, see 30, p. 122.

Then there came a three-year hiatus, marked by an incident so famous that it has become a popular subject for film and TV dramatization, most effectively in the epic *The Emperor and the Assassin* (1998),[5] directed by Chen Kaige, one of the 'new wave' or 'fifth generation' of Chinese filmmakers, who had won international recognition five years previously with the intimate, restrained *Farewell My Concubine*. *The Emperor and the Assassin* was the opposite – a vast canvas, huge personalities, epic battle sequences. Leaving aside the love interest, provided by the delectable Gong Li, Chen Kaige's main source was Sima Qian, whose account is as vivid as a film synopsis. Here it is, with his words as dialogue:

The back-story:
Prince Dan, the heir apparent of Qin's neighbour once removed, Yan, lives in fear of King Zheng. Two states have already fallen, and his is next in line. Dan and Zheng have known each other as young men. Moreover, Dan was a hostage in the Qin court, where he was so badly treated that he fled. Not long before, a Qin general, Fan Yuqi, defected, and is now under the protection of Prince Dan. The general needs all the protection he can get, for Zheng has offered a reward of a city plus 250 kilos of gold ($5.25 million, at today's rates) for his head.
We open on Dan's tutor warning him of trouble:

TUTOR:
This will not do! Violent as the King of Qin
is, and with the resentment he nurses against

---

[5] Two others are Quentin Tarantino's martial arts epic *Hero* (2002) and *The Emperor's Shadow* (directed by Zhou Xiaowen, 1996).

Yan because of your escape, it is already enough to make one's heart run cold.

Zhou has just fallen, he says, Qin troops are massing on Yan's border, and the only way to stop Zheng's meteoric rise is by finding an assassin to kill him.

(In Chen Kaige's film, the plot is all carefully orchestrated by the emperor, who wants to inspire an attempted assassination to give him a reason for declaring war on Yan. This is where Gong Li comes in. She is the king's favourite concubine, the love of his life, and it is she who decides to initiate the plot by having her face branded, then pretending to defect to Yan, her branded face giving her an apparent motive for betraying the emperor. It is she who then finds the assassin, with whom, in another twist, she falls in love.

Back to Sima Qian:)

The emperor's death will surely spark revolt from the dispossessed feudal lords, and Zheng's Legalist revolution will be reversed. A young adventurer named Jing Ke is chosen for the task. He is an ice-cool character of high intelligence, who likes 'to read books and practise swordsmanship'. He refuses to quarrel: if offended, he simply walks away.

Jing Ke is too smart to agree at once, but his reluctance is overcome by being made a minister and given a mansion. Knowing he has no chance of getting close to Zheng without a good excuse, he approaches the renegade Qin general, Fan, with an extraordinary suggestion: if only he can have the general's head, he will go to Zheng offering Yan's surrender, with the head as a sign of good faith. He will also have a map of Yan territory. These two items will gain him access. Inside the rolled-up map he plans to

conceal a poisoned dagger, with which he will stab Zheng.
The general finds this an excellent plan –

GENERAL FAN:
Day and night I gnash my teeth and eat out
my heart trying to think of some plan. Now
you have shown me the way!

– and obligingly cuts his own throat.
Head and map gain Jing Ke and an accomplice entry into
the court, and an audience with the king. At this moment the
accomplice has an attack of nerves, leaving Jing Ke to go on
alone. Watched by a crowd of courtiers, Jing Ke unrolls his
map, seizes the dagger, grabs the king by the sleeve, and
strikes. The king leaps back, tearing off his sleeve, and Jing
Ke's lunge misses its mark. Zheng flees with the assassin in
pursuit, while the unarmed courtiers stand back, appalled,
watching their lord and master dodging around a pillar, try-
ing in vain to untangle his long ceremonial sword from his
robes. A doctor has the presence of mind to hit Jing Ke with
his medicine-bag, which gives the king a moment's grace.

CROWD:
Push the scabbard around behind you!

Even as Jing Ke comes at him again, the king manages to
untangle his sword, draw it and wound Jing Ke in the leg.
Jing Ke hurls the poisoned dagger, misses, and falls back as
the king strikes at him, wounding him again. Jing Ke, seeing
he has failed, leans against the pillar, then squats down,
alternately laughing hysterically and cursing the king. The
crowd moves in and finishes him off.

This is a terrific story, perhaps Sima Qian's best, and one which he claimed to have from the horse's mouth – friends of the doctor, Xia Wuju, who hit Jing Ke with his bag, thus becoming the only one among the emperor's lily-livered courtiers to do anything, and probably saving the emperor's life. The two friends 'learned from him exactly what happened', writes Sima Qian. 'I have therefore reported everything just as they told me.'

To bridge the intervening century is a stretch, but possible. The assassination attempt was in 227 BC; the (young) doctor might have lived until (say) 180 BC. Imagine him as an old man telling his story to two open-mouthed teenagers, who could have lived until 130 BC. In their old age, the two could have passed on the tale to the future grand historian, who would have been a teenager himself when he heard the story.

An insatiable desire for security in an uncertain world now further fuelled Zheng's drive to national unity. Campaign followed campaign, all justified (as is the way of conquerors) by reference to broken promises and perceived acts of aggression. With attacks, counter-attacks, setbacks and final victories, Wei fell in 225, Chu in 223, Yan – the source of the head, the poisoned dagger and the would-be assassin – in 222, and finally Qi in the far east in 221.

The First Emperor thus came to be lord not only of six other kingdoms and their cities, but of dozens, scores, probably hundreds of tribal peoples, a few of whose names survive in the records: the Sushen of the bleak north-east borderlands; the nomadic Donghu of the northern grasslands; a dozen groups of south-western 'barbarians', both settled and semi-nomadic; the half-dozen tribes of Sichuan, among them the slave-raiding Po and the Zuo, named after the bamboo-and-rope bridges they built to span Sichuan's ravines; the hunting-and-fishing Yue groups of the south-east – the whole patchwork of peoples that foreshadow today's 56 nationalities.

Qin became recognizably the core of today's China, for Chinese and foreigners alike, though under different names. Those in the heartland, roughly the seven rival states united by the First Emperor, had long referred to their lands as the centre, the 'Central Nation' or 'Middle Kingdom' (*zhong guo*). So it has remained. But not to foreigners. Now unified from the borders of Tibet to the Pacific, from the Inner Mongolian escarpment to the South China Sea, this region was gradually equated by outsiders with its dominant power. Thus, as the name passed from language to language across Eurasia, did Qin become China.

6

A RUTHLESS FRENZY

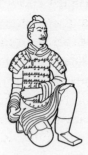

THIS WAS TO BE A NEW AGE, AS THE FIRST EMPEROR DECLARED:
'Insignificant person that I am, I have called up troops to
punish violence and rebellion. Thanks to the help of the
ancestral spirits, these six kings have acknowledged their
guilt and the world is in profound order.' Qin had succeeded
Zhou as the nation's heart and soul, with consequences far
beyond mere military conquest. Now would begin what
Germany's Nazi regime called *Gleichschaltung*, the central-
izing process that seized total control over all aspects of
society.

It started, as Nazism did, with a title. How was the king
to be addressed now that he was sole ruler? As everyone
agreed, never before had such a huge area been unified;
never before had laws proceeded from a single authority.
Only the grandest title ever conferred on a king would suit:

Greatly (*dà* /大) August (*huáng* /皇), one of the legendary emperors who had founded Chinese civilization some 2,000 years before. But Zheng, emperor by the grace of Heaven, did not like the idea of a precedent, understandably, because legend spoke of three emperors, or five, or somehow both. The five were known as the Wu Di, the Five Emperors, and they were considered to be the embodiments of wisdom and purity. Di was also a term for the highest supernatural power. Zheng came to the logical conclusion: 'We will drop the Greatly, keep the August and adopt the title used by the emperors of high antiquity': Huang Di, often translated as August Emperor, thus declaring himself imperial ruler, god, sage and ancestor all in one.[1] Moreover he was to be the first, the beginning, the *shǐ* (始). His heirs would bear the same title with their number added – Second, Third, Fourth – unto the ten thousandth generation of Qin emperors. Many books call him by his full title: Qin Shi Huang Di, The First Qin August Emperor. Some academics would like to call him a 'thearch', on the grounds that he headed a thearchy or theocracy, a god-ruled state, which is unlikely to catch on, partly because it is obscure and partly because it encourages lesser mortals to call him The Arch. For the sake of simplicity, let's go with 'the First Emperor'.

The First Emperor, raised on the fringe of the Chinese heartland, was not noted for his intellect, and he had just achieved something that must have seemed miraculous. Heaven was surely with him. To understand himself, his achievement and his future, he turned to those who claimed to know the ways of Heaven.

According to a popular line of Daoist thought, each

---

[1] This gets even more complicated, because Huang Di sounds the same as a different *huáng*, meaning yellow, recalling by a pun one of the legendary Five, the Yellow Emperor.

historical age was dominated by one of the five elements: earth, wood, metal, fire and water, which overwhelm each other in a fixed cycle, like a cosmic version of the children's game of scissors–rock–paper. Zhou had ruled through the power of fire. Its successor, Qin, would be the age of water, which extinguishes fire. Water had certain attributes, its colour being black, its number six. So flags became black, six the preferred unit of length for measuring almost anything, from the height of hats to the width of chariot-axles.

Then there was a public statement of the emperor's achievement to be made to his own people, and thanks to be given to the spirits of Qin for victory. This involved a royal progress to Qin's western border, 470 kilometres away, and up a sacred mountain, Qitou, an expedition that served as a trial run for tours to more distant parts of the new empire a few years later.

This was all very well as a way of beginning a dynasty. But how was one to avoid its dissolution? Only by ensuring control of the forces that governed the sequence of ages. This did not mean, as is often assumed, living for ever in this life, but ensuring immortality in the next. Daoist mystics, self-proclaimed sages who called themselves True Men, claimed to know how to achieve this by finding and drinking a certain elixir. Sima Qian wrote of one famous mystic called Zou Yan, whose followers practised his arts, but could not understand them: 'Thereupon there arose innumerable persons who were skilled in extraordinary prodigies, in deceiving flatteries, and who knew how to win people over' – in particular, this new and superstitious emperor.

Remember that Sima Qian was aiming his barbs at his own emperor, Wu, who was also prey to quackery and dreams of immortality; so some of this must be taken as deliberate exaggeration. You get a sense of what is unreliable when he becomes vague. But the Grand Historian backed these generalities up with a convincing detail. A team of 'magicians' submitted a memo suggesting a research trip: 'In the middle of the sea [by which they meant the Pacific somewhere between China and Japan] there are three super-natural mountains called Penglai, Fangzhang and Yingzhou. Immortals dwell there. We beg that after we have been purified, we may, together with young boys and girls, go there to seek for them.' At once, the First Emperor dispatched the expedition – other sources speak of 3,000 boys and 3,000 girls, though Sima Qian offers no numbers. Anyway, they were never heard of again. It was rumoured that the expedition ended up in Japan. Undeterred, the First Emperor sent out another equally useless expedition six years later.

The same year the First Emperor ordered a revolution in administration. Out went the old kingdoms and their feudal hierarchies; in came three dozen centrally controlled commanderies, under a chancellor, three deputy chancellors and nine ministers, all mirrored by a parallel military hierarchy. The commanderies were subdivided into several hundred prefectures (about the size of counties), and on down to districts, cantons and hamlets. Each commandery had both a civil and a military administrator, together with tax collectors, judges and officials, all of whom reported directly to the emperor.

Former ruling families – 120,000 of them, according to Sima Qian – were all moved to Xianyang, the Qin capital, where the First Emperor could keep an eye on them. But wait: 120,000 *families*? That's about 600,000 people. But Xianyang was never *that* big. Frankly, it's incredible: another of the extreme 'statistics' that Sima Qian throws into his text to exaggerate the emperor's authoritarian policies. Then come more startling numbers: from all the six defeated states, weapons were collected and melted down to make bells and twelve vast statues of barbarians, each weighing a conveniently round 1,000 piculs (about 30 or 50 or 60 tonnes, for sources vary; again, a figure to be taken with a large pinch of salt).

So much had been confused when China was divided. Each of the seven states had used different measures of area, different widths for cart-axles, different laws, coins, weights, measures, styles of clothing, and scripts. Under the direction of the great Li Si, all were now collated, unified and imposed nation-wide. From now on, for instance, vehicles had a standard gauge, with results that you can see today on the stone floors of many old gateways, like Cloud Terrace beside the Great Wall outside Beijing, worn away in two deep ruts by the passage of countless wagons and their evenly spaced wheels.

The revision of the script and its widespread imposition was perhaps the one change that ensured China's future unity, because governments could issue edicts that everyone everywhere could read, even if their pronunciations varied wildly. Away went the old script variants, with their curly lines, replaced with what came to be called the Small Seal script. It was this script, with its straight-line brush-strokes, that evolved into today's. As a result, as Derk Bodde puts it, 'China has suffered political disunity, but never has there been a time when she has lost her cultural continuity, a fact which explains why, of all the great civilisations of antiquity, hers is the only one to survive today.'

Labour now became available on an unprecedented scale, not only because of the empire's vastly extended population but because hundreds of thousands of soldiers had been freed by the ending of the wars of conquest. Peasants had always been liable to forced service as soldiers and labourers in their own kingdoms. Now they were called up nation-wide. Every male between 15 and 60 was eligible for labour on state projects; so a population of about 20 million could provide a workforce of perhaps one or two million a year (one prime source of labour being criminals), with many older men left to work the fields – without which the economy would collapse. Over the next decade, a national system of paved roads arose, including an 800-kilometre north–south highway of rammed earth across the Ordos – and this at least is backed by evidence, because parts of the road are still visible today, as are the remains of five royal palaces, nine command depots and numerous beacon-hillocks. Other roads fanned out from Xianyang, adding up to a grand total of some 6,750 kilometres.

Supposedly, the grandest of the First Emperor's projects was the Great Wall, the most massive state enterprise since the building of the pyramids, with millions drafted in to build it, and millions dying in the process. I say 'supposedly' because the evidence is scanty, consisting of a few lines in the only source, Sima Qian's *History*.

The project was under the command of Meng Tian, one of the emperor's top generals. In 215 BC, six years after unification, Meng Tian took an army of 300,000, headed north across the Ordos, chased out two barbarian tribes and 'set about constructing the Great Wall, following the contours of the land and utilizing the narrow defiles to set up frontier posts'. When finished, it extended 'for a distance of over ten thousand *li*', about 5,000 kilometres. Reading most non-specialist sources, you get the impression that the First Emperor built the Great Wall as it exists today north of Beijing, but stretching all the way across the empire's northern border. Not so. The *wàn* (10,000 / 万) is not an exact distance, but a frequent synonym for 'very large number'; and it is unlikely that any of this wall was of stone. Whatever was built from scratch was of rammed earth, and most of it has now vanished or been incorporated into other, later, walls. There is a stone section labelled 'Qin Great Wall' north of Baotou, but it was probably built by the king of Zhou around 300 BC, some 80 years before Meng Tian hijacked it and made it the Qin frontier. Nor did the First Emperor build a single Great Wall from nothing. What he did was to repair and join up a collection of little walls; a project which, considering its 2,500-kilometre length, was quite enough to keep his million-plus workforce employed between his accession and his death. It seems that the First Emperor's Great Wall, if we are talking about one structure built on his orders, is a figment of later imagination, made to seem solid by confusion with later and earlier walls, and given spurious historical roots in history by Sima Qian's vague words.

Oppression, brutality, excess and barbarism: these were the elements that formed the dynasty's later reputation, confirmed (so later generations believed) by two acts in particular. They are known as the Burning of the Books and the Burial of the Scholars. To destroy the records of the past and to bury alive one's intellectuals would indeed call forth condemnation. But, bad as the First Emperor was, it is possible he was not quite as bad as is generally believed.

The book-burning comes first. The story started at a banquet in the palace in Xianyang in 213 BC. Scholars and officials delivered eulogies to the empire. But one conservative, bolder than the rest, warned of trouble. Previous emperors, he said, had rewarded their sons, younger brothers and meritorious ministers with estates. Not so the First Emperor, who had broken with the past by destroying feudalism. This was bad news, for 'I have never heard of any undertaking that failed to imitate the example of antiquity, and yet was able to endure for long!' He went on to speak of the emperor's 'error', and of the disloyalty of his flattering ministers.

The man must have been out of his mind, for the emperor had come to absolute power by doing the exact opposite. The emperor's leadership training would have told him to make no reaction, to retain his mystery at all costs. So it was his bulldog, Grand Councillor Li Si, the second most powerful man in the empire, who responded, in a furious memo to the emperor:

In the past, the empire was in confusion and fragmented. Why? Because rulers disparaged the present by 'declaiming on antiquity'. They didn't see the need to sweep away the old, as His Majesty has done. His Majesty has unified all under heaven, yet still there are those who criticize and debate, which they can do because they have access to the opinions of others. And they're proud of it! If such behaviour is not prohibited, 'then in upper circles the authority of the ruler will be compromised, and in lower ones cliques will form'. The answer is to ban works of literature and poetry, historical documents and 'the sayings of the hundred schools of philosophy'. They should all be destroyed, Sima Qian has him say in one chapter (87, Li Si's biography), and anyone failing to destroy such books within a month should be branded and subjected to forced labour. In another chapter (6, 'The Basic Annals of the First Emperor'), the punishments are much more dire. Li Si demands that

all persons in the empire daring to store [these books] should go to the administrative and military governors so that these books may be indiscriminately burned. Those who dare to discuss the *Odes* and the *Histories* should be [executed and their bodies] exposed in the market place. Those who use the past to criticize the present should be put to death together with their relatives.

The emperor agreed to this Orwellian attempt at mind control. The books would be destroyed 'for the purpose of making the people ignorant', and so that no one should 'use the past to discredit the present'. So it happened. The poetry books and the historical sources, which were all in the royal archives, 'were all destroyed. How regrettable! How regrettable!' This was the act known as the Burning of the Books, for which the First Emperor has been demonized as the destroyer of China's literary heritage.

But hang on. How bad was it really? Much was to be spared, as were certain people: the records of Qin; books on medicine and pharmacy, divination, arboriculture and agriculture; the 70 officials of the Bureau of Scholars of Wide Learning. True, the poetry and history in the royal archives vanished, but most of the poetry books survived in private hands. 'Destroy' becomes 'burned' from one chapter to another, almost as if Sima Qian were keen to make bad into worse. There is something particularly nasty about burning books: it is a symbolic, public act of reducing information and opinion to nothing, used by other totalitarians, particularly religious zealots, in attempts to destroy a competing religion, or a heresy, or unacceptable behaviour.[2] Sima Qian knew that book-burning was on the Legalist agenda. Remember Han Fei's account of how Lord Shang taught Duke Xiao of Qin about informants, and his advice about burning books of poetry and history? There is no evidence that Xiao actually burned any books, but it was

[2] Perhaps the most infamous example was the burning of 20,000 Jewish books by the Nazis in Berlin on 10 May 1933. A Wikipedia article lists 50 other examples, including Muslims burning Salman Rushdie's *Satanic Verses* and three Christian churches in the USA burning Harry Potter books.

THE FIRST EMPEROR AS ICON

No genuine portrait survives of the man who first unified China, but modern artists agree informally on looks suitable for a conqueror. All over China, but particularly at the heart of his empire around Xian, his stern features and imposing figure make him instantly recognizable.

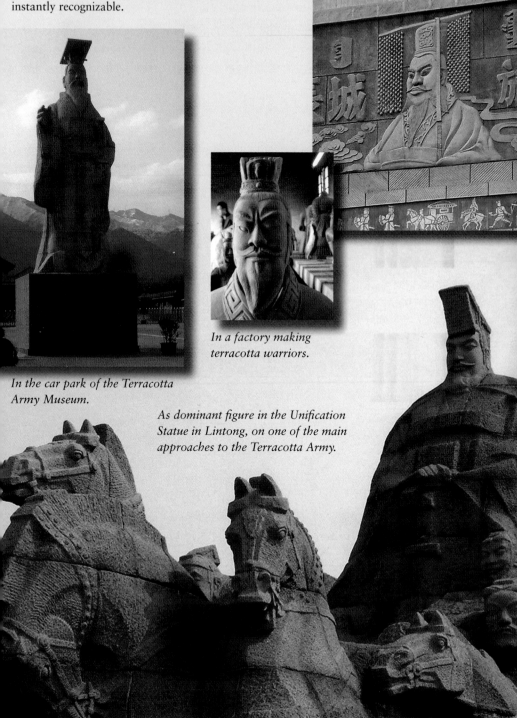

On a plaque marking the Great Wall north of the Yellow River.

In a factory making terracotta warriors.

In the car park of the Terracotta Army Museum.

As dominant figure in the Unification Statue in Lintong, on one of the main approaches to the Terracotta Army.

AN ENDURING PRESENCE

For over 2,000 years, the First Emperor's tomb-mound has stood against the backdrop of the Qin Ling mountains. Its covering of trees is recent, as the 1914 inset photograph shows, clearly revealing the pyramid's stepped shape and flat top. The colour picture was taken around 1990 while today's encircling walls were being built.

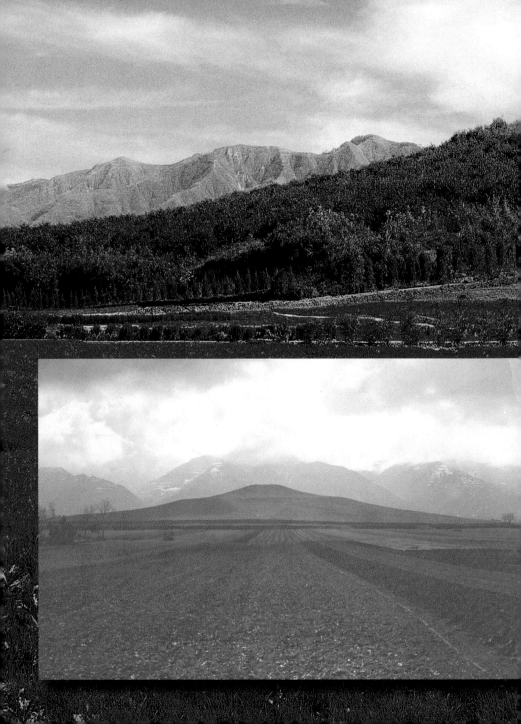

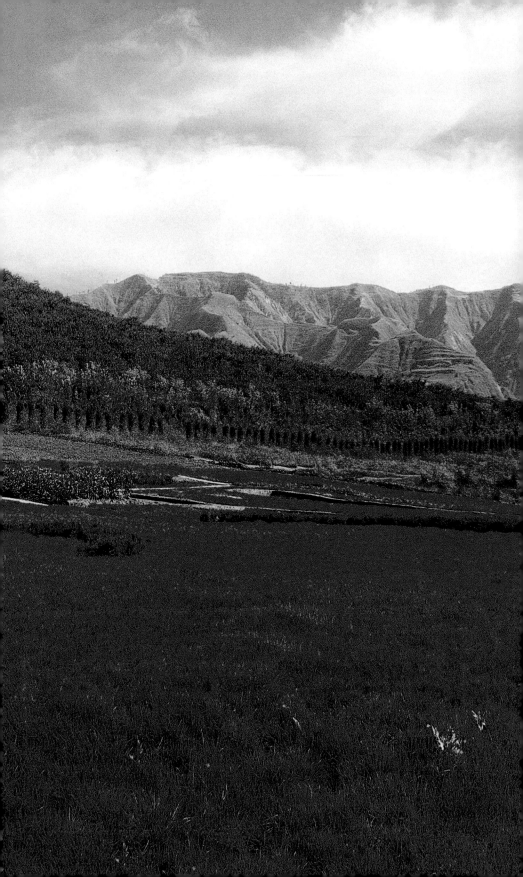

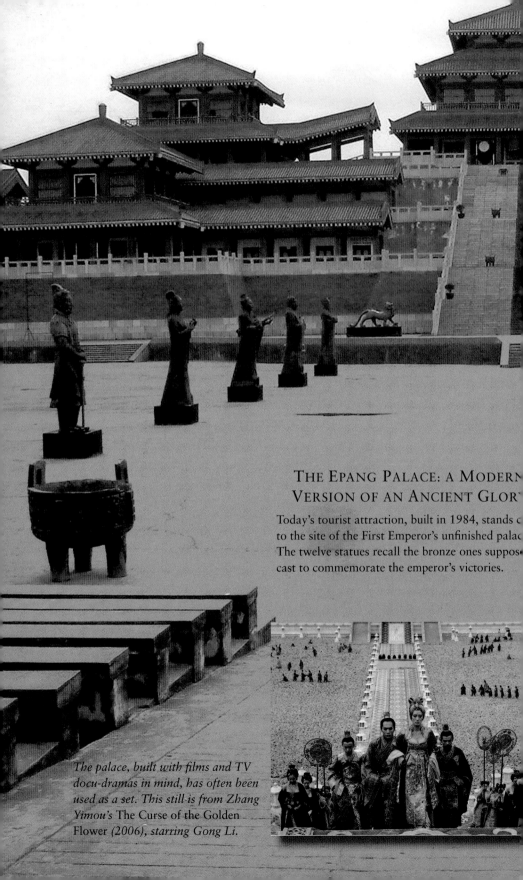

THE EPANG PALACE: A MODERN VERSION OF AN ANCIENT GLORY

Today's tourist attraction, built in 1984, stands close to the site of the First Emperor's unfinished palace. The twelve statues recall the bronze ones supposedly cast to commemorate the emperor's victories.

The palace, built with films and TV docu-dramas in mind, has often been used as a set. This still is from Zhang Yimou's The Curse of the Golden Flower *(2006), starring Gong Li.*

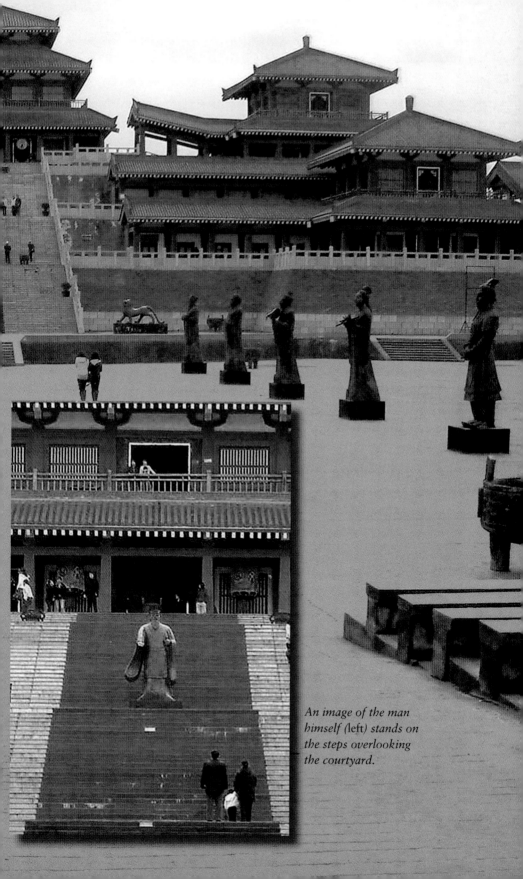

An image of the man himself (left) stands on the steps overlooking the courtyard.

REVELATION IN PIT NO.1:
A SHATTERED ARMY FOUND AND RESTORED

The discovery of the Terracotta Army in 1974 was due to luck, timing and expertise. Several statues had emerged from other pits over the years, but the six farming brothers who unearthed the first warriors might have kept their finds hidden if it had not been for local archaeologist Zhao Kangmin (*below left*). He attracted official interest in Beijing, which led to long-term attention by teams of technicians under scholars like Yuan Zhongyi.

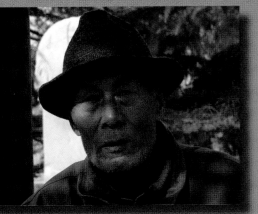

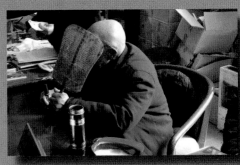

Yang Zhefa (above), one of the original discoverers, has remained a modest man wary of the attention he and his brothers attract.

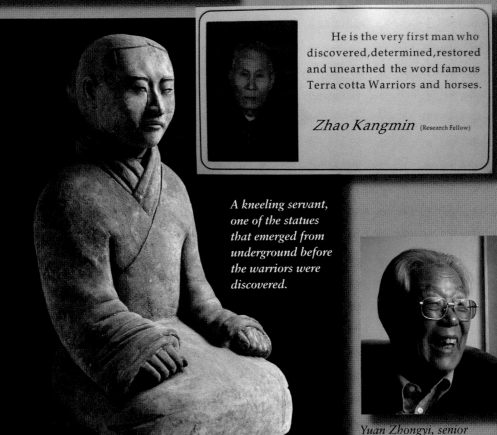

He is the very first man who discovered, determined, restored and unearthed the word famous Terra cotta Warriors and horses.

Zhao Kangmin (Research Fellow)

A kneeling servant, one of the statues that emerged from underground before the warriors were discovered.

Yuan Zhongyi, senior archaeologist.

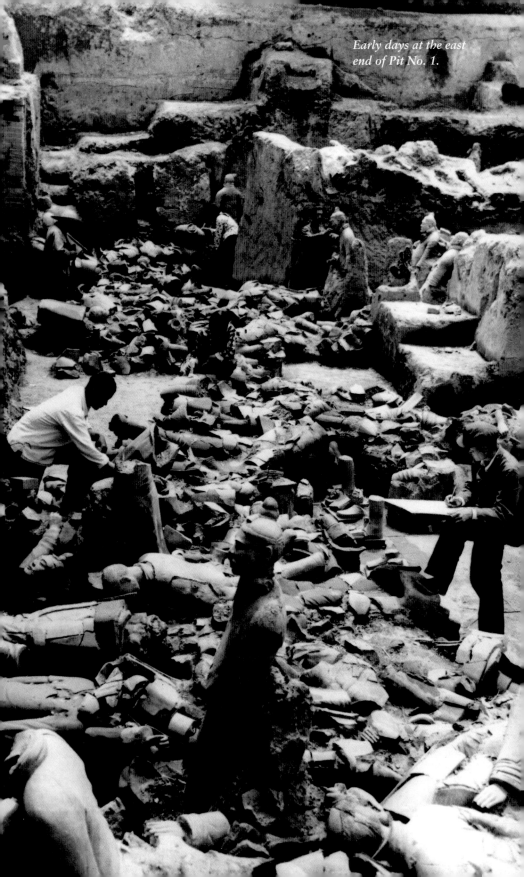

Early days at the east end of Pit No. 1.

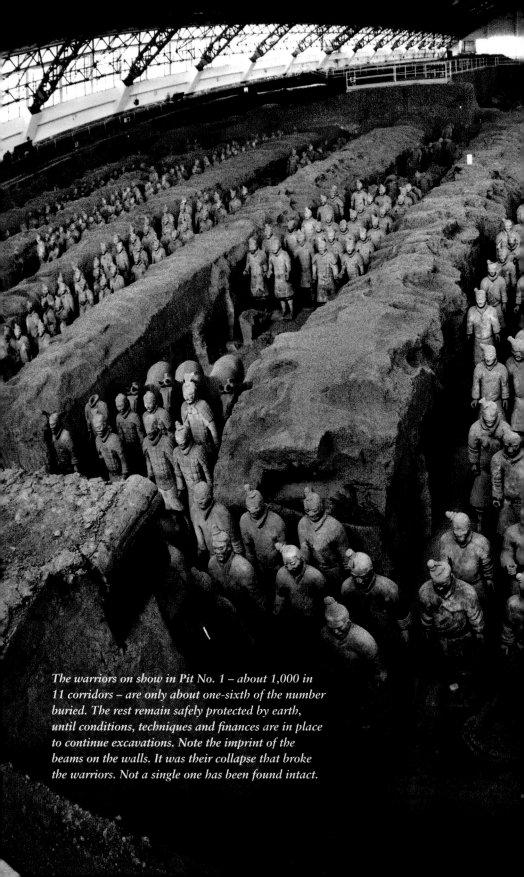

The warriors on show in Pit No. 1 – about 1,000 in
11 corridors – are only about one-sixth of the number
buried. The rest remain safely protected by earth,
until conditions, techniques and finances are in place
to continue excavations. Note the imprint of the
beams on the walls. It was their collapse that broke
the warriors. Not a single one has been found intact.

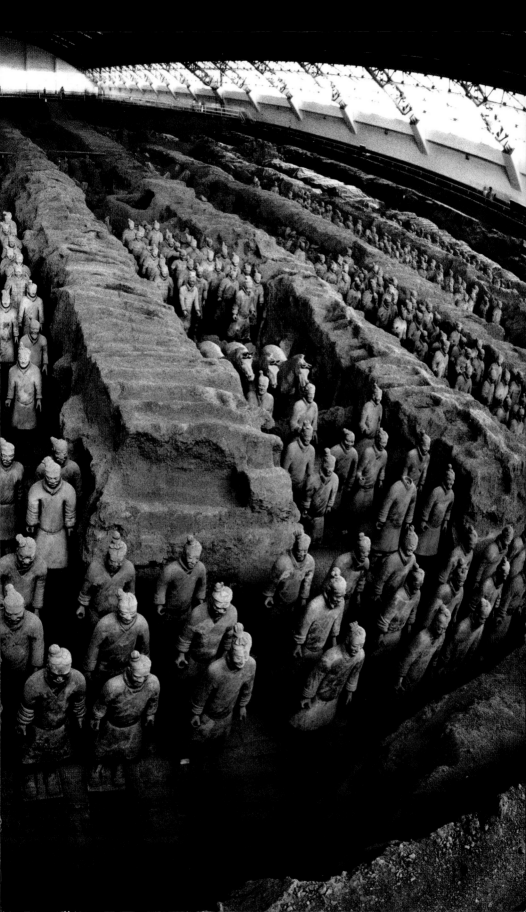

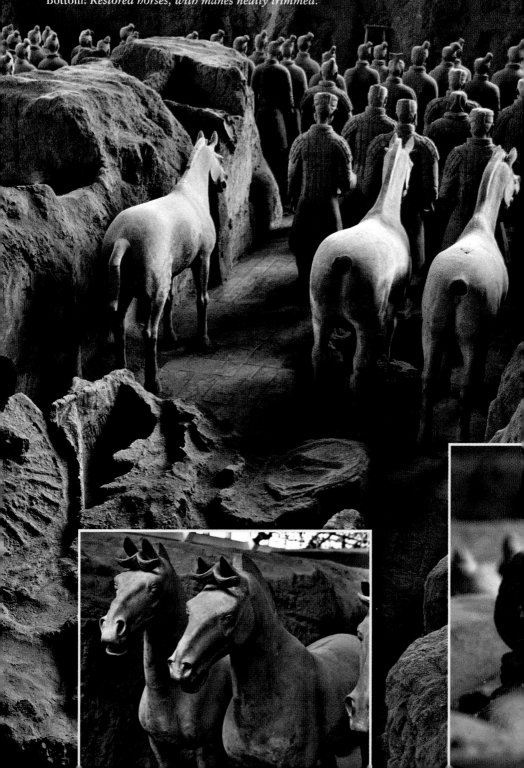

The wooden chariots were also crushed by the falling roof, but often left their remains imprinted in the soil. This has provided enough information to reconstruct them, and to allow the correct amount of space for them and their four horses, three of which are shown here as models.

Bottom: *Restored horses, with manes neatly trimmed.*

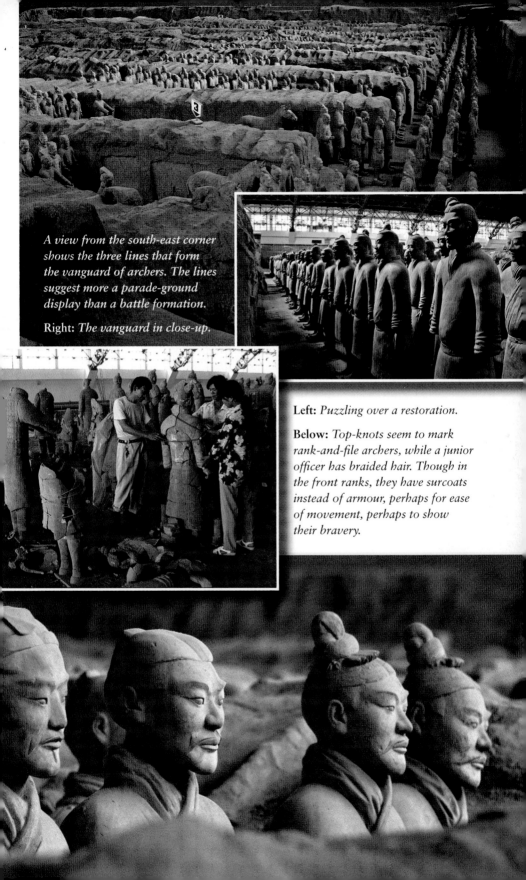

A view from the south-east corner shows the three lines that form the vanguard of archers. The lines suggest more a parade-ground display than a battle formation.

Right: *The vanguard in close-up.*

Left: *Puzzling over a restoration.*

Below: *Top-knots seem to mark rank-and-file archers, while a junior officer has braided hair. Though in the front ranks, they have surcoats instead of armour, perhaps for ease of movement, perhaps to show their bravery.*

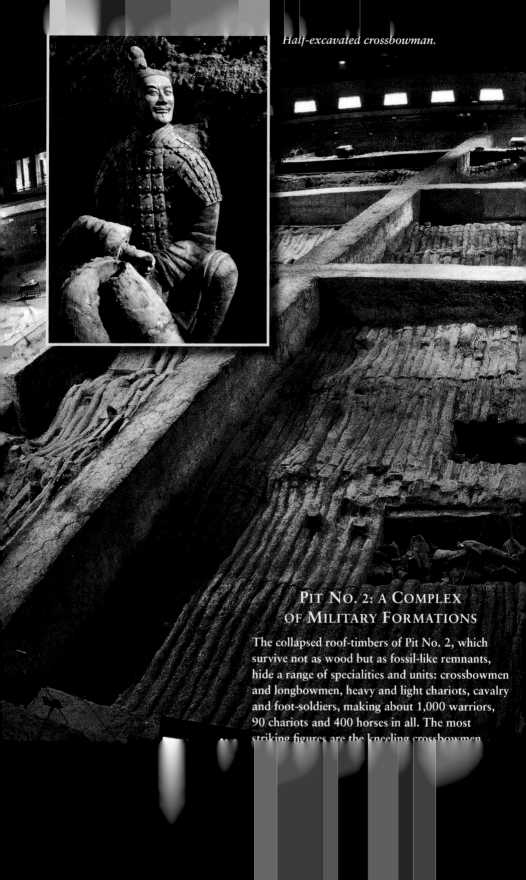

Half-excavated crossbowman.

PIT NO. 2: A COMPLEX OF MILITARY FORMATIONS

The collapsed roof-timbers of Pit No. 2, which survive not as wood but as fossil-like remnants, hide a range of specialities and units: crossbowmen and longbowmen, heavy and light chariots, cavalry and foot-soldiers, making about 1,000 warriors, 90 chariots and 400 horses in all. The most striking figures are the kneeling crossbowmen.

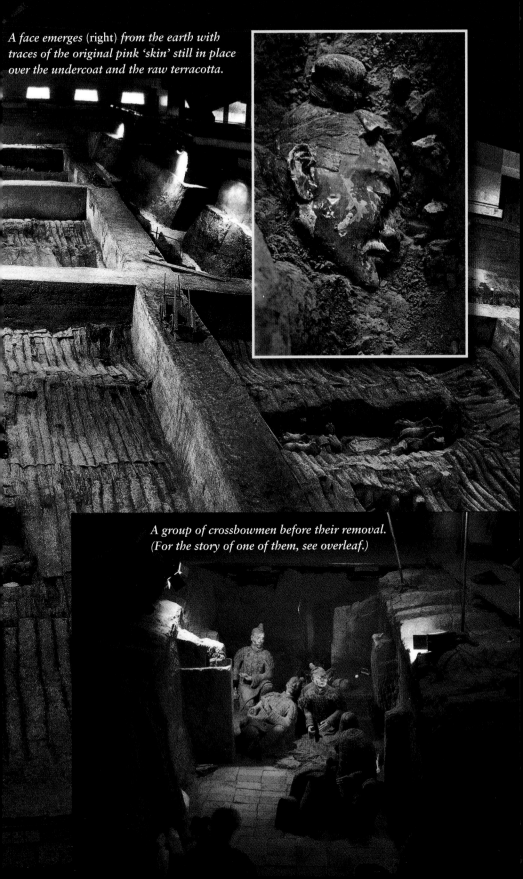

A face emerges (right) *from the earth with traces of the original pink 'skin' still in place over the undercoat and the raw terracotta.*

A group of crossbowmen before their removal. (For the story of one of them, see overleaf.)

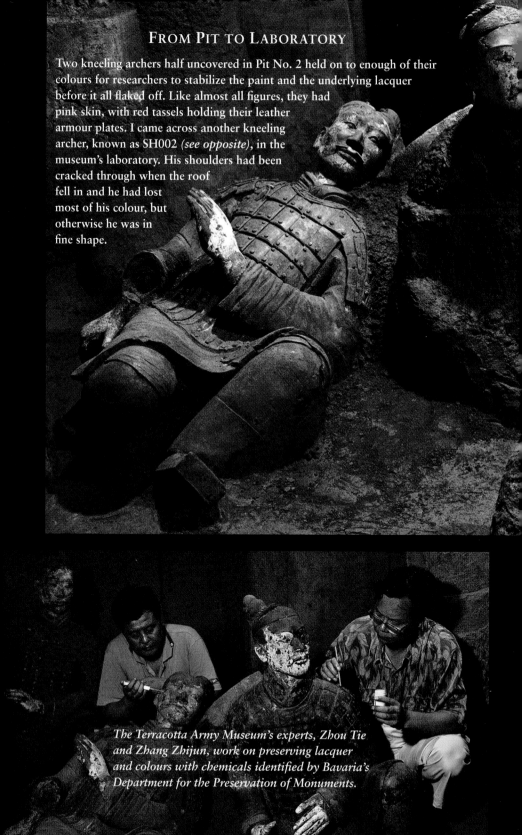

FROM PIT TO LABORATORY

Two kneeling archers half uncovered in Pit No. 2 held on to enough of their colours for researchers to stabilize the paint and the underlying lacquer before it all flaked off. Like almost all figures, they had pink skin, with red tassels holding their leather armour plates. I came across another kneeling archer, known as SH002 *(see opposite)*, in the museum's laboratory. His shoulders had been cracked through when the roof fell in and he had lost most of his colour, but otherwise he was in fine shape.

The Terracotta Army Museum's experts, Zhou Tie and Zhang Zhijun, work on preserving lacquer and colours with chemicals identified by Bavaria's Department for the Preservation of Monuments.

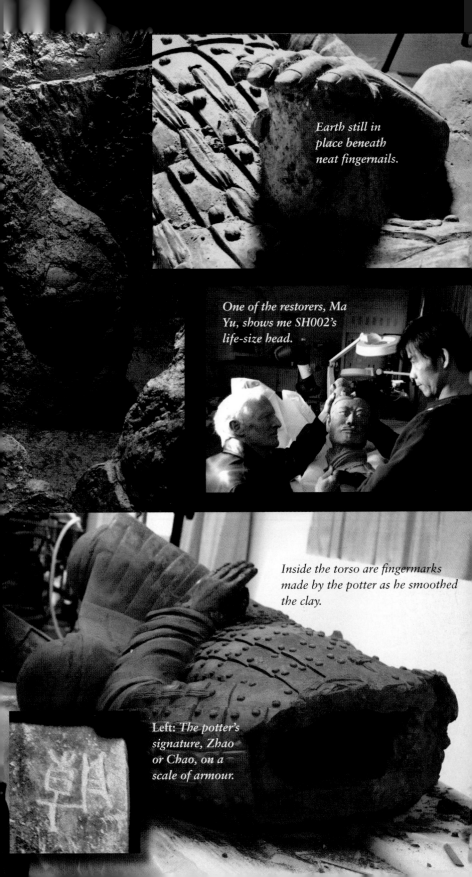

Earth still in place beneath neat fingernails.

One of the restorers, Ma Yu, shows me SH002's life-size head.

Inside the torso are fingermarks made by the potter as he smoothed the clay.

Left: The potter's signature, Zhao or Chao, on a scale of armour.

A GENERAL, VIRTUALLY RESTORED

As the result of collaboration between the museum and German specialists, computer software can re-paint one of the most famous warriors, a general unearthed from Pit No. 2. Though the colours themselves are well understood, their significance is not. Possibly the expensive 'Chinese purple' of the coat indicates high status, but what of the green tassels and red trimmings? And what of other details like the crossed hands and the raised index finger?

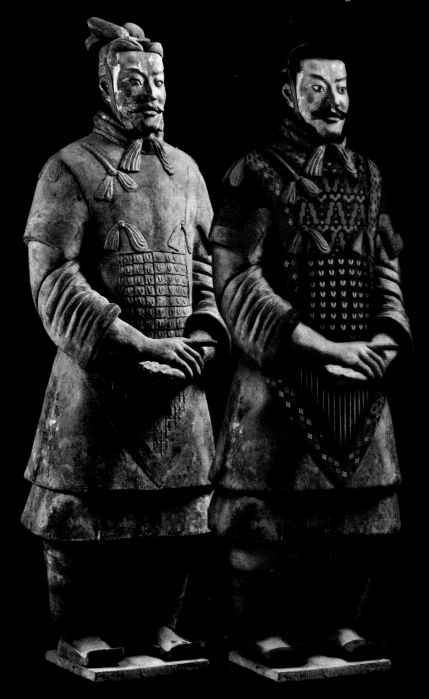

an idea Sima Qian could tap into in order to discredit the First Emperor. Many scholars agree that this was less total destruction than an attempt to impose a state monopoly on certain subjects.

Derk Bodde, my main source for this analysis, even finds a silver lining to this cloud: the fact that books were destroyed made the Chinese inordinately conscious of their heritage. 'The result has been the development of what may almost be called a cult of books in China, and a tremendous reinforcement of the interest, already strong, of the historically-minded Chinese in their historical records . . . Thus did Li Si's aim defeat itself!'

Anyway, the destruction was nothing compared to that unleashed when the dynasty fell, or to the gradual loss of material later as century succeeded century: Bodde points out that of 677 works listed in the Han imperial library – the first Chinese bibliography – 524, or 77 per cent, vanished not by wilful destruction but simply through carelessness and decay.

And what of the punishments? Sima Qian does not say; there is no evidence that anyone was actually executed for the possession of banned books. That raises a point about the harshness of Qin law. It was indeed severe in principle, but how was it applied in practice? Until recently, no one could say, because neither the laws themselves nor the sentences were known; all that survived were adverse comments by later writers. But in 1975 workers digging a drainage canal in central Hubei province discovered some graves, one of which was that of a Qin official named Xi who was buried in about 217 BC. It contained 1,155 strips of bamboo – the standard material for writing on in those pre-paper times – half of which recorded Qin laws, court cases and punishments.[3] These show that justice could

---

[3] This analysis is based on Hulsewé's *Remnants of Qin Law*.

indeed be harsh, with death sentences that included beheading, being torn apart by carriages, boiling to death in a cauldron and quartering, and lesser sentences like banishment and mutilation (amputations of the nose and of one or both feet, removal of kneecaps), which might or might not be combined with hard labour (especially wall-building). In 1973 nine neck-irons were unearthed near the emperor's tomb; these were used to fetter prisoners who had served their gaol terms, during a three-year stint of forced labour on public works.[4] Castration seems to have been reserved for the privileged, which was lucky for the underprivileged.

It sounds grim. But perhaps it was not *that* grim. The actual case records show that in practice Qin law was rather more lenient than its code suggests. Investigations were meticulous. A report on a man found murdered by the roadside describes the exact location, the wounds, the clothing, and the shoes found at some distance from the body. Investigators were told to exercise patience with suspects, and avoid torture, which produced inferior evidence. Those convicted could ask for a retrial. Officials had to consider precedents that modified the written law. A distinction was made between manslaughter (punished by a heavy fine) and murder, for which the killer unsheathed a weapon (long-term forced labour, please note, not execution).

In general, the laws reveal a complexity and sophistication rather at odds with Qin's reputation for barbarism. It was not so much the laws that oppressed as their abuse, as the First Emperor's demands drove the Qin economy into crisis.

Xianyang was now a capital of unprecedented wealth, with grand Qin-style houses for the newly tamed aristocracy and

[4] Ledderose and Schlombs, *Jenseits der Grossen Mauer*, pp. 212–13.

others in the styles of the conquered territories. But it had
not been conceived to be this size. And the original palace on
its platform overlooking the flood plain of the Wei was not
really impressive enough for the emperor of all China. 'In
view of the large population of Xianyang,' writes Sima
Qian, 'the palace of the former kings of Qin was too small.'

Nor was it in quite the right place. The First Emperor
looked south and east, across the Wei, towards present-day
Xian. He had good reason to do so. Xian was well supplied
with little rivers, but was not hemmed in by large ones; it
had a big river (the Wei) to the north and mountains to the
south, which meant that from the point of view of
geomancy, it had good *feng shui*. In addition, it was within
easy reach of the burial grounds of the First Emperor's
immediate ancestors. In 212 BC he gave the order to start
work on an immense new project, his palace in Epang.
Already, as we shall see in more detail in chapter 8, an army
of labourers were working on the tomb in Lintong.
Together, says Sima Qian, the workforce totalled 700,000,
all criminals – 'persons condemned to castration and convict
labourers' – a figure that is surely inflated tenfold or more.

Xianyang, Epang, Xian, Lintong: these four places are
linked by roads which swoop between them as if traversing
the base of a bowl some 70 kilometres across. Given the
phenomenal rise in tourism to Xian and the Terracotta
Army, and given that airborne visitors land at Xianyang air-
port, all four will eventually be linked by a light railway. To
the First Emperor this would have seemed right and proper.

We will be returning to the tomb and its army many times
in the following pages, but first let me take you in the
opposite direction: to Epang, the site of the emperor's new
palace on the western outskirts of Xian. It's a little hard to
find, partly because there is so much disagreement on how
to pronounce it. Locals say 'Er-pang', but in E-pang the first

character (阿) may also be pronounced 'ah', and the second one is a rare sign that looks like *fang* (房 / house), so that's what outsiders say and what many maps record. Epang, Er-pang, Ah-fang, even O-pang, if you follow the old Wade–Giles version – it's very confusing, especially as no one seems sure what it means either. Some claim it means 'Next to', i.e. next to Xianyang. I have even been told that the emperor had a concubine called Epang, and this was a palace dedicated to her. Best to avoid speculation: it's the name of the place and the palace, period.

Epang was intended to dwarf the First Emperor's Xianyang palace: some 690 metres long and 115 metres wide, according to Sima Qian.[5] Could this be true? At 79,000 square metres, it would have been larger than the modern world's most extreme expression of megalomania, Nicolae Ceauşescu's Palace of the People. Above a ground floor with 11-metre ceilings, its upper hall was to seat 10,000 people. Apparently, work was started on this immense project. Stone was quarried from the northern hills, timber brought from the south, and 'an elevated walk' built across the river Wei to Xianyang, some 25 kilometres away.

There is a site marked on some maps, so I could check on the First Emperor's ambitions. We – my driver Wang, Tony and I – turned down side-roads in the suburbs of western Xian, and pulled up by something that looked promising: a huge structure of pyramidal stone bases topped by wooden towers with austere roofs in the Qin style, lacking the usual upturned eaves. It called itself the Epang Palace. Well, not exactly. It was built in 1984, and it doesn't face south, as a palace should, because it has to welcome the tourist cars and

[5] 500 *bu* long (1 *bu* = 1.38 metres) × 50 *zhang* wide (1 *zhang* = 2.31 metres), according to Loewe, *Records of Han Administration*.

buses that come along the road to the north. It is guarded by twelve statues recalling the 30- (or 50-, or 60-) tonne ones supposedly made from the weapons of Qin's conquered states, and by two mythical animals that embody fierceness, each with the head of a lion, an eagle's claws, a wolf's body and a tiger's tail. Inside is an amphitheatre, and a giant stairway to a hall where an actor playing the First Emperor is regaled by dancing girls. It is not too surprising to learn that the place was built as a film set, and features in practically every film and docudrama about the First Emperor, except Chen Kaige's.

Its only claim to authenticity is that it stands opposite the site of the original Epang Palace, which at first glance was far less inviting, being a cross between a rubbish tip and a ploughed field. Still, we could drive in, because the mess was crossed by 200 metres of new road, the first step in some grand new plan yet to be realized.

We knew we were in the right place because, beside a sad collection of bushes that served as a visitors' toilet, a stele – an engraved stone pillar – laid claim to forgotten grandeur: 'This is one of the most famous traditional complexes in China,' it began, 'the location of the first political centre in Chinese history.' Moreover, it continued, archaeological research suggests it was even bigger than Sima Qian claimed: 1,270 metres from east to west and 426 metres from north to south, which means – the stele concluded – that 'the front hall of the Epang Palace was the largest basement to survive in China, if not the world'. You could hardly find a greater contrast between the grandness of the claim and the poverty of the site.

Where the palace itself had stood was unclear at first. It was only the fact that something was being planned here that drew me on, past a dip that was going to be a lake, and an unfinished basketball court. Beyond was a steep bank of earth about 3 metres high, topped by orchards. That was it: it had to be, because, as we climbed the bank, we emerged on to a plateau. This was a platform, which, like old Xianyang, was an ideal base for a palace, with a fine view southward. A glance east and west showed it was at least a kilometre long, as the stele said. Imagination turned the earth platform and fruit trees into a palace under construction: a line of arches below, a great assembly hall above, several hundred thousand workers landscaping and laying foundations.

But that was about as far as things got, because two years later the First Emperor died and work ground to a halt. It was supposedly finished by his heir, and then burned to the ground in the revolution that threw out the Qin. Sima Qian says the flames lasted for three months.

But here's a strange thing: when archaeologists probed the site in the autumn of 2002,[6] they found no trace of fire. 'We found burned red soil and traces of ashes during our excavation of the Xianyang Palace, but we've found nothing of the kind at the site of the Epang Palace,' the team leader Li Yufang told the Beijing-based *Guangming Daily*. They didn't find much else, either. 'We found tiles of the Qin Dynasty,' she said, 'but not a single piece of eaves tile, which was the most common part of buildings of the period.' Floor-tiles, no roof-tiles, no ashes, no fire-hardened earth: it all suggests that the palace was started, but never completed.

Tony and I wandered round among the fruit trees. A hundred metres away was a long plastic polytunnel that might have been covering an archaeological dig, but was in fact shielding vegetables. An old farm worker dozed in the

---

[6] The team was from the Institute of Archaeology of the Chinese Academy of Social Sciences (CASS), in cooperation with the Xian Municipal Archaeological Research Institute.

shade of a peach tree in a reclining chair, soothed by a radio blaring – I could hardly believe it – Qin opera.

'Did you know that China invented ice-cream?' remarked Tony. 'Actually, it was the First Emperor. When the archaeologists were here, they found a hole that went down very deep and ended in a little room. It must have been an ice-well, which they filled with ice in the winter so the First Emperor could have ice all through the summer.'

It seemed a bit of a leap from hole to ice to ice-cream, but the find supported the general idea that this had been a dream-palace. What we were standing on was the foundation not just of the palace, but of a myth – that the Epang Palace was the hugest ever built, that it was not only the fount of political power but also the expression of unprecedented wealth. It has also been seen as an expression of egomania, a vast waste of national resources, and a symbol of oppression that inspired revolution and the end of a dynasty that was to have lasted 10,000 generations. Some of this was true: referring to the Second Emperor, who restarted work on the palace, Sima Qian quotes Li Si as saying, 'For the making of the Epang Palace, he has exacted taxes throughout the empire . . . without regard for the expenditure.' Plans and taxes never added up to a palace. It was not this unfinished enterprise that became the focus of discontent, but the tomb and its spirit army.

Yet with hindsight the idea of building such a structure with such a workforce suggests that the First Emperor was becoming somewhat divorced from reality – and not without reason. He was emperor by the grace of Heaven, yet he was surrounded by enemies, not just Confucians eager to turn back the clock, but also would-be assassins. The suspicions that must have dogged him ever since the Jing Ke episode were confirmed by an odd incident that had its roots in that affair.

On the conquest of Yan, the First Emperor had initiated a drive to uncover all those who had been part of the plot five years before. One of them, a certain Gao Jianli, went into hiding, changed his name and became a simple labourer. It happened that he was an accomplished lute-player, a talent that came to the attention of his master. Eventually, his fame spread to court, and he was invited to play before the emperor. A mistake. Someone recognized him, and he would have been put to death, had not the emperor admired his talent. So he got off lightly: his eyes were put out, and he was kept on as a court musician. Gao, though, wanted revenge (more than ever, I should imagine, having been blinded), and dreamed up a plot almost as remarkable as that of Jing Ke's: he fixed a piece of lead in his lute, and when next playing close to the emperor, he tried to club him to death. Not surprisingly, he missed. This time there was no reprieve: he was 'summarily executed, and after that the emperor never again permitted any of the former followers of the feudal lords to approach his person'.

Living increasingly in a world of his own, the First Emperor was encouraged by his 'magicians' to give more and more thought to their ideas about how to become an immortal. One of them told him they had looked every-where for the herbs that would make the Elixir of Immortality, but had so far failed because they were blocked by evil spirits. So the emperor had better take action.

The magic arts teach that the ruler of men should at times move about in secret to avoid evil spirits. If the evil spirits are avoided, one can reach the status of a True Man. If the whereabouts of the ruler of men are known to his ministers, this hinders his spiritual power . . . Do not let others know

where you are. Once that is done, I believe the herbs of
immortality can be obtained.

'I shall imitate the True Men,' promised the emperor.
Then, if Sima Qian is to be believed, he ordered that the
roads connecting Xianyang's 270 palaces should all be
walled and roofed. He would travel between them in secret,
and anyone who divulged his whereabouts would be
executed. One day, at a certain palace, he expressed concern
at the number of Li Si's carriages and horsemen. Soon afterwards, Li Si cut his entourage. Obviously, said the emperor,
someone had passed on his opinion without his permission,
which he interpreted as treachery. Of those who had been
with him, no one owned up, and in a rage the emperor had
them all killed. 'From this time onward, whenever he moved
about, no one knew where he was.'

There soon came a time when even his two top
'magicians' could no longer stand the emperor's erratic and
despotic behaviour. Telling each other that he had become
remote, brutal and surrounded by flatterers, they fled. In a
fury, the emperor turned upon his officials, or intellectuals, or
'scholars' as they are usually called, and subjected them to
'investigation'. Accused of violating 'prohibitions', they
accused each other, as the accused often do when interrogated
by secret police, and 'over 460' of them were . . . what?

There follows a much disputed word, *kēng* (坑 as it is
today), which is sometimes translated as 'executed' but is
traditionally rendered as 'buried alive'. That is certainly one
meaning in modern dictionaries. Given that the word also
means 'a pit', it seems more than possible. But the sign has
changed, and possibly the modern meaning merely reflects
tradition. There is a vagueness here that plants doubts: '*over*
460' scholars and unnamed 'prohibitions'. And 'burial alive'
does not appear as a form of execution on the bamboo strips

in Xi's grave; nor are there any other recorded examples. Whatever the fate of the scholars, there was nothing furtive about it. The emperor 'made this act known throughout the empire as a warning'. Would a Legalist emperor, even a furious and unbalanced one, have resorted to such well-publicized brutality? Many modern scholars doubt it. As Burton Watson remarks, 'buried alive' is the translation preferred by 'commentators anxious to emphasise the satanic nature of the First Emperor'.

There remained one vital task to complete the confirmation of the new era. The First Emperor had to assert his rule not simply in Qin (he had done that already) but over the whole empire. This he did between 219 and 211 BC with ritual tours of inspection during which he set his mark on seven sacred mountains – acts that were the political equivalents of a lion marking his territory. The marks were made in a totally original way: by placing on each mountain stone pillars, or stelae, engraved with poetic statements singing his praise.

He seems to have got the idea by combining two traditions. Previous kings had toured their territories, and had commissioned commemorative inscriptions on bronze cauldrons, on 'stone drums', and in a couple of cases on stones. But there had never been anything on this scale. The mountains honoured by the First Emperor include one in the far north near Beijing, three others down the east coast, and a fourth 200 kilometres from the coast in the far south. Nothing could have been more explicit. All emphasize conquest, the foundation of the new empire, the arrival of a new social order.

Previous rulers wishing to make political statements with a spiritual dimension had made sacrifices. These were known as '*feng* and *shan* rituals'. Sima Qian devotes a long chapter to the subject. These hugely significant rites were performed from the earliest times, at least 2,200 BC. Unfortunately, rulers had to qualify to perform them: 'When each dynasty attains the height of its glory, then the *feng* and *shan* are celebrated, but when it reaches a period of decline, they are no longer performed.' So there had been long gaps of hundreds of years, or even 'as many as a thousand', between enactments of these rites, with the result that 'the details of the ancient ceremony have been completely lost'. Confucius himself said he had heard that over 70 rulers had performed the sacrifices, but 'it was impossible to say much about them'. By Qin times no one had a clue. It was as if Christians knew they should be taking communion, but had forgotten about the bread and wine.

Never mind. Something had to be done to mark the momentous nature of the First Emperor's achievement; so when he and his entourage arrived at the most sacred mountain – Mount Tai in Shandong province – he summoned 70 scholars and demanded rituals. (As an aside, note that these were experts in history and ritual, Confucians not Legalists, who had obviously not been buried alive: the First Emperor needed such scholars to help him assert legitimacy. What he didn't need was outright opposition.) They ummed and aahed and argued, until he lost patience, dismissed them all and decided on his own private ritual, namely the placing of engraved stelae, followed by an announcement that he had succeeded in performing the sacrifices. Obviously, he hadn't. But no one was to know that. 'The directions for the ritual were sealed and stored away, being kept strictly secret.' Thus was an ancient tradition revived in theory, if not in practice.

There were other, lesser, sacrifices as well – to mountains, rivers, springs, the Eight Spirits – but the engravings were what mattered. In the words of one scholar, it was the stelae that 'completed his conquest by inscribing the reality of his power, in the newly created imperial script, into the sacred landscape of his new subjects'.[7] The stones themselves have long vanished, but six of the seven inscriptions were recorded by Sima Qian, and all were copied several times in manuscript or rubbings.

This was history as the First Emperor wanted it: Qin history, without the competition, and with him spotlit in glorious perfection. The stelae were the equivalent of posters and newspaper headlines in modern dictatorships, the cult of personality at its most extreme, rivalled only by a select few: Stalin, Mao, Kim Jong-Il. Like them he claimed to bring the blessings of strong rule: wisdom, peace, the rule of law, the elimination of evil, the promotion of virtue, and care for the reverential and obedient common people.

Here is the sort of thing his fawning officials wrote for him, in rhyming lines of four signs each:

> They [his officials] record and contemplate the times of
> chaos:
> When they apportioned the land, established discrete
> states,
> And thus unfolded the impetus for struggle.
> Attacks and campaigns were daily waged;
> How they shed their blood in the open countryside.
> *(Inscription on Mount Yi; trans. Martin Kern)*

That was then. How much better things were now:

In his twenty-sixth year
He first unified All under Heaven –

---

[7] Lewis, *Writing and Authority in Early China*.

There was none who was not respectful and submissive.
He personally tours to the distant multitudes,
Ascends this Great Mountain
And all around surveys the eastern extremity.
The attending officials meditate upon his feats,
Trace the roots and origins of His deeds and achievements
And respectfully recite His merits and virtuous power.
        (Inscription on Mount Tai; trans. Martin Kern)

Seven sacred mountains, seven pillars, seven grand statements about how wonderful the new regime was. The last, set in place in 211 BC on Mount Kuaiji, on the coast east of Hangzhou, declared 'His virtuous power and favour is permanent and lasting.'

Had he never heard of tempting Fate?

II

BEYOND THE GRAVE

7

THE WORLD TO COME

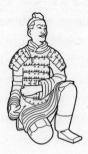

MEANWHILE, WHAT OF ZHENG'S TOMB? IT HAD BEEN A dominant focus of his attention right from the time of his accession at the age of thirteen. That was when work started, so Sima Qian tells us.

Nothing remains of the original conception, for reasons that will soon become clear, but you can get an idea of what it was for by considering the fundamentals – what the teenaged Prince Zheng and the twenty-something King Zheng believed, and how other kings planned their existence beyond death.

Here is a rough, brief guide to 3,000 years of Chinese belief and practice concerning the afterlife:

The dominant ideas in the remote past were that we have souls; that souls live for ever; and that we should make provision for them. But by the time of the First Emperor these ideas had evolved. Now it was believed that we have two souls: the 'spirit soul', which inspired thoughts, virtues and artistic abilities and which flew off to the land of the immortals at the moment of death; and the 'earth soul', which was at that point left behind, in some way attached to the corpse, to be buried with it. Both souls needed care and attention, so that the one could travel freely, and the other find peace rather than roam the earth, lost, restless and hungry.

We don't know much about the afterlife, but we assume a general principle: as below, so above. The spirit world was ruled like a Chinese kingdom, under the direction of the Yellow Emperor, one of the mythical five founder-emperors, with teams of messengers and powers and bureaucrats who kept tabs on the lives and deaths of individuals. In attendance were the spirits of ancestors, who were joined by the newly dead, forming a sort of community of the spirits. It was this belief in a 'spirit community' that injected into China a deep concern with the afterlife; a concern, an *obsession*, as powerful and as thoroughly human as that of almost any other culture you care to mention. No one except a few sceptical philosophers doubted that there was a hidden reality, the world of the dead, and that there were deep patterns connecting that world, with its various guides and entities – gods, forces, ancestral spirits – to this one. There was, however, much uncertainty about the nature of that connection, how to make contact with the spirit world, and how best to deal honourably with it or control it. In temples devoted to the ancestors, priests did their best with rituals, sacrifices and offerings, which would draw ancestral spirits down from the sphere of the highest god, Shang Di, as he or it was named. Oracles revealed the spirits' will to the living.

One thing everyone seemed to 'know' from time

immemorial – back at least to 3500 BC – was that the dead could use things in the next life that they had used in this. The dead, particularly its senior members, should therefore be properly housed in lavish tombs, protected either by huge mounds of earth or by rock into which the tombs were cut. With them were buried the things they would need in the afterlife. Naturally, the richer and more powerful the person, the more stuff they needed. Graves of the rich contained ceramic cups and vases, (later) bronze containers for food and wine – for the dead would need to conduct their own religious ceremonies – as well as bells, objects of jade and gold, parts of chariots, weaponry, and wonderfully weird creatures in bronze which were probably to ward off evil spirits. One fifth-century BC tomb was found to contain some 15,000 artefacts.

Traditionally, also, rulers and other aristocrats were given an entourage of servants, concubines and lesser relatives, who were either killed first or buried alive. Sima Qian mentions a certain Duke Mu who was buried in 621 BC with 177 of his staff; the sixth-century BC tomb of an early Qin duke contained 166 skeletons. In Qin, this grisly practice was largely suppressed in the fourth century BC, though it remained in occasional use for almost another 2,000 years, being formally abolished only in the fifteenth century AD.

All this was necessary, because it was the most realistic way of fulfilling the dead person's needs. It was realism that was the key (or at least had become the key by the time of the First Emperor) – realism, though, not quite in the western sense. Flesh-and-blood was not enough, because it decayed. Nor was function important. Real objects as used in this world were included; but often the objects would be made deliberately non-functional – carriages without their fittings, earthenware made too thin for use. Size was not significant either. What was crucial was a certain sense of detail. So real people – and animals – were replaced by small figures in wood, clay, bronze, stone and jade; and real sacrificial vessels in bronze were increasingly replaced by 'fake' ones in pottery, so-called 'spirit vessels', which did not even have to be baked hard. They were, in a sense, toys. In the words of the German scholar of Chinese art Lothar Ledderose, 'The tomb represents, idealizes and perpetuates the reality of life on earth.'

The toy artefacts, together with a rich array of everyday and ritual objects, provided the elements from which spirits were expected to recreate the living world. As Jessica Rawson, the Warden of Merton College, Oxford, and a noted scholar in Chinese art and archaeology, puts it, 'If an image was convincing, that is, if it had the correct features, then these features gave the image the powers of the thing or person depicted.' In some sense, once in the grave, the image became the thing itself: the statue of a servant was a servant. The aim was to provide the means to recreate life in all its essentials, complete with music, banquets, entertainments, hunting and fighting. If the grave was a place of solemnity, it was also a place for fun. In addition, grave-builders aimed to provide a cosmic setting, with images of the two spirit worlds, above and below; the sun, moon and constellations; and the animals associated with all of them. In brief, as Jessica Rawson says, 'Each tomb was an entire universe centred on its occupant.'

How could one ensure that one's souls did not simply dissipate, and that one could therefore remain in this hidden world? Answer: only by becoming an immortal.

The idea that immortality could be achieved seems to have arisen slowly from the idea of longevity, the commonest term in the most ancient prayers for blessings. Since we age slowly, some more slowly than others, it did not strike Daoist philosophers as impossible that the process could be made slower still, indeed extended indefinitely. In the words of an old saying, 'The sage evolves but undergoes no sudden change.' By the time of the First Emperor, it was widely believed that there were men who had freed themselves from mortality, and would live for ever. How to achieve this was the subject of countless musings. Objects and places 'of Immortality' were commonplace. In the words of Joseph Needham, 'a mountain, a country, a land, a wilderness, a river, a people, a tree, a herb, a drug – all were very attractive, if only one could get there, or find the medicine'. All might enable one to become a *xiān* (仙), an immortal. Poets wrote of the lives of the holy immortals, those who had 'departed from the flux of change and vanished from the sight of men', as one said, before describing how he himself learned to journey through earth and heaven until he merged with the universal spirit. Would-be immortals could aim to join one of two groups: those who remained on earth and those who roamed the heavens, with clouds as their vehicles and rainbows for canopies.

As always when belief combines with wishful thinking, no amount of experience undermined faith. Han Fei tells the story of a certain philosopher who taught the Prince of Yan something of the art of immortality. The prince sent off some men to study with the philosopher, who unfortunately died before they could complete their studies. The prince scolded the students for their slowness, rather than drawing the conclusion that a philosopher who died was hardly qualified to teach deathlessness.

For ordinary people, aiming for immortality required long-term commitment to demanding practices. But emperors had no time for all that. What they wanted was a quick fix: rituals that would persuade the gods and immortals to bestow deathlessness, and/or an elixir of immortality.

The taking of elixirs was a dangerous business, justified only by the supposed rewards. To experiment not only with gold and mercury – the favourites – but also with arsenic, lead, copper and tin was to poison oneself. Here, too, experience was no match for optimism. To quote a sixth-century text that ticks off an array of metal-poisoning symptoms:

> After taking an elixir, if your face and body itch as though insects were crawling over them, if your hands and feet swell dropsically, if you cannot stand the smell of food and bring it up after you have eaten it, if you feel as though you were going to be sick most of the time, if you experience weakness in your four limbs, if you have to go often to the latrine, or if your head or stomach violently ache – do not be alarmed or disturbed. All these effects are merely proofs that the elixir you are taking is successfully dispelling your latent disorders.

The theory behind these practices, wildly eccentric though they sound to outsiders (and sounded back then to Confucians), was mainstream among Daoists for centuries. The elixirs were supposed to somehow rarefy or aetherialize the body (an idea that may have derived from the trance-inducing 'magic mushroom' potions taken by Siberian shamans and ancient Indian mystics), the purpose being to generate a new self that was immortal though still physical. Adepts took elixirs during life to prevent decay after death. Indeed, arsenic has precisely this effect, presumably because it poisons not only the victim but also the bacteria that cause decay. Death thus becomes a doorway to immortality. The corpse of the successful adept would remain incorruptible, and emerge like a butterfly from a chrysalis to dwell with the immortals. This (it was believed) was hard to achieve, but possible; certainly it was possible to take a few steps in the right direction. Japanese monks of the Shingon sect make themselves into 'self-mummified Buddhas' by avoiding cereals and eating only chestnuts, pine-tree bark or grass roots. Then, after death, as Needham says, incorruptibility can be seen as proof of coming immortality.

Now, a few paragraphs cannot possibly do justice to such ancient and complex beliefs. This was not a coherent system, any more than Christianity is wholly coherent (as anyone knows who has tried to come to grips with the Trinity, the Resurrection or the way communion wine is supposed to turn to blood). Contending philosophies and religions – Confucianism and the various mystical strands of Daoism – made conflicting claims. Sages struggled to make sense of it all by exploring patterns of cyclical change, by linking the seasons with bodily organs, by applying complex astronomical and calendrical systems, by imposing concepts of alternating Yin and Yang forces, and by using divination, notably the *Yi Jing* (*I Ching*). How this world interacted with the next was a matter of much dispute. Some rivers were seen as spirits, and so were some mountains. Here one could get direct access to the spirit world – hence the First Emperor's mountain-climbing tours and the shape of his tomb and those of his immediate ancestors: they were artificial mountains where the spirits would feel at home. Either the dead person's soul would visit spirits in their own realm, or the spirits would visit the tomb, or both.

One thing even a thirteen-year-old would have known: as king, he would need a tomb suitable for his status. It may seem strange that a new young ruler should be so keen on preparing for the world to come, but he would have believed that the very process of building a 'living tomb' conferred longevity. This was to be an ongoing project right up until death dictated its end. Lü Buwei, father-figure and chancellor, would surely have advised His youthful Majesty that, life being uncertain and death certain, it would be best not to delay, especially as it would have been obvious where the tomb should be.

Back then, before the growth of Xian and the coming of industrial haze, the young Prince Zheng could have stood on his private veranda on the third floor of Xianyang Palace and seen a dim line of hills fringing the southern and eastern horizons. This was Qin's old frontier, beyond which lay mountain barbarians and the hostile kingdom of Chu. One of the mountains, Mount Li, had particular significance, because it was there that Lao Zi, the founder of Daoism, had lived and taught in the sixth century BC. So people say. They also say that he met Confucius here. Maybe it is true, maybe not. Who can tell?

Even after all this time, and even though you will take the cable-car and climb the new cement stairs to the summit, old ways and spirituality linger in the air, inclining you to believe. Li Shan, which means Black Horse Mountain because that's what they say it looks like from a distance, is protected, revered even, as a notice suggests in two quirky, poetic phrases: 'Caress Mt. Li, breath green.'

People had cause to remember the mountain from long before Lao Zi's day. Tony told a story as we climbed the nice new steps through fir trees, part of the Green Great Wall of forests planted all across north China to control the sand-storms that sweep in from the Gobi. It is the local equivalent of 'The Boy Who Cried "Wolf"'.

The Smile That Cost a Kingdom

This happened long, long ago [the eighth century BC, if it happened at all], when Qin was young and threatened by southern barbarians called Quan Rong. For this reason, there was a beacon fire on the top of Mount Li that was lit when the barbarians approached. The king had a beautiful concubine whom he loved very much, but he was unhappy because she always had a long face and never smiled. So he said, 'Anyone who makes her smile will be rewarded with a thousand gold pieces.' A certain official said, 'Your Majesty, you could make her laugh by playing a joke. Light the beacon fire and your feudal lords will come running to defend you. Then you can tell them you fooled them, and send them home.' The king thought this was a great idea. The fire was lit, the lords came running, the king had his joke at their expense, they complained bitterly – and the lady smiled, and the official got his 1,000 gold pieces. But (of course) later there was a real attack, the beacon blazed a warning, and the feudal lords said 'Oh, another joke!' and stayed put. The lady was captured, the king killed and the dynasty fell. Moral: don't let your heart rule your head.

I had been hoping for a view of the First Emperor's tomb, but we were in clouds. Beyond the beacon tower – no, not the original, but a newish one occupied by fire prevention officers – the forested hills rolled away into mist. From the invisible town of Lintong below came the sound of traffic and the distant crackle of fireworks celebrating a wedding. Below I could see, through trees, upturned eaves and a courtyard – a Daoist temple, which, I hoped, would recall the days when Lao Zi walked here.

On the way down, at a bend in the track, an old man in a blue jacket and track shoes sat on a folding stool, looking at me through vast spectacles. He beckoned. 'I can see you are good at solving problems!'

'How do you know that?'

'I am an expert in the *Yi Jing*!'

Once a schoolmaster, he was now a fortune-teller, with the

tools of his profession on the ground before him: a sheet of paper, strips of inscribed wood. 'Come, it will only cost ten yuan, but do not pay me yet. You sit here, on my left, because you are male. Now, your left hand.'

He began a long monologue, speaking with absolute conviction for 20 minutes. This is the condensed version: 'Oh, a ring on your middle finger, so you have many ideas . . . this finger is longer than usual, so your brain is a computer, and if this little finger is long' – he measured it with a little plastic ruler – 'oh, yes, it is; so you will live longer than ninety-three years. The second finger is shorter, so you are a little bit obstinate. The thumb is long, so you will be rich. Your ears go backwards, so you have power, and you are pink, so you don't worry. Now I have to give advice.' He became serious, a Chinese Polonius. 'Insist on your principles. Do not lend money, and don't borrow too much either. Buddha will protect you, and you will lack accidents while travelling. There, that is your life. Why do I not ask for payment in advance? Because then I would tell you only good things! I suggest you pay fifteen yuan.'

I gave him 20 (£1.35), because it looked as if I was going to be his only client for many hours.

'Why do you sit up here, when there are more people down below?'

'Up here is better. It is easier to see the truth. The higher you are, the better the view.'

That, I supposed, was why a temple had been built here, 668 steps below the fortune-teller (I know this because Tony and I bet on the number, and I counted). Not this precise temple, which is pristine – a plaque states that rebuilding finished in 2001 – but the original, which supposedly marked the birth-site of the legendary Grandmother who made humans out of mud from Mount Li's yellow soil.

Steps led up to a temple of grey bricks, in which stood

three statues of fierce warrior-protectors. Through a soft drift of incense, I wandered out into a paved yard and across into another temple, this one of blue-patterned beams, red pillars and pink tiles. Three goddesses presided inside, wearing expressions of beatific calm. A gentle bell turned my attention to one side, where a woman attending a postcard stand had just struck a bowl with three holes in it. She was dressed in a blue jacket, padded blue trousers, white gaiters and black shoes. 'A nun,' whispered Tony. 'Blue, black, white: the colours of Daoism. Look, here is another.' The two muttered together for a moment, until I approached to speak to them. The first turned away shyly, but the second, a sturdy figure with confident brown eyes and her hair in a chignon, was content to talk. Content was the word. She exuded peace, calm and timeless contentment, perhaps because she was not at all concerned with time. 'I have no age,' she said when I asked. 'We have no concern for age.'

There were about 20 living in the temple at present, she said, but they came and went, for everywhere and anywhere could be their home. Their purpose was to understand the pains of the world through study. No, there was no teacher. They had their books, and studied any time, any place. The only guidance they needed was Buddha.

I asked about the goddesses. 'They are immortals, ancestors of humans, who make our lives happy. We show them respect, for all immortals know our thoughts. If you have evil thoughts, they will know and punish you. We should trust them, for if you really trust, they will help.'

To recreate the earlier mood, I wanted to hear the sound of the bell-bowl again.

'If you wish to hear, you should pay your respects to the Grandmother. She is in charge of longevity.' She nodded to the central figure. 'Go to her, hold your hands in prayer, kneel and bow three times.'

So I did. And, as the bell-bowl softly rang three times, one for each bow, and the incense drifted up around the Grandmother's face, I lost myself in a moment of peace, then returned to the nun and thanked her. I'm not sure why. For a brief glimpse of tranquillity, I suppose.

'You will have a longer life,' she said. 'Because this religion is about longevity. Of all religions, it is this that makes it perhaps the most practical.'

It sounded good. Maybe learning more about Daoism would help me in my work, give me some sense of why the First Emperor chose the site below for his tomb.

'I am very certain he was here, because here was a temple to the Grandmother of all humans. She would have been like his own Grandmother. He must have decided that this, of all places, was the place to ensure safety in the afterlife.'

I asked if she minded if I took her picture, to help me remember her. She waved a finger to say no. 'We have no interest. You must keep these things in your heart.'

I lacked practice in using my heart to remember things, so outside the temple I turned to take a picture through the doorway, only to find that the camera would not stay switched on. It was old for a digital camera, and had developed some odd little quirks, but I found it strangely coincidental that it had chosen this moment to give up the ghost. So I have no goddesses to print out, no Grandmother, no nuns, only scattered images that drift like incense between heart and mind.

As we walked back down to the cable-car, the mood lightened. Tony recalled Daoism's roots in a combination of mysticism, folklore, extreme physical techniques and alchemical experiments to discover elixirs of immortality. 'Did you know that gunpowder was invented by Daoists trying to find medicines to extend life?'

We agreed that life is full of little ironies. You try to take forbidden pictures and your camera breaks. You try to live longer, and blow yourself up instead. Somewhere below, in the industrial haze that clouded Lintong, an emperor had sought immortality by burial, and was achieving it by un-burial.

So King Zheng needed a tomb, and here was an excellent spot, because that was what his ancestors had thought. Niu Xinlong, a young archaeologist from the Terracotta Army Museum, was eager to show Qin's ancestral burial ground to me, Tony and Tony's boss, Stephanie, who packed a great deal of intelligence, curiosity and dynamism into a very small space.

If you drive west out of Lintong, then turn north under the new expressway to the Terracotta Army, after about 5 kilometres a small concrete road leads uphill to the left. This is farm country of deep earth, terraced fields and orchards. The road turns to a track. Where the slope flattens out, the track slices through the top of a hill in a 100-metre cut.

Except, as Mr Niu pointed out, it is not a hill but a Qin tomb. No one knew this until 1986, long after the road had been cut straight through it, and an orchard planted on it, and a house built on its flank.

Did anyone know whose it was?

'We think so. Sima Qian says the First Emperor's ancestors were buried here. That was why we came looking. When we found these two fish-backs, as we call them' – he indicated this tomb-mound and a next-door one I hadn't noticed – 'they didn't look natural. This one has passageways, which give it the shape of *zhong* [中 / 'middle'; the sign that is the first element in the Chinese for China, Zhongguo, Middle Kingdom], so we think it belongs to the First Emperor's grandfather.'

It is still unopened and its contents unknown, but by drilling down from the surface and recording how the soil changed, archaeologists have mapped the tomb. It is like an upside-down pyramid with a flat floor and four entrance ramps. Not that outsiders get a hint of this at first glance. To my eyes it looked just like a normal hill, so Mr Niu was at pains to show how, if you get up close to the earth at the side of the cutting, you can tell the difference by the cracks. If it's rammed earth, and therefore artificial, the cracks are horizontal; if ordinary undisturbed earth, then they're vertical. Yes, I could see. The cutting had allowed us to stroll right to the top of the southern edge of the First Emperor's granddaddy's grave.

You can make tombs like this – deep holes, with big mounds – because this rich, reddish earth, typical of the farmland all over northern China, is so deep.

How deep? I was about to learn. For there were other tomb-mounds in the area – a couple of other Qin ones, and several built later under the Han dynasty. Mr Niu directed Wang to drive up a side-track, past a lone house, to a set of handkerchief-sized fields a couple of hundred metres beyond, and pointed to a steep-sided mound.

Our presence attracted a farmer, a fit and voluble 60-year-old in a flat hat and many shirts. It was his house, his land, and we were welcome. The mound? Of course. He would show us. We struggled over an apricot orchard and soft fields of winter wheat, until he could point to a hole at the base of the mound. 'A few years ago someone came and blew this up, thinking they would rob the grave. Then archaeologists came and drilled down seventeen or eighteen metres, and they didn't find anything either, no bottom, no treasure. People started to come almost every year to dig, so we volunteered to protect it.'

As he talked we had climbed the mound, from the top of

which there was a good view over orchards to his house. It looked remarkably nice for a farmer's house. Instantly, he invited us to visit, to see how he lived with his family: his burly wife, his thirtyish son and his beautiful three-year-old granddaughter.

But it was not so much the house that attracted attention as what was beside it. The ground rose steeply, and into the slope was cut a square, brick-lined arch, which led into a tunnel, with light at the end. Following the farmer, I found myself in a huge pit, a good 8 metres high, with sheer sides. Into the sides had been cut three semi-circular arches, each with a door and a window. This was where the family had lived before they had the house – a little village of caves dug from the deep, red earth. A pig snuffled at one end of the pit, beside another cave that was both a sty and a barn.

I stood, astonished, by the labour involved, by the novelty (to me) of the sight, and also by its charm. It was like being held in a loving embrace, and an ageless one.

'Even my father could not remember how many generations ago we made this,' he said. 'It was seven or eight at least' – which took its creation back a good 200 years. Proudly, he showed us inside one of the little dwellings. It was like walking into a huge store-cupboard with air-conditioning, its temperature stabilized by the mass of the surrounding earth. The ceiling was carefully smoothed clay. There was a table, a couple of chairs and a sleeping platform, with room for a stove underneath, big enough to keep a whole family snug in cold weather, all lit by a couple of bare electric bulbs. 'It's warm in winter, cool in summer, which is why we still use it. And it has an upstairs, too,' he said, pointing to a back room, with a ladder climbing into darkness.

And, moreover, there was another crater-village

immediately next door. Not long ago, this had been a whole community.

'Are there many families who still live like this?'

'Some. But most have moved into houses.'

He seemed to feel some nostalgia for the old days, and I'm not surprised, given the sad story that came out as we went around the new house. Large, with echoing tiled rooms and much unused space, it was built ten years ago, 'the same year Hong Kong came back to China'. In the son's room, Tony and Stephanie saw a woman's photograph. 'Oh, the woman of the house,' said Stephanie, at which our host glanced away, obviously upset. 'That was the past,' he said. 'Don't ask any more.' So it was Mr Niu who revealed to the rest of us what had happened, for it was general knowledge in the area. The young man's wife had come from a distant province to this new house far from the nearest village. Despite her beautiful little girl, she was unhappy. Neither she nor her daughter had friends. One morning, without any warning, without speaking of her loneliness, she killed herself, leaving this close and hospitable family shattered.

Outside, as the wife pressed on us handfuls of small bread rolls, baked as hard as biscuit, Tony pointed to a mirror over the door, too high for anyone to use. It was to ward off Evil, he said later. 'If Evil comes to the house, he will see his face in the mirror, and Evil, who has never seen his own face, will be scared away.'

Well, it hadn't worked. I was left pondering about time and earth. This modern house and its tragedy, the blink of an eye at the end of two centuries of community living beneath and inside the soil; the leap back two millennia to the unplumbed Han tomb; and back a few more centuries to the Qin royal tombs – all succeeding each other on these few acres, thanks to this deep, red earth.

*

So there could have been no doubt that King Zheng should start preparing his grave somewhere close by present-day Lintong. They made a start where Mount Li's lower slopes level out into ravines and orchards and wheat fields. By comparison with what followed, this was not a huge operation, because at that pre-imperial time the labour force came only from Qin, no doubt including teams of prisoners captured in the incessant cross-border raids.

Imagine a few thousand men, summoned by the order of Lü Buwei on behalf of the king, beginning to clear soil from Mount Li's lower slopes, presumably living in a small town built nearby. The spot must have been chosen with care: close to the sacred mountain, high enough to ensure that the water from Mount Li would run off down into the lowlands below, low enough to be on relatively level ground.

As it happens, archaeologists have identified the actual spot of this first excavation. It lies some 700 metres south of the edge of the tomb, higher up the mountainside. Not many people know this, except people like the head of the province's archaeological department, Duan Qingbo, a master of the technical surveys done all around the tomb, who brought a laptop bearing a collection of diagrams along to my hotel to brief me on his research. 'How do we know the original site? We discovered it by soil analysis and gravitational studies. This part had an anomaly in the consistency of the soil. The only possible explanation is that this part had been dug out and refilled. It's not at all like the surrounding soil.'

OK. But what about Sima Qian's words: 'When the Emperor first came to the throne' – that is, in 246 BC – 'he began digging and shaping Mount Li', with the implication that this was the beginning of the massive mound we see today? Well, Sima Qian may have tweaked the truth in order to get at his own boss, Emperor Wu, who notoriously ordered work to begin on his own tomb just two years into his rule – work that continued on and off for the full term of his reign, 53 years. Work may have started in Lintong in 246 BC; but it was not work on the real thing. It was a first attempt, a small-scale excavation, suitable for a boy-king.

And it was in the wrong place.

As Duan Qingbo said, 'It was too close to the mountain, so the soil was not deep enough and they hit rocks.' That would have presented a problem, and a choice: either to dig out a grave in rock – possible, but expensive for a boy-king with an uncertain future – or to put everything on hold until his death or until his rule was more secure.

Probably, then, work was stopped. It was simply left, a hole in the stony ground, with its rocky bottom, until the flow of events told the young king and his chancellor Lü Buwei what to do.

8

DIGGING THE TOMB

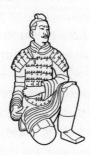

IMAGINE THE SUDDEN CHANGE INSPIRED BY UNIFICATION IN 221 BC. The lower slopes of Mount Li would have been a mess – the beginnings of a hole, a square of earth outlining the base of a pyramid-shaped mound, piles of overgrown soil carried off by the army of labourers ready to cover the tomb when the time came, the nearby town abandoned. But now, suddenly, came the need for a new vision, with the prospect of virtually unlimited manpower. This presented an opportunity – no, a necessity – to do something far more ambitious than anything that had been done so far. As ruler by Heaven's will, the First Emperor had clearly been given a mandate to do more than follow old ways; now he must add to them, and improvise new beliefs and practices suitable for his 10,000-generation empire.

There is no blueprint of his plans. But we can get an idea

of what he was aiming at from the tombs of the Han dynasty, which took over from the Qin empire, inheriting the Qin belief system and accepting much of it. Han tombs – some scholars argue – therefore suggest what the First Emperor had in mind.

The easy, bland approach is to take the expressway due north of Xian for half an hour. The more interesting one is to follow the cliff from Xianyang and the site of the First Emperor's palace, eastwards along the base of the cliff, past the new double-gated houses built with cash sent by the citified young to their farming parents, then steeply uphill to the top of the plateau, where you will find one of China's more staggering pieces of modern architecture. It is Yangling Museum, created from the tomb-mound of the fourth Han emperor, Jing Di (188–141 BC), and it hints, in glistening, space-age terms, at what the First Emperor had been aiming for 70 years previously.

There are in fact two mounds, belonging to the emperor and his wife, a his-and-hers of the afterlife surrounded by 200 cemeteries containing 10,000 graves of Han nobles. His has been turned into a wonder, a suitable memorial to an emperor who presided over a time of peace and prosperity. 'Everyone was well-off,' wrote the historian Ban Gu 200 years later, 'all the granaries and barns bursting with grain, government repositories teeming with money.' Opened in 2006 after 16 years of work, the tomb beneath its 31-metre mound is an air-conditioned glory of light and space in which you walk on glass over everything considered necessary to make the afterlife comfortable, in vast quantities – 50,000 objects have been unearthed so far, and estimates for those unfound range up to half a million. The finds include several thousand terracotta attendants, soldiers, even female equestrians, and animals by the hundred – goats, dogs, sheep, horses, oxen, pigs and chickens, all painted appropriate colours. The human figures look a little odd because their clothing has rotted away, along with their wooden arms. But they are impeccably modelled, walking, kneeling, running, many with cheerful expressions – smiling, quizzical, humorous – for the emperor would be in need of good cheer in the afterlife. All are painted, with red skins and black eyebrows. All have small but perfectly formed genitalia – all except the eunuchs, who are also impeccably modelled in their own way. With the figures are thousands of objects in bronze, gold and clay: seals, bells, axes, spears, swords, ovens, pots, chariots, ploughshares, granaries filled with grain, farm implements, agricultural carts, and more, always more.

All of this is extraordinary; but even more so is the fact that the people, the animals and the objects are, on average, one-third life-size. In fact, some are even smaller: a tiny copper crossbow is only 6.7 centimetres long, complete with front sight and trigger, both of which move. We are in a world of dolls. Clearly, accuracy of modelling – realism, if you like – was of more importance than size or consistency of material. The artists might, for instance, have modelled clothing in clay, as the makers of the Terracotta Army did. But instead they chose to cover their figures in silk or hemp, presumably draping it over the wooden arms.

There is one other thing about Jing Di's tomb that suggests something about the First Emperor's, and helps explain the existence of the Terracotta Army. The purpose of the exercise was to provide the deceased emperor with his entire realm, not simply by giving him figures, animals and objects, but by providing the means to organize them: the tomb is surrounded by 81 satellite pits, each one representing a government department.

'How do we know this?' asked my guide (who called

himself Sean) rhetorically. 'Every pit we found had a seal,[1] so we know which department is symbolized. Here is the Department to Punish Prisoners' – we were walking slowly along heavy glass, looking down at the remains beneath our feet – 'here the Department for Sacrifices. And here all the figures are eunuchs, so this is the Eunuchs' Department, and this, Number Sixteen, you see the animal bones, the fat animals for eating – this is the Royal Kitchen. And here, the blackened grain shows we are in the Grain Preparation Department.'

It is fair to assume that Jing Di inherited and developed the idea of recreating this world for the next from the First Emperor. Since the First Emperor now ruled 'all under Heaven', all under Heaven had to be taken into account: the universe, the physical world, the spirit world, together with all spirits, demons and deities and the ways by which they travelled – all had to be modelled in the new tomb.

But no one had done this before. What exactly might it mean? The emperor was spoiled for choice, for the answers were now to be sought all over the new empire and beyond its borders, as we know from the contents of tombs in newly conquered areas. Gold was imported from the lands beyond the western deserts (Iran, Scythia, Siberia) and used to decorate weapons and make small animal motifs. Images of new deities – winged beasts, fighting animals – arrived along these same trade routes. From western Asia too came fashions for lamps, mirrors and lions, which were unknown in China. Somewhere in unexplored lands to the north or north-west lived the Queen Mother of the West, whose

[1] A slight exaggeration. Only a few seals have been found, but scholars would agree that he makes a fair assumption.

legendary cave-palace ought perhaps to be a model for a royal tomb. From the state of Chu came the new tomb tradition, according to which the tomb should have several rooms – for ceremonies, for entertainment, for attendants, for weapons. Chu rulers (notably Marquis Yi of Zeng) had a preference for ordinary household goods, for musical instruments and for attendants of all kinds to create banquets. Life in a Chu tomb would be one long party, if the models were accurate enough. Possibly, the Qin had also come across ancient tombs in Zhejiang on the east coast, in which there were numerous jade discs with holes in them; these both conferred protection and allowed the soul to escape. All these possibilities and more were available to the First Emperor as he contemplated the design of his tomb. In the words of Jessica Rawson, 'It would seem that the unification of the empire had brought within reach of the court a concern with the full sweep of the universe and all that lay within it' – a universe that was no longer foreign, but part of the unified realm that the emperor sought to control.[2]

Following more recent fashions, the First Emperor would have naturally opted for a mound covering several rooms, as if the tomb were a sort of house, like his grandfather's tomb outside Lintong, and like the Han dynasty tombs to come – but grander than anything to date. His tomb was to be a symbolic representation – a reflection, a microcosm – of the physical world, representing an imperial city: outer wall, inner wall, *inner* inner wall, many buildings and a palace, this one being underneath its vast four-sided pyramid, doubling as a tomb.

The first step was to choose exactly the right spot for the tomb itself, for on its position depended a multitude of other

[2] Rawson, 'The Eternal Palaces of the Western Han'.

projects: housing for those who would look after the rites, the many kilometres of walls, the additional buildings, the pits that would contain officials, animals, chariots and eventually the clay warriors that would protect the emperor in the afterlife. This time, there would be no mistake. Planning and scheduling would have been meticulous: designs drawn on wooden boards, lists made on bamboo strips (timing, numbers of workers, food supplies, artisans). There would, I imagine, have been a number of test digs until engineers settled on a site 700 metres further downhill from the first, where the soil was deep enough for the emperor's underground palace.

Sima Qian gives a hint of the preparatory work, saying that the labourers 'dug down to the third layer of underground springs' and put in drains to carry the water clear of the tomb. This sounds a huge operation. How huge, I wonder? Sima Qian, in his casual way, says that 700,000 men were involved from the First Emperor's accession in 246 BC. That's the number that is unthinkingly quoted in almost all accounts. But this vague figure includes the force working on the Epang Palace, and is anyway hugely exaggerated, both in time (as we know from the false start) and in numbers. It would be far larger than the population of any city in the world at the time. Where would such numbers live? How would they be fed? A computer simulation would be welcome, but so far there isn't one. To introduce a sense of realism, we must resort to some back-of-the-envelope calculations.

These suggest a slow start, a long pause, and then – only on the emperor's death – a big push with an army of labourers, large to be sure but still far short of Sima Qian's numbers.

'A slow start' means work on the palace foundations. But at once we are in a much disputed subject-area, for beginning work on the palace foundations means having an idea of the size of the palace, which will have to fit beneath the funeral mound, which means we have to know – right now, in advance – the size of the mound. The base of the mound today measures about 350 × 350 metres, and its height something between 50 and 75 metres, depending on which side the measurement is taken. That gives a volume of 1.8–2 million cubic metres. Many sources quote the official history of the Han dynasty, which says that the original height of the tomb was 'more than 50 *zhang* [115 metres]'. They almost always add that in the subsequent 2,200 years 'erosion' brought it down to its present size. Really? This sounds to me like a pseudo-explanation, because erosion has not affected other mounds anything like that much.

Even more problematic are assumptions made since 1981, when a number of trial drillings struck brick and rammed earth. It seemed, as Yuan Zhongyi writes in his archae-ological survey, that what had been found were walls; and if so then these walls must belong to the underground palace. Joining the dots and extrapolating them beyond the area of the drillings suggested an immense structure of 460 × 390 metres. This is considerably larger than the base of today's mound, and was considered 'proof' that the mound must have been much larger in the past – *much* larger; something like 500 × 500 metres, and 115 metres high. But doubling the height and adding one-third to the length of each side does very peculiar things to the volume: it makes it 8.6 million cubic metres – *five times* the size of today's mound (and almost four times the size of the Great Pyramid).

It makes no sense. If the palace is really larger than the base of today's mound, either its outlines should be visible, which they are not; or the whole thing would have to be beneath ground level, which it isn't, because the probes did not go that deep. Indeed, some 'walls', if that is what they are, lie some 40 metres from the top, which means that the 'walls' are at least 10 and perhaps 18 metres high, depending how far below ground the foundations lie.

The fact is, the only thing everyone agrees on (backed by one other vital piece of evidence that we will get to later) is that something big is under there. No one knows how big. Most likely, as the archaeologist Duan Qingbo insisted to me, the standard assumptions are wrong. 'From our research, it seems the hundred and fifteen metres was just the *planned* height. When the emperor died and they started to pile earth on his tomb, it was almost the end of the dynasty. They did not have time to complete the plan. Probably the tomb we see today was just like it was over two thousand years ago.' His view makes his conclusion persuasive: 'We know there is an underground palace beneath the tomb. It is about eighty by fifty metres in size, surrounded by a stone wall.'

It seems slightly odd to place a rectangular building beneath a square mound. Let's assume an upper limit for the palace of half the size of today's mound: 175 × 175 metres, rising about 10 metres above ground level, with foundations that go down perhaps 5–7 metres below ground level. This is about as large as it could be, bearing in mind that the walls and the roof must be covered with earth thickly enough to deter vandals.

Now to return to the starting point: If the pit went (say) 7 metres below the surface, then the workers would have had to shift some 200,000 cubic metres, or 300,000 tonnes, of earth (always working in very round numbers).

In what time? And with what size of workforce? These are questions that Li Si's quantity surveyors would have needed to answer in order to estimate their needs for tools (mainly spades, hoes and two-man, earth-carrying slings-on-poles), food and housing, a schedule and countless other planning details.

Compared to the problems to be faced later, the foundations of the underground palace were a minor challenge. As a first step, assume that the earth must be carried well clear of the site, not with wagons and horses, because they are expensive, but by men with two-man teams, because men, especially criminals, are cheap. A man with a spade takes up (say) 2 square metres, so you could fit a theoretical maximum of 15,000 labourers in the foundations. But with that number nobody could swing a shovel, and there would be no room for the earth-carriers to move between them. Further constraints are imposed by the speed with which the earth is removed and the numbers needed to move it. Today, quantity surveyors work on the assumption that the average digger can remove 1 cubic metre (about 1.5 tonnes of soft earth) in 2.7 hours. But at that rate, especially with slave-labour conditions, you will work your men to a standstill pretty quickly. Assume 5 tonnes per day per digger. Let's pick several other round-number assumptions out of the air: that the two-man earth-carriers carry their earth in three different directions (i.e. not uphill); that every team makes three journeys back and forth to their dump every day; that each dump is 2 kilometres away; and that each two-man sling carries 40 kilos. Imagine three double lines of earth-carriers plodding back and forth on three roads, which gives us 8,000 two-man earth-carrying teams. Digging his 5 tonnes daily, one digger supplies 35 teams.

The slightly surprising conclusion is that the 16,000 earth-carriers will be supplied by just 200 diggers, who will shift 1,000 tonnes a day, digging the underground palace's foundations in 300 days, or ten months. (If the palace is smaller – 80 × 50 metres, as suggested by Duan Qingbo – that brings the total tonnage of soil down to a mere 42,000 tonnes, which hardly counts as labour at all by comparison.) The real labour will come later, after the emperor's death, when the mound will have to be built and the surrounding walls finished in double-quick time.

It's not quite that simple, though, because the foundation, whatever its size, demands meticulous design. It needs access ramps, probably four of them; not too steep, because earth-carriers must go up and down, come rain or shine, and later processions bearing coffins and grave goods will need to make stately progress. The whole thing will eventually have to be divided into several different compartments, floored with clay tiles (like those on which the Terracotta Army stands) and lined somehow to prevent the walls collapsing. The floor-tiles will number up to 1.2 million, depending on how much of the floor space is taken up with pillars and rammed-earth walls, which will be needed to support a roof of sturdy timbers (more about them in chapter 10).

It is perhaps during the preliminary survey for the excavation that the Qin engineers make an unpleasant discovery. There is a stream, the Sha (still there today), which, after heavy rain, careers down from Mount Li, and will, if it floods, threaten the grave – if not now, when it is nothing but a hole in the ground, then some time in the future, literally undermining the whole project. Perhaps they realized the danger when the first attempt at the grave was made, but the implications were so dramatic that nothing, it seemed, could be done. The answer, in fact, is to build yet another wall, the Wu Ling (Five Hills) Dam, to deflect the water away from the tomb's south-east corner. Some dam: 1.5 kilometres long, 30 metres across and perhaps 10 metres high. I'm guessing the height, because if you go there today, working your way uphill along muddy tracks, past small-holdings, through a couple of villages, you will find that the First Emperor's dam is a fine, raised foundation for what will soon be a new highway running from Lintong to the mausoleum. I can vouch for the dam's width: the smooth earth, scraped flat by bulldozers, was easy to pace. The dam adds another 450,000 cubic metres – 675,000 tonnes – of earth to be moved. This is over twice the volume and weight of the grave's foundations. Yes, a formidable challenge – Where does the earth come from? How does the work dovetail with the grave-digging? – yet, once the logistical problems are solved, our 16,000 labourers, shifting 1,000 tonnes a day, could handle the job in just under two years.

Of course, the labourers will need to be supplemented by additional contingents of families, overseers, engineers and troops to keep control. Li's new township will have a population of perhaps 25,000 – which, so far, is a fraction of the number mentioned by Sima Qian. The notion of construction stretching over 30 years is pure hogwash.

All of this is mere infrastructure, a stage set waiting to be filled with life when the emperor dies. No one knows in advance what lands the emperor will rule, what he will possess, what the governmental departments will be, whether his queen will still be alive, how many concubines he will have, what children, what other nieces and nephews, princes and princesses, high officials, horses, carriages, and treasures of bronze, jade and pottery he will have around him when he dies. But whatever he has will somehow have to be either buried with him or buried in separate pits, even as he is reverently placed to rest and the vast task of sealing the tomb begins. That lies in the future.

Meanwhile, someone has dreamed up the idea of making an army of full-sized warriors, and the emperor likes it. As Lothar Ledderose writes, it was as if the emperor had said: 'Make me a magic army. It must never decay, but protect my residence for eternity. It must look like a real army in all respects. Only then will the magic work!'

The warriors will have to be buried, somehow, somewhere; but that can wait, because their pit is only 75 per cent of the underground palace's foundations, and, as our time-and-motion study on those foundations suggests, that pit could be dug in not much over six months.

The statues, however, demand immediate attention. Qin artisans were terrific at bronze casting and making substantial bits of pottery, but no one had made a clay statue on this scale, let alone an army of them. In workshops and kilns far removed from the creation of the tomb, work started on an unprecedented operation.

9

MAKING THE ETERNAL ARMY

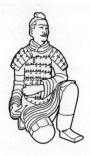

THE TERRACOTTA ARMY WAS A ONE-OFF CREATION, ORIGINAL IN both concept and execution, unmentioned in any source, no sooner buried than destroyed and forgotten. Seen from the viewing platform of Pit No. 1, lined up in their geometrical columns, with their calm expressions, the warriors seem at first sight as enigmatic as a regiment of sphinxes. Why so realistic? Why this many? Why full-size? Why clay? So many questions – and now, after three decades and much specialist attention, some answers.

The initial inspiration was the need to duplicate a new force, of which the main element was infantry, conscripted from the emperor's newly acquired masses of peasants, and protected not with custom-made armour but with scales of leather and simple, standardized weapons. It was the combination of archers, infantry and charioteers, this particular

balance between officers and men, that had enabled the First
Emperor to unify the nation. Since the next life was thought
to reflect this one, and since soldiers would anyway be part
of life in the tomb, unity would have to be achieved and/or
maintained in the afterlife as well. Unification and the army
would be honoured together. To reflect the novelty of what
had been achieved by the emperor and his army, a new level
of realism was called for. How better to achieve this than by
giving the spirit army real weapons, which already existed
by the ten thousand and which could be topped up by long-
established manufacturing techniques? And if the weapons
were real, clearly they could not be held by anything but
full-size figures.

Then there is the question of the numbers. If realism was
the key, then they had to represent a real army. No army
could be called an army unless it was a *wan*, 10,000 strong
– not, as we have already seen, that a *wan* was an exact
number. It was a word that evoked a very large number, as
'zillion' does. The Great Wall was a *wan* of half-kilometres
(*li*) long, the Epang Palace could hold a *wan* of people, and no
doubt if Sima Qian had recorded the Terracotta Army he
would have said it consisted of a *wan* of soldiers. So far, count-
ing all pits discovered to date, archaeologists estimate there are
about 8,000, which is close enough to count as a *wan*.

Achievement, status and logic all combine to dictate size
and numbers. But what of the material? That too springs
from the First Emperor's requirements. Think of the alter-
natives. The First Emperor might have opted for human
sacrifices; certainly, he would not have hesitated if he
thought it necessary. But he himself, as a commander,
would have instantly seen three major drawbacks: men
dispatched into the next world cannot fight in this one;
such old-fashioned practices, long since condemned as
barbaric, were not suitable for a new, forward-looking

dynasty; and bodies rot – this army was to be eternal.

Other considerations were cost and speed of manufacture. No point in an ambition that could not be realized in something like the time it would take to build the tomb – a few years. And no point either in decreeing full-size figures made in bronze, say, or jade, let alone gold. Even in bronze, several thousand full-size figures would stretch the Qin budget beyond breaking point, even if the expert artisans could be gathered. The figures could conceivably have been made of wood. But the labour of carving each figure would have been immense. What was required was a way of mass-producing the figures, fast. That left only one possible medium: clay.

All of China's diverse cultures understood clay. There were and are beds of it all over north China, so it was cheap, widely available and easily worked. Moreover, clay had been used in mass production techniques for well over 1,000 years.

The greatest artefacts of the ancient Chinese, their huge bronze vessels, depended on their skills in making the clay moulds in which the bronzes were cast. This was a process of great sophistication, brought to perfection in the Shang dynasty (eighteenth to twelfth centuries BC). For instance, a four-legged food cauldron, probably made around 1200 BC, weighs 875 kilos – the largest bronze vessel discovered so far – and was cast in six moulds (four sides, top and bottom). Each mould holds the shape to be cast, plus any decorations, in reverse; that is, if the finished vessel is to have a raised pattern – 'in the positive', as it is called – then that shape must be pressed or cut into the mould to create the same pattern 'in the negative'. This could be done directly by the artist; or the artist could make a model of the finished object in clay, raised decorations and all, which could then be used to make a mould. Then the pieces were joined, and molten bronze poured in. Once the metal was cool and the moulds removed, you then used the same moulds to make the next vessel, and the next. You could also change designs by using different decorated blocks to stamp the clay, or attaching additions – an animal here, a handle there, three legs instead of a single stand – that had been cast separately. It took time to refine the process, but by the sixth century BC several great foundries had mastered the factory-line mass production of bronze vessels, with the possibility of personalizing any product by the addition of details.

Henry Ford, who introduced the world's first moving assembly line to produce his Model T cars in 1913, would have understood exactly what a Chinese bronze works was up to in the second millennium BC. Mass production meant specialized workmen. Some prepared the furnaces, some the bronze, some the clay, some the basic designs, some the moulds, each man an expert in his own field. There must have been constant pressure from management to lower unit cost and increase volume. The end result was the same for 1,000 years: high quality; efficient, regular, fast production; and no room for individuality and creativity. All the foundries lacked was a moving assembly line.

No one had ever thought of making full-size figures before, but Li Si would have brushed objections aside. Every element was to hand – clay, furnaces, artisans, and labourers ad infinitum. The challenge was not in the artistry, the techniques or the expense; it was in the scale. As Adele Schlombs, Director of the Museum of East Asian Art in Cologne, says, 'The production of life-size figures in this enormous number set a new level in terms of practicality and organisation, which was neither foreshadowed nor matched later.'[1]

---

[1] 'Die Herstellung der Terrakotta-Armee', in Ledderose and Schlombs, *Jenseits der Grossen Mauer.*

Astonishing, therefore, that word of it did not filter down to Sima Qian. Perhaps it was because of the routine nature of the work. Perhaps people got so used to seeing the warriors that no one commented. Besides, there were so many vast projects – the Wall, the palaces, the road-systems, the canals, the tomb itself – that perhaps the true scale of the operation only emerged when the time came to bury them, just when the project was overshadowed by the closure of the tomb and the chaos unleashed by dynastic collapse.

Whether it was low-key, or officially concealed, or simply forgotten, the business of making the figures was a huge operation. How huge? What does it take exactly to produce figures on this scale? There are no historical sources to consult. But it is possible to consult the next best things: the reproductions.

They are around the museum like a halo, the grey ghosts of the real things, haunting every step of your approach. They are present on every scale, from chess-pieces weighing a few grams – 'Hey, mister! One dollar one box!' – to the full-size ones crowding courtyards and roadsides and show-rooms and tourist-traps. Some are so amateurish that you wonder why anyone would bother to set them up. But they exist in such numbers (greater even, surely, than the original army), that I became curious to know more about the busi-ness. I thought I would learn only about the local equivalent of tourist tat. Far from it. I was led straight to the heart of an operation that would have been strangely familiar to the First Emperor.

On your way to Lintong, the expressway leading through Xian's eastern suburbs takes you across the river Ba, a muddy swirl running down from the mountains between a chaos of ruts cut in times of flood. If you turn off left, aim for the tall chimney stacks, and penetrate the haze along Power Plant Road, you come to the Xian Art Ceramics and Lacquer Factory. It makes and sells many things, including silk carpets and reproduction furniture, but what greets you as you go into the first hall is a line of full-size terracotta warriors, perfect except that they have no heads, the heads being made separately. They flank a dozen tables where employees work to produce small-scale warriors in many different sizes.

I had questions, not so much about the small copies, but about the full-size figures, which looked just like the originals. The factory's manager, Li Junyi, took me into his office to brief me, speaking in Chinese through my guide, Tony. In a thick smoker's voice, Li said he had been here since before the discovery in 1974, when this place had been a ceramics factory. The reproductions business had started almost at once. Now they did about eight million dollars' worth of trade annually, half of which was in reproductions. They sold 200,000 of the small statues every year, and about 200 of the full-size figures, at $1,200 a piece, insurance and shipping included. A pretty good deal, I thought, considering they weigh up to 200 kilos each.

'What on earth do people do with them?'

'They put them in their gardens to protect their families. If they have a business connection in China, they use them as advertisements.'

At this point his young, handsome, crew-cut deputy 'Jerry' Wong took over, in very good English, his looks, western name and language skills reflecting the several tens of thousands of foreign tourists who come here every year. He led me round the workshop to see how the copies were made. It's pretty simple, really. You take raw clay from a pile dumped near the entrance (wonderful dark brown stuff, thick and smooth as well-rolled plasticine). You go with it to your desk. You pummel it to get the air-bubbles out; squeeze it into the right size mould or moulds, depending on the size of statue you are making; let it harden for a few days; prise the mould(s) off and make the finishing touches – a few hairs added with a stylus, a stroke or two to smooth an imperfection – and off the statue goes for firing in kilns alongside the factory.

The same principle applied to the full-size statues, some of which were standing around clamped into their moulds (ten for the body, another two for the head). After setting for several days, they would be stripped and taken to a kiln for firing.

'Why are the heads done separately?'

Because when you make a life-size warrior, said Jerry, you have 1.8 metres of clay, so you have to consider how to keep it balanced. It was the same 2,000 years ago. There are three ways. One is to make a base, which is what some of them have. Another way is to make them kneeling, like the kneeling archers. The third way is to make sure the legs are heavy and the rest of the body is light, so you give them solid legs and a hollow chest. That's how most of them are made.

And if the statue has a hollow chest, what happens when you put it in the kiln with the head on?

'The air expands, and it would blow up. So we leave a big hole for the neck and add the head afterwards.' I think perhaps he was joking. All you would have to do is leave a *small* hole or two somewhere. 'And of course there is another reason. The clothes don't vary much, but the heads do, so it makes them seem like individuals.'

The factory did not provide all the answers. For one thing, its seven coal-fired kilns could not be used all the time because in Xian's suburbs there was already too much pollution. So most of the full-size figures on display had been produced in other kilns out in the countryside.

In terms of production, this factory was just a sideshow.

Second, copying statues with moulds was not hard. Where did the moulds come from? Were they, perhaps, allowed to make casts from the original figures?

'Er, no.' His tone told me how ludicrous the idea was. The terracotta warriors were untouchable, sacrosanct. 'We have experts. They make an original copy, not with a mould. That is a most important job.'

Indeed it was; absolutely fundamental. His words gave me a sudden insight, making two things clear:

- First, that the techniques for making these copies were almost identical to the original techniques. By studying the reproductions business, I would learn how the originals had been made.
- Second, that *it was actually impossible to make exact copies*. The 'copies' that I saw all around me were not like xeroxes, more like artist's versions of the original.

Who, then, were these experts? Where did they work their magic?

If you like to see patterns in lives, here is one. As a six-year-old boy Wang Lianyuan was playing around the orchards where the warriors were found in 1974. He saw an older friend gather arrowheads for sale at the scrap-metal shop. He saw the heads and torsos lying around in the field before the arrival of the archaeologists. I'm tempted to say he was inspired, because now, three decades later, he is the top man in the four-million-dollar-a-year reproductions business. Dressed in a casual-chic black leather jacket and driving a top-of-the-range 4×4, he was taking me to his main factory a few miles north of Lintong.

In fact, he explained, through a steady flow of cigarette smoke, there was no direct inspiration. It was just luck, a combination of the emergence of the warriors and his own rare mixture of commercial and artistic aptitude. At heart, he is a sculptor, having trained as a teenager in the Xian ceramics factory. By the time he was eighteen, he was a master of his trade, able to copy any statue.

I imagined that it would be possible these days to store images in computers and apply software that would somehow help out with making the copies.

'No, I do it all by eye.' Later, he showed me his old references – battered photographs torn from picture books and a set of detailed measurements scribbled alongside – but he scarcely needs even these aids. 'The images of all the warriors are stored in my brain. I don't need the pictures now. It's like a concert pianist, I don't need the reminders.'

'So you must know them better than anyone.'

'Well, I still come to study them, wondering if there are ways to make my copies closer to the originals.'

'Do you get the impression they are portraits of real men?'

'I think some are. Did you notice that, among the thousand warriors you see in Pit Number One, they all have moustaches – all except one?' (No, I hadn't. I've been trying to find the clean-shaven one in pictures ever since, but so far no luck.) 'What strikes me is the craftsmanship. From the style I can tell that one man was responsible for many of the warriors.'

We crossed the Wei and turned left along a muddy road, into the little town of Bei Tian, ordinary square brick houses backing on to fields of winter wheat and vegetable gardens. Wang turned through rickety iron gates, beneath a sign stating we were entering the Qin-Style Eighth Wonder Reproduction Factory (more about the 'eighth wonder' later), and into a courtyard that was a chaotic cross between a building site and an open-air art gallery. It was the most basic, grubby, hands-on, practical place you could imagine. Standing in random clumps were scores of headless, full-size terracotta warriors. Buildings in various stages of dilapidation edged the yard – tin-roofed sheds with open fronts apparently filled with discarded pottery, two workshops filled with shadowy figures, a house with a veranda where two women were attending to an extremely cheerful baby built like a miniature sumo wrestler, and four smoking kilns dug into a bank of earth.

Wang proudly showed me into the first workroom. The figures I had glimpsed from outside were contingents of warriors newly released from their moulds; one still encased and bound looked like a giant Easter egg on a stand. The figures were all the colour of the original clay, toffee in the shadows, more like caffè latte where the sunlight spilled on to them through the dusty window. Some were still supported by wooden struts to keep the soft clay firm against the pull of gravity. Two men were at work, smoothing armour plating, heightening details. Obviously they were not direct copies, because two of the figures were not soldiers at all, but two versions of the First Emperor himself, his ceremonial sword strapped round his paunch. And at a bench a woman in a red jacket was working on a dozen officers in miniature sizes, which of course had no counterpart in 210 BC.

I still hadn't quite grasped the essence of this operation. All these full-size statues came from moulds, of which there were many, still enclosing statues, or lying about on the floor. But there were several different statue designs: emperors, officers, soldiers, kneeling archers – ten of them in all.

'Where do all the moulds come from?'

'We make them. From the original statues.'

'But who makes *those*?'

'I do.'

By hindsight, I was being incredibly dim. 'Wait a minute. You make the originals, then use those to make moulds, and from the moulds come all these statues?'

'Yes.'

'So where are the originals?' I wanted to see the foundation, the starting point of the process.

'Oh, once I have made the moulds, there's no point in keeping them. Perhaps I have a few left. I will show you.' And he led me out, past a smaller shed where the clay was stored, and into his own workroom, which was as basic as a prison cell. A couple of rough branches stuck up from a stand to act as a frame for the clay. A head stood on a shelf, along with dozens of small moulds. He showed me the tools of his trade: a little polystyrene box containing three wooden styluses, three small trowels, two loops of wire on handles, a tape measure, a ruler. That was all.

Let me get to the bottom line here rather more quickly than I managed to understand what Wang had created. Around me in the sheds were reproductions of 10 different styles of warrior in 10 different sizes, from 6-centimetre miniatures to full-size ones. So Wang had made 100 original statues, copying by eye, his only references being photographs and his own memory. From his originals moulds had been taken, and from the moulds, with the help of his 20 workers, came the litter of statuary I saw around me – the piles of pottery in the open-fronted sheds at the far end of the yard turned out to be miniature warriors by the thousand – and the scores on display at the museum and the ceramics factory and the other tourist outlets around Xian.

Making the statues was a slow and steady business. New statues must be left to harden for a few days, carefully protected from the elements in a darkened room, with no windows open. Then the firing takes a week on low temperatures to ensure regular heating, then a couple of days at high temperatures, up to 1,000°C. Several figures could be fired at once, the gaps between them being filled with dozens, scores, hundreds of smaller statues, the numbers depending on the sizes. In this way, Wang's workers produced several hundred full-sized figures – up to 1,000 was possible, he said – and some 10,000 of the smaller figures every year.

I felt I was almost down to bedrock. One more thing: where did the clay come from? For without the clay there would have been no spirit army, none of Wang's artistry, no reproductions business. Most of it came down by the tractor-load from Mount Li, Wang said, where we could not go because spring rains had made the track dangerous, even for a 4×4. But there was another smaller source in a village just outside Xian. Wang had never been to the spot, which for some reason I assumed would be by a river. But after many side-roads and several phone calls we were met by a local farmer who led us along a track leading into the middle of fields green with young wheat. Ahead, down a muddy slope torn up by tractors, was an open-cast pit about 10 metres across which ended in a wall some 4 metres high.

While the others held back, wary of the mess, I started forward, and at once understood why this clay was ideal for sculpting. It was the stickiest stuff imaginable. Every step sucked up more of it, until I was struggling in slow motion, and getting taller as well, like the Qin opera singer I had seen the night before parading on platform shoes. This rich, thick, even-textured, chocolatey gloop was mined by hand, then prepared by a sort of baling machine, which swallowed it and cut it up into brick-sized slabs. That was the only nod to modernity. Otherwise, the clay that clogged my track shoes was the same now as then, and so was the whole manufacturing operation: natural materials worked by nothing but artistry and heat.

That night a thought leaped out of my dreaming mind and punched me awake. I had assumed that every terracotta soldier was an individual creation. Not so: once an original had been created, and once moulds had been taken from it, this was a mass production, factory-based operation which could produce – how many soldiers? In what period of time? What were the constraints, the upper limits? Using Wang's experience as a guide, it should be possible to do a time-and-motion study on the whole Terracotta Army and come to a new understanding of what it was all about.

So Wang agreed to perform a thought experiment, talking in the reception area of the museum. First I wondered what would limit the production of warriors: the amount of clay, perhaps, or the number of kilns available?

No, the clay would not have been a problem. Wang has used about 150 tonnes a year for the last 10 years – 1,500 tonnes – and he foresees no problems in supply for many years to come. The Terracotta Army needed between 1,200 and 2,000 tonnes.

Kilns? It takes about ten days to build a kiln out of bricks, said Wang. 'But they didn't have kilns like ours. The topography round here is special. We have many places with cliffs of earth. The kilns were dug into cliffs.' Yes, like the cave-houses I had seen not far from Lintong. There is no shortage of hillsides and deep earth. The making of kilns would not impose restraints.

He thought the number of craftsmen would be the biggest problem. After all, he was the only designer and artisan in his factory.

'So how long does it take you to create one full-size figure?'

His reply was instantaneous: 'Twenty days.' (Incidentally, it takes almost as long, fifteen days, to make a smaller figure.) So his ten full-size designs represented a little over six months' work for one man.

Now, Wang does not have to live under the pressure imposed by the First Emperor, who would surely have wanted work completed as quickly as possible, with the greatest possible variety. This could only have been done by making many small moulds for various parts of the body – hands, legs, heads, ears – and thus producing a range of interchangeable parts. An analysis of the warriors reveals some 80 different moulds. Even assuming that all these were as complex as Wang's (they weren't), the original statues and sections of statues from which the whole army was made could have been completed in under five years by one man. In fact, of course, there would have been many. A team of, say, 80 master sculptors – and surely such a team could have been assembled, given that the emperor had the whole of his newly formed empire to choose from – could have had the moulds for the whole army ready in three weeks. OK: master craftsmen do not grow on trees. Let's say they could only find 20. Even so, all the moulds would be ready in three months.

What about the numbers of Qin workers and their output?

There would have been no shortage of clay-workers in Qin times, because armies of potters were used to produce drainpipes, floor-tiles and roof-tiles, not simply for the emperor's new Epang Palace but for all the palaces built in Xianyang after unification. Co-opting a few dozen trained workers, even a few hundred, would make hardly any difference. Bearing in mind that Wang employs 20 people, who could produce 1,000 full-size statues a year, let's put 200 on the job, which boosts production tenfold – to 10,000 full-size statues a year. At that rate, the 8,000 statues needed to fill the main pit and all the others with full-size statues would be ready in under ten months.

I'm guessing, but my guess is pretty much in line with another, very much more expert, estimate by Yuan Zhongyi, one of the Army's top excavators, whom I went to see in his Xian apartment.[2] Yuan points out that it was common for potters to sign their names on their products, as part of quality control, so that overseers would know whom to blame for shoddy work. The same is true of the warriors. And signatures on some of the tiles from the Xianyang palace match those on some of the warriors, so it is fair to infer that the techniques used to make the warriors were familiar to potters. More: on 1,383 warriors and 132 horses examined by Yuan, there are 477 stamps and incisions, mostly serial numbers, but also the names of 87 foremen, who often identified themselves by their place of work or residence. One, for instance, was Gong Jiang (Jiang of the Palace, the state factory); another, Xianyang Ge (Ge of a local factory in Xianyang). The arguments are highly technical and uncertain, but serial numbers suggest that figures were worked on and counted in multiples of five, which in turn suggests that sculptors worked in teams of ten. Suppose that these foremen also produced most of the other unrestored warriors, but let's add fifteen more for the sake of argument, which gives us a workforce of 1,000. Suppose it takes a ten-man team two weeks to complete their five figures. That means the 1,000 artisans will, in one year, produce 12,500 figures.

Often, you will read that this operation involved 'hundreds of thousands' of workers, but that is to confuse the tomb as a whole with the Terracotta Army, which was

[2] His work is also summarized by Lothar Ledderose in *Ten Thousand Things*.

by comparison a small-scale affair with the potential for huge production figures, rather like a modern car factory.

You see where I am going – as Wang did, because he was smiling gently.

The emperor clearly wished to have a spirit army that would represent his real army. But his real army was numbered in the tens of thousands. Why would he be content with the 7,000–8,000 that are buried near his tomb?

'If you are the First Emperor, and you say: "Give me my whole army in terracotta," is anyone going to tell you that you cannot do it for this or that reason?'

Wang's smile grew. 'No. It is possible.'

'What I'm wondering is: why is the Terracotta Army so *small*?'

I went on, improvising. On the basis of Wang's work with reproductions and Yuan's calculations, it seemed that, allowing (say) a year for the fundamentals – the creation of figures to make moulds, the building of kilns – by the time of his death in 210 BC, after a decade of work, the emperor could have had not 8,000 warriors but over 100,000: enough to produce not only an army facing east, but others facing west and north (not south: it's uphill and too rocky).

It seemed to me that Wang's work had opened up a line of thought that was entirely new. The Army is presented as a pinnacle of achievement, the greatest of the First Emperor's works, only to be matched perhaps by the tomb when it is finally opened. But what if it is not a pinnacle? What if it was only a beginning?

And why had no one else examined this idea? At the time, I strongly suspected it had something to do with a glass wall between academics and artisans. The academics look to archaeologists for their evidence, which lies in the ground and must be dug up with extreme care and skill and reported in journals in the proper way and then turned into a tourist industry through government departments. But Wang's world was utterly different. It was a world of mess, and hands-on artistry, and simple labourers doing simple things, and making money privately. I suspected a barrier between officials and academics on the one hand and workers and artisans on the other. I thought: it's time for the academics to pay Wang a visit, get some mud on their shiny shoes, and learn something about the past by studying the present.

Well, by hindsight, I was being a little hasty, because I had not yet realized the importance of colour. More about that in a moment.

Work on the statues began. Not that it was precisely the same as Wang's in every detail. The Qin sculptors did not use moulds to make the heavy legs, or many of the torsos. These they built up by rolling the clay into long, thin cylinders, coiling these on top of each other and then smoothing out the dents and bumps, the same way as potters make a pot freehand. In some broken figures, the strips of clay are clearly visible. Nor does Wang make horses, which had solid legs, for strength and balance, and bodies that were also made with coils of clay.

Still, the essence of the operation depended on the moulds: ten for heads, four for boots, two for legs, three for shoes. From the modular production process, heads, boots, bodies and legs emerge, still soft from their moulds. Now details must be added; these may be produced from smaller moulds (ears, moustaches, buckles, hairstyles and shoes) or by hand, achieved (as by Wang's workers today) by refining noses, beards and eyes with scrapers, shavers and sharpened bamboo sticks. In this way, realism is heightened. Indeed, when the figures first came to light the realism seemed so astonishing that it was widely claimed – still is, in the more unthinking brochures – that the warriors were actual portraits of every man in the First Emperor's army.[3]

That would be truly astonishing, for the Chinese had never developed a tradition of portraiture to match Greek or Indian art. There were animals modelled in clay, carved in stone or cast in metals; there were masks; there were superb bronzes, even the occasional figure. Then, later, artists became adept at portraying movement, hairstyles and clothing. But the figures were heavily symbolic. A figure might represent the essence of kingship, but it never occurred to any ruler or any artist to capture the actual features of the king.

Or of the individual soldier. What the sculptors and production workers had to capture was the essence of military ability, which meant exactly the opposite of individuality. As Eleanor von Edberg says, 'In these heads there could be no place for any thought other than military discipline and duty. To act as an individual would be gross insubordination.' Of course, the emperor's recruiters would have selected the best, rejecting the super-tall, the undersized, the lame, the diseased, the weak. But even for cannon-fodder, or in this case arrow-fodder, entry standards into the real army would have been lower than perfection. Yet in these warriors there are no deformities, no faces disfigured by smallpox, no pimply teenagers, no earless or one-eyed fighters, no gnarled ancients, not a single wound. The army would surely have recruited from every newly conquered land, incorporating for example the tough little horse-riders of the steppes, yet you would be hard-pressed to find racial differences (which are well represented in the little figures in the Han tombs at Yangling). Impeccable hair,

[3] The definitive statement on this matter is by Eleanor von Erdberg in 'Die Soldaten Shih Huang Ti's'.

neat eyebrows, trim moustaches, every eyelid delineated: they are all suspiciously good-looking, as idealized as a Michelangelo Christ, with expressions, or rather lack of them, to match – inscrutable, calm, with hardly a frown or a smile to sully those perfect features.

Take their heights: the rank-and-file soldiers range between 1.66 metres and 1.87 metres, with an average of 1.77 metres (5 feet 10½ inches), which may or may not mirror the average height of the emperor's real army. But officers average 1.9 metres (6 feet 3 inches), while a general is an imposing 1.96 metres (6 feet 5½ inches), though he is in boots and on a little tile. In the real world, generals are not necessarily taller than their men, and some are notoriously shorter. The differences are further evidence of idealization.

The intention was to capture a deeper reality. For this army, like all armies, depended on group actions, group loyalties, total obedience. As anyone knows who has watched *An Officer and a Gentleman* or been through an old-fashioned English public school, basic training in the hands of sadistic sergeant-majors and housemasters involves stripping away individuality to create the group. That is what is being idealized here: the group, composed of individuals all made obedient and calmly ready for whatever fate lies in store.

Yet in real life men and boys do not become indistinguishable one from another, no matter how they are depersonalized. They are *not* like pawns on a chess-board, because differences can never be eradicated. Reality would not have been served by making them identical. In these idealized faces and bodies, there had to be individuality – but only *apparent* individuality. For an artisan to take the next step, to become (in western eyes) an artist, to portray a real individual, would have been unthinkable.

This variety was intended to achieve far more than the

appearance of individuality: it also stated differences in rank and speciality. If personal variation is suggested by a dozen different face-shapes, combined with varieties of eyebrow, moustache, beard and lips, difference in status is indicated by distinguishing headgear, collars, belt-buckles, armour and tassels, providing extraordinary insights into Qin military uniforms. Armour, for instance, was all made of leather, either in large pieces or in plates tied together with little straps. Some had sleeve-armour, some didn't. Charioteers wore full armour; cavalry not much, to ensure lightness and speed. Lower ranks had larger leather plates (between 119 and 147 of them, according to the statues), which made their armour less flexible, while officers had up to 229 nice little flexible ones. All officers wore caps. These gradations suggest seven divisions: high-ranking officer (seven so-called 'generals'), middle-ranking officer, armoured soldier, unarmoured soldier, charioteer, cavalry-man and archer (kneeling or standing).

Under the armour soldiers wore coats, shirts, vests, trousers, puttees and shin-pads, which the soldiers had to supply themselves. The main item was the long wraparound coat (always closed with the left side overlapping the right),[4] a relatively new style adopted from the horse-riding Xiongnu the other side of the Great Wall. Evidence that soldiers had to provide their own undergarments comes from a Qin grave unearthed in Shuihudi (near Yunmeng, Hubei). Here archaeologists found a wooden tablet written by a third-century-BC soldier named Hei Fu: 'Mother, would you please check when the silk in Anlu is reasonably priced and then make me a couple of unlined skirts and coats? Send them to me together with the money.' Hei Fu was lucky to

[4] If you did the opposite, you showed you were in mourning, because it imitated the northern barbarians and meant 'turning your back on life'.

be able to ask for light summer wear. Most soldiers had to make do with coarse hemp material. Cavalrymen, though, had tunics with narrow sleeves and a smaller overlap, to give them better freedom of movement, if less warmth – and not much protection: surprisingly, the warriors lack shields. No one knows why. Perhaps because they slowed reactions, or were considered effete, or were simply omitted by the sculptors to assert the macho qualities of their creations.

Qin hairstyles were of particular importance, as revealed by bamboo scrolls found in the Shuihudi grave. Question: How should a man be disciplined for severing another's hair-knot? Answer: 'Forced to build walls,' for four years. Even tearing out another's hair in a brawl was a 'hair-crime'. And what if things get really bad – if, during a fight, the victim's hands are bound and his eyebrows and beard torn out? Not a common crime these days: it implies some sort of ritual way of causing grievous bodily harm combined with an outrageous insult. Anyway, the answer is the same: building walls, for four years. To be condemned for any serious offence meant being shaved – head, beard or both.

Clearly, then, the warriors' hairstyles were of great social, military and aesthetic significance, which is why they were modelled in such detail: hair-knots on the top right side made from one, two or three plaits bound or tied in a dozen styles; flat hair-knots made without plaits or with a single, six-stranded plait; knots that are held with pins, slides, caps or scarves. Most, but not all, infantrymen had the top-knot on the right, a fashion that was conventional in the past, but dropped out of use in later dynasties. Those infantrymen with flat knots presumably wore helmets. Officers, cavalrymen and charioteers favoured flat knots on the back of the head.

The Qin cared equally about their beards and moustaches, which were marks of beauty and status. Beards could be worn as side-whiskers, 'three-drop' beards (with three little tufts), half-shaved, divided, full (one warrior has a beard down to his chest) or residual; moustaches could be upturned crescents, down-turned, arrow-headed or flat, all in large and small versions. Varying the styles and combinations of moustaches and beards offered scores of different possibilities.

And this pseudo-individuality was guaranteed to perfection by the modular process. The operation was a three-dimensional version of the children's book in which pages of heads, bodies and legs can all be turned over separately to make a huge variety of different figures, with underlying similarities further disguised by the fact that similar figures are separated to intensify the impression of endless human variety.

Then there are the colours. Colour turns out to be a matter of much complexity and labour. It was not shortage of clay or kilns or sculptors, I think, that placed a limit on the number of warriors, but the drive to apply colour.

For non-specialists, the fact that the warriors were painted is both strange and disturbing, for it flies in the face of the evidence as you see it today. We have all got used to the terracotta warriors looking like terracotta. But they weren't like that at all when they were made. They were lacquered, and bright with reds and blues and greens and purples – not just the uniforms, but the faces too. You have to imagine one of the most famous figures, the towering 'general', as he is known, with painted patterns on his tunic and armour, green and purple clothing, and bright green shin-protectors. And a pink face, like virtually all the warriors: a gentle pink created by mixing red and white, even gentler for the more senior officers, perhaps because (then as now) a pale skin suggested upper-class status, whereas a weather-beaten skin indicated the hard outdoor life of the common soldier.

Why the colour? I turned to the German conservator Catharina Blänsdorf, who holds the Chair of Conservation in Munich's Technical University and has been masterminding colour conservation at Lintong since 2003. She answered the question by widening it, then turning it on its head.

First, colour was all the rage in the ancient world, in the West as well as the East. The Parthenon, the Elgin Marbles, the Venus de Milo – all were originally a riot of colours. Weather and the passage of time stripped them; and it is to this process that we owe our view that Greek statues should be earth- and clay- and marble-coloured. The Romans avoided colour, as did Renaissance sculptors, so that remained the fashion defined by the art historian Edward Strange as 'the solemn grandeur of the international Classical style'.[5] It was an attitude strengthened by determined 'restoration'. The Elgin Marbles were robbed of most of their remaining colours when they arrived in London in the early nineteenth century, and subsequent cleanings removed the rest. That is why browns, greys and whites are seen as 'noble', 'tasteful' and therefore 'authentic'.

It's an attitude that will be hard to change. When I was at the reproductions factory in Xian, I asked about the colours. Surely true authenticity ought to mean that the reproductions should be painted? Jerry Wong, who was showing me round, reacted as if I had made an improper suggestion. *Paint* them? Of course not! It would run counter to the expectations of the customers. Everyone knows the warriors are 'really' grey-brown, earth-coloured. That is the way they expect them to be. In fact – I am looking at Wang's

[5] The 'Lacquer' entry in the *Enyclopaedia Britannica* from 1922 onwards, now incorporated into 'Decorative Arts and Furnishings'.

miniatures as I write this – reproductions of all sizes have mud rubbed on to them, to suggest that they have just come out of the ground. This is crazy, since the only true originals were full-size figures that were crisp, sparkling, coloured – and totally unmuddy until their roof fell in. I look again at the array of little figures Wang gave me: miniatures, unpainted, artificially dirty – how inauthentic can you get?

An *authentic* warrior was a brightly coloured warrior. As Catharina Blänsdorf says, to ask why is to look at the matter the wrong way round. 'As so many objects of the antique world were painted – in the West as well as the East – and especially the sculptures, the question should rather be: why *not* paint them?'

The fact is that Chinese adored their colours, mainly because they were hard to come by, hard to make, expensive, and therefore symbols of luxury. It would have been inconceivable *not* to paint the statues, never mind that this would add labour, management, time, expense and complexity, and never mind that this was in a sense frivolous. The colours did not reflect reality, for ordinary soldiers would not have invested in colour. If officers did so, it would have been a personal indulgence. As Yuan Zhongyi writes in a long analysis of the warriors' looks: 'Differentiation between various ranks is not possible on the basis of clothing colour alone nor is differentiation between the various military units.'[6] This is art for the sake of art.

Take the lacquer, a remarkable substance which was vital to seal the clay and act as the foundation layer of the paint. Hard and lustrous, lacquer had been known for 3,000 years as a protection against acid, water and mould – 'the most ancient industrial plastic known to man', in the words of Joseph Needham. Though common enough even in the

[6] Yuan Zhongyi, 'Hairstyles, Armour and Clothing of the Terracotta Army'.

West, it is a mystery to non-specialists, like me before I researched it. Lacquer is the thick, light-grey sap of the lacquer tree (or varnish tree, as it is sometimes known),[7] obtained in egg-cup amounts – 10 grams per tree on average – by cutting through the outer bark and bleeding the sap into a cup, rather like gathering rubber, or maple syrup. Trees have to grow for six years before they are ripe, and they can be tapped only during four months, June to September (carefully, because the sap is toxic and causes a nasty rash if touched and a violent reaction if inhaled). The lacquer, which turns black on exposure to humidity and warmth, has to be stirred, beaten and sieved to make it pure and even. If many coats are needed, each has to 'dry' before the next is applied. The quotes are there because the sap doesn't exactly dry, but reacts chemically with the water in damp air to harden into something like enamel. It can be used on almost anything: it seals wood, bamboo, even cloth, and was used for centuries to make wooden dinner services that resisted the heat of cooking as effectively as metal. One hundred coats applied over many months create a surface thick enough to carve. Even lesser-grade lacquer-work – of the kind used to seal the warrior statues – takes weeks, and a lot of lacquer: each statue would have been sealed using the sap from up to 25 trees. In all, the 8,000 warriors would have needed the sap from 150,000–200,000 trees.[8] At a production rate of 1,000 statues a year, that's 20,000 trees annually to be tapped, and the sap processed and stored. Often, tapping the tree kills it, which means that this operation killed whole forests, creating a

[7] Botanical note: *Toxicodendron vernicifluum*, as it is now, after years of dispute about classification. The lacquer tree is related to other toxicodendrons, e.g. poison ivy and poison sumac. Strictly speaking, lacquer goes under paint, varnish over it.
[8] Cristina Thieme, 'East Asian Lacquer', in Blänsdorf et al., *Qin Shihuang*.

shortage in the following dynasty noted by Sima Qian.

Catharina Blänsdorf took part in a lacquering experiment, though she did not watch the work closely because, after three severe reactions, she realized she was highly allergic to the lacquer. Two Chinese painters, using slightly diluted raw lacquer, took a day to cover one statue, which took five days to harden. She suggests that an untreated statue would have needed three coats (one to prime, two to seal), over the course of about three weeks, depending on the time of year. We have just added 3,000 to the warriors' workforce and quadrupled the production time to a month per statue.

Of the colours used – red, white, green, black, brown, blue, purple – each has a story, the last being the most extraordinary. Known as 'Chinese [or Han] Purple', because it was made only in China, it was an unlikely combination of minerals. No one knew the details until recently because Chinese Purple fell from use over the next few centuries. Experiments in the 1980s revealed the formula: barium, copper, quartz and lead melted together at 900–1,100°C, which (not coincidentally) was the temperature at which the terracotta warriors were fired. The process was so complex that it must have been the result of many experimental trials and errors.

But why perform the experiments? A few years ago, a seven-man team of American physicists undertook a research project to find the answers, and in January 2007 they published their results.[9] The team noted that the process was like that used in glass-making, which developed at the same time, from about 500 BC onwards. Glass production was of great interest to Daoist monks, mainly because they were obsessed with making artificial jade,

[9] Liu et al., 'Influence of Taoism on the Invention of the Purple Pigment Used on the Qin Terracotta Warriors'.

which they believed to be a vital ingredient in any possible elixir of immortality. During countless experiments over many years, they discovered that adding barium to glass makes it turbid, resembling jade. Lead, which was anyway an ingredient of red and white pigments, was routinely added to reduce the melting point of other minerals. Inevitably, over the course of such experiments with these ingredients, someone would eventually, by chance, stumble on 'Chinese Purple'.

(As additional evidence for this idea, the American scientists also note that Chinese Purple fell from use in the following dynasty, the Han, as mystical, alchemical Daoism gave way to down-to-earth Confucianism, 'a striking example of how cultural changes affected scientific developments in ancient China').

All this should revise the standard view of the production process. First, we have to include the lacquer-men and their back-up army of sap-collectors. Then we also need teams of alchemists, in particular one dedicated to the highly specialized task of brewing up Chinese Purple.

Other colours are almost as demanding. Whatever the original material, it had to be ground to exceptional fineness. The red, for instance, was made with cinnabar, a rare mineral of red crystals which, when processed, produces mercury (of peculiar interest to the First Emperor, as we shall see). A major source was some 200 kilometres south, where an enterprising widow named Qing had made herself rich running a cinnabar mine – a hazardous occupation for the miners, since mercury is poisonous. To produce red pigment for paint, it had to be ground into the finest of powders by hand.

No wonder the First Emperor wanted his figures coloured. In real life, his warriors were dressed in drab materials, so would the emperor not wish something better for his spirit army? Something lavish? Something extremely expensive and difficult to produce? To make the spirits happy with their lot, and even more eager in death than in life to fight for their generous emperor? Of course he would.

Meanwhile, the warriors' own tomb had to be prepared. There is absolutely no mention anywhere in the ancient texts of the Terracotta Army's pit, or indeed any other. This could surely be only because they were all lesser operations compared to the gigantic task of covering the tomb-mound. Lesser, yes; but still vast compared to the work achieved to date. Some department head in the Qin administration must have known how many men it took to dig a pit of such and such a size, and how long it would take them. In the case of the Army pit, they had a size in mind, because they knew what sort of an army would be required – soldiers, officers, chariots, infantrymen, archers – and already had most of them in storage.

Let's see what would have been involved. The pit is 260 metres long, 62 wide and almost 9 deep: 145,000 cubic metres. First, labourers had to shift 217,000 tonnes of soil, which was about two-thirds the amount dug for the main tomb's underground palace. It is also less demanding in design terms. Let's assume 200 diggers (again) and 16,000 earth-carriers shifting the same 1,000 tonnes a day. Could be faster, because there are no surrounding walls to hem in the earth-carriers. Even at this slow rate, they could dig this pit in just over seven months.

With good planning, the two operations – the Army pit and the underground palace's foundation – should be happening simultaneously. In that case some of the earth could have gone into the tomb's walls, the rest being kept to be returned to the Army pit in the form of the rammed earth walls that will bear the rafters and make the 11 corridors in which the soldiers will stand. That's 30,000 cubic metres – 45,000 tonnes – of earth to be rammed into 3 kilometres of walls 5 metres high and 2 metres across.

This had to be done because the Qin, who did not build in stone, did not know about arches and used horizontal beams for all their ceilings. This would have to be a strong ceiling, with each beam supporting 5 tonnes of earth. The beams would be rough-hewn, some 425–450 millimetres across, sawn into 5-metre lengths (saw-marks have been found on several). These are big beams, twice as thick as telegraph poles, weighing 500 kilos – half a tonne – each. There will be 575 beams per aisle, over 6,000 in all – 3,000 tonnes of wood! And that's just Pit No. 1. It needed to be as carefully planned as a military campaign. You would not want to forget the floor, sealed with grey-blue bricks, 256,000 of them. Who makes them? When? Where?

Final question: When would the roof be added? After the warriors were in place? That's risky, because a dropped beam would mean broken statues, let alone the engineering problem of raising a half-tonne beam to enable the broken warriors to be replaced from above – lifting out broken pieces and carefully lowering new ones into position. Or was it the other way around, with the warriors placed after the roof was finished? That would surely be even worse, for they would all have to be carried along dark, narrow corridors (always with the risk of breakage) and placed in very restricted spaces. Once roofed, no corridor could see over into the next. Yet the rows match up pretty well. It seems to me that the Qin surveyors would wait for the emperor's death, and then place the warriors and roof the pit in a joint operation, putting a few warriors in position at a time, then roofing that small section.

Meanwhile, production continues. As the figures emerge

from the kilns, the painters get to work on them. Some acquire two layers of soft pink, to give them the glow of healthy skin. Blackened hair shines against red headbands. Eyes with darkened pupils stare with piercing gaze, very different from the blank look of the warriors today. Brightly coloured clothes contrast with the scales of the leather armour, lacquered as they were in life, the connecting fabrics that stitched them together coloured in white, orange, green and ochre.

And as other specialists work on their own creations – bronze-workers producing animals and intricate, perfect models of chariots, stone-workers wiring flakes of stone into dozens of suits of mock-armour, and tens of thousands labouring on the tomb itself – the terracotta figures in their garish colours are placed under wraps or in storehouses to await the day, years in the future, when the emperor's body will release his spirit, and the whole massive enterprise will shift gear to prepare his final resting place.

10

SUDDEN DEATH

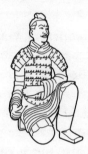

WE LEFT THE FIRST EMPEROR UP MOUNT KUAIJI, FURTHERING HIS own personality cult. It was the end of 211 BC, with winter well advanced. He was approaching 50, and was as keen as ever to maximize security and minimize risk.

There had been bad omens. The previous year a meteorite had fallen on which someone had engraved, 'The First Emperor will die and his land will be divided.' The emperor ordered an investigation that ended without result, except that the locals were all executed and the offending rock destroyed. A stranger had given a royal envoy a jade disc inscribed with the enigmatic words, 'This year the primal dragon will die.' Did he mean the First Emperor? Could be. The emperor had his magi consult the *Yi Jing*. A journey, they concluded, would be propitious, which suited the emperor, because he wanted to make another tour – the fourth – of his new dominions.

Hence this immense journey, with most of his government in tow (for he needed to be as much in control as ever) – nine ministers and unknown numbers of assistants and families, all in scores of four-horse chariots, with who knows how many troops and herds of replacement horses. Besides the emperor himself, this mass of people included the following *dramatis personae*:

- Li Si, chancellor. In office for 37 years and now in his early seventies.
- Huhai, one of the emperor's younger sons (18th of 20). Aged 20. Ineffectual, compliant. He needs to be brought on stage, because it is he, in the end, who will supervise the burial of the Terracotta Army.
- Zhao Gao, the villain. Transport chief, responsible for carriages and communications. He doubled as Huhai's law tutor, and was also the most senior of a small group of eunuch attendants.
- Meng Yi, chief minister. Zhao's enemy. He is the brother of Meng Tian, the great general who is guarding the northern frontier and building the Great Wall.

This was more an official migration than a procession, fraught with all the tensions of government at home. In particular, the villainous eunuch Zhao Gao and Meng Yi loathed each other. Zhao Gao had once been accused of committing some crime, probably corruption of some kind, which is quite possible given that his mother was a long-term prisoner, though with enough freedom to bear Zhao and several other sons. It was chief minister Meng Yi who had had Zhao tried and condemned. Even though Zhao was a senior official, as a good Legalist, Meng Yi argued for the death penalty. But Zhao, as young Huhai's tutor and himself a legal expert, was a slippery lawyer, and persuaded the emperor to pardon him. Zhao never forgave Meng Yi, and nursed a bitter resentment against both brothers.

Almost certainly, given his well-justified paranoia about assassins, the emperor was travelling in any one of several identical carriages. This would have been a basic precaution for many years, and an effective one: a third assassination attempt seven years earlier had failed because the assailant attacked the wrong carriage. Each carriage in this group would have been like the bronze one now on display in the Terracotta Army Museum: topped with a huge round roof that overlapped walls with small sliding grilles for windows, and driven by a single man armed with a crossbow. All were designed to keep warm in winter and cool in summer, all were equally discreet.

The immense retinue, moving sedately at an average of only 15 kilometres a day, worked its way 600 kilometres south-east to the Yangtze, another 500 kilometres downriver in a fleet of boats, then cross-country again for 250 kilometres to the sacred mountain of Kuaiji, near Shaoxing, famous for its wine, where, in the long-ago dreamtime of semi-mythical founders, Yu the flood hero had succeeded in controlling China's waters. Here the emperor claimed to be Yu's heir by sacrificing to him, then left the pillar promoting his own power, purity, beneficence and popularity. 'The officials in his retinue praise his brilliance, begging to inscribe this stone,' concluded the text. 'May its glorious message shine through the ages.'

The emperor might then have turned homeward. But he was drawn to the sea as the route to the islands that were the supposed source of the immortality drugs promised by his entourage of Daoist mystics. He had sent out two expeditions, remember, and nothing had been heard of any results. So instead of going home he headed north along the coast for some 700 kilometres, to two mountains where he had previously erected stelae. First stop was Mount Langya, where he had placed a stele eight years before. He had loved it there, so much that he had 30,000 families resettled nearby.

He must have had high hopes, because it was from near here – today's Jiaonan, a river port a few kilometres inland – that his Daoist adviser Xu Fu had dispatched the last expedition to find the elixir of immortality. On arrival, he questioned Xu Fu. Had he not promised that the elixir existed on islands in the middle of the sea? Had he not spent years searching, at huge cost? Xu Fu replied that indeed the islands could be seen afar off, but unfortunately – the excuse is so ludicrous as to be laughable, except that the emperor had never been to sea and would apparently believe anything – unfortunately 'always there are large fish that cause difficulty, and therefore we are unable to reach the island'. Xu Fu had a solution to hand: what they needed was a skilled archer with a repeating crossbow so that they could shoot any fish they saw.

The emperor's response seems to have been an intense mixture of hope and doubt. He was by now, perhaps, almost (but not completely) in thrall to his paranoias and obsessions. He dreamed that he was wrestling with an ocean-god. When he asked one of his advisers what this meant, he was told that his opponent, though real, could not be seen except in the form of a 'large fish or dragon'. That did it. All doubt vanished. It was him versus the fish. The emperor ordered that his seamen should carry with them nets and lines to seize any huge fish, while 'he himself carried a repeating crossbow and watched for a great fish to appear so that he could shoot it'.

He then proceeded along the Shandong coast and round its peninsula for some 350 kilometres to another of his mountains, Zhifu, near present-day Yantai. On the beach there, so Sima Qian says, he actually saw some large fish and shot one of them. It's an unlikely story, which suggests an image of a deranged emperor urged on by obsequious courtiers and firing all the arrows in his repeating crossbow at a non-existent target out at sea, to be hailed by the watching crowd as a master bowman.

He then continued west, perhaps via Penglai, because this was also the name of one of the fabulous islands where the elixir of immortality was supposedly to be found. It is a place that inspires fantasy, first because there are a number of islands offshore, some close enough to be seen; and second because it is famous for occasional sea-mirages, in which mountains, trees, even people seem to float on the horizon (you can find recent accounts of this mirage by Googling 'Penglai'). He then set off for home, minus any elixirs.

But after some 500 kilometres, suddenly, at a place called Sand Hill on the flat and river-rich expanses of southern Hebei, he fell ill. It was high summer, and Xian locals tell you he went down with heatstroke. That seems unlikely, given his well-shaded and well-aired carriage. No source reveals his disease, which suggests no one knew what it was. In any event, he went downhill fast.

Fearing the end was coming, he dispatched Meng Yi home, with orders to make life-saving sacrifices along the way. Then he turned to the succession, a matter he had been avoiding and no one else had dared mention because he hated the very idea of death. He had exiled his eldest son Fusu to the northern frontier as a punishment for criticizing the execution of the 460 Confucian literati, but Fusu was still his heir. The emperor wrote him a peremptory letter: When mourning is announced, go to Xianyang and arrange the funeral. Few words, yet a huge order – work on the tomb to be resumed, subsidiary pits dug, horses and concubines and officials designated for suicide or execution (for there would be some human sacrifices to be made), the Terracotta Army to be retrieved from storage and buried, countless other artefacts to be gathered, all the correct rituals to be organized.

By implication, this letter confirmed Fusu as the next emperor. And there was another implication: Fusu had been seconded to the great general of the northern frontier, Meng Tian. When he came to take up his inheritance, he would have the empire's toughest army at his back.

Having handed the letter over to his communications chief and senior eunuch, Zhao Gao, the First Emperor died.

At this point, the top officials faced a problem. So far, not many people knew what had happened. The emperor's hold on his new estates was tenuous. That was, after all, why he was making this long journey, to show his restless people that the empire was there for keeps. What might the reaction be when they knew he had died – and died, moreover, far from Xianyang and the mass of his armies? Dreadful prospects loomed, dark imagined futures: uprisings, revolution, an end to the Qin empire, and back to the bad old days of seven states and eternal wars.

This was one of those rare moments when history held her breath. Not even Prince Huhai knew the emperor was dead. The only ones who did were the eunuch chief of carriages, Zhao Gao, the chancellor, Li Si, and a few other trusted eunuchs. To tell or not to tell? The high stakes, the few characters involved, their moral dilemmas, their fears, the rising tension of the next few days – once again, we are in the realm of high drama. As far as I know, there is no film. There should be; there could be, because Sima Qian wrote the script, or at least some powerful dialogue. He's not so good on scene-setting. Where do these intense and secretive exchanges take place? Back and forth between carriages on the move, presumably. These are mere details. More important are the plot, the characters, and the outcome.

But is it history? In his long biography of Li Si, on which this account is based, Sima Qian does not give his sources. Remember his agenda: to discredit his own emperor by discrediting the First. In this case, he is dramatizing treachery in order to condemn it. The empire is about to go to hell, thanks to plotting and the imposition of an illegal heir. This must somehow be explained, and the cause lies in the *éminence grise*, Zhao Gao, who, as a eunuch in charge of eunuchs, was head of a group suspected through all Chinese history of being malign and self-serving. Real events and outcomes provide a sound historical framework, but it is the invented dialogue and characterization that fill it with life.

It was eminent, trustworthy, elderly Li Si who took the first step, perhaps with the best intentions: namely, to gain time to work out the best policy. He secretly had the body placed in the imperial carriage, which no one could enter without the permission of the attendant eunuch. I imagine Li Si, Zhao Gao and Huhai in adjacent carriages, hemming in the emperor's along the narrow mud roads as the great procession moved slowly westward. Ministers continued to deliver state papers for the emperor's approval, cooks delivered food. Inside, a second eunuch placed the emperor's seal on the papers, and handed them out. For a couple of days – it could hardly have been more, given what happens to dead bodies in the height of summer – business continued as usual.

Zhao Gao still had not handed the emperor's last letter to

a messenger. He had a motive for delay, because he loathed the whole Meng family. If the letter was sent, then Fusu would take over – Fusu the pro-Confucian, the man who had defended the Confucian scholars and criticized his own father. And what then? An outcome almost as bad as revolution and imperial collapse, at least from the Legalist point of view. Out would go the long-standing chancellor Li Si and minister Zhao Gao, their extensive families and all their retainers. If they were lucky, they would be allowed to commit suicide; if not, their deaths would be almost as unpleasant as being buried alive. In would come Fusu and Meng Tian and their Confucians, and all would be set at risk. It was Zhao, therefore, who took the next crucial step.

Zhao had only a few hours to act. Perhaps he told himself that there was no treachery, for the emperor had written to Fusu, 'When mourning is announced . . .' Well, there would be no mourning announced. Zhao Gao seized the moment, strode up or down the line to Huhai's carriage and broke the news, with its stark consequences: The emperor's dead, and there is no will securing the position of any prince, except Fusu; if Fusu becomes emperor, 'you will be without so much as a foot of territory. What will you do?'

Huhai was too young and too distraught to be an instant convert to treachery. It's obvious what I have to do, he said. Nothing. There's nothing I can do, nothing at all.

Not so, said Zhao Gao, and laid out for him the decision before them, in words that make Sima Qian seem to foreshadow Shakespeare. He did not quite have Zhao say 'There is a tide in the affairs of men which, taken at the flood, leads on to fortune,' but that's what he meant: 'At this moment the decision of who shall take control of the empire lies with you, me and the chancellor alone. I beg you to think of this! To make others your subjects or to be a subject of others, to rule men or be ruled by them – how can the two be discussed in the same breath?'

Huhai, still the good son, hesitates. An elder brother betrayed, a father's edict ignored by a man like me, so lacking in ability – it is unrighteous, it is unfilial, the empire would never consent, the altars would not accept my sacrifices . . .

Zhao Gao, still the prince's tutor, seizes his pupil, shakes him, and snarls sense and treachery together in his face. Other princes have done worse, actually killed their fathers, and no one said they lacked virtue! 'Great actions do not wait on petty scruples, abundant virtue does not trouble with niceties! Only dare to be decisive and the gods and spirits will step aside! I beg you to see this through!'

Zhao Gao sees he's on the verge of winning, and changes tack. Look, he says, we have to see the chancellor about this.

But how is that proper, argues querulous Huhai, seeing as how the death is still hidden, the mourning rites not yet performed?

'Now is the time! Now is the time!'

And at last Huhai buckles. Zhao Gao locks him into the plot by giving him the emperor's letter. He then seeks out Li Si and brings him up to date. Now that Huhai has the letter, 'The choice of an heir apparent depends solely on your say, my lord, and mine. What do you intend to do?'

Li Si is shocked to his core. 'How can you speak words that might destroy the nation!'

There follows a series of exchanges in which Zhao Gao convinces the upright Li Si to back his treacherous scheme.

My lord, consider, says Zhao Gao. If Fusu rules, he will be backed by Meng Tian and his border army. Can you compare with Meng Tian in ability, merit, strategic planning, allies, or friendship with the emperor's eldest son?

Li Si admits that on none of these counts can he match

Meng Tian. Why does Zhao Gao want to labour the point? To humiliate him?

Zhao Gao reviews his own 20-year career in the service of the emperor, then adds the clinching argument: never has he heard of a minister who was able to pass on his estates to the next generation. 'All in the end have been condemned and put to death.' So it will happen to Li Si. If Fusu becomes emperor, Meng Tian will be his chancellor, and you, my lord, will be impoverished. Now consider Huhai, his pupil for many years. He is kindhearted, generous, thinks little of wealth but much of his men, reserved, punctilious, respect- ful – in brief, an ideal emperor. He, not Fusu, should be the heir.

Now it's out in the open. Here's how the debate continues, adapted from two sources, Sima Qian and Derk Bodde:

Lɪ Sɪ (*aloof*):
Please return to your post. I will honour the command of my sovereign and heed the Mandate of Heaven.

Zʜᴀᴏ Gᴀᴏ:
What is secure may become perilous, the perilous can become secure. Choosing between security and peril – that is wisdom.

Lɪ Sɪ (*increasingly distressed*):
I was but a commoner who through imperial favour rose to become chancellor and mar- quis. I have been entrusted with the nation's preservation or its ruin. How can I betray that charge? A loyal subject does not reach perfection by shunning death, a filial son does not heed peril. Each man has his own duty. I

beg you say no more, for you would force me
to do evil.

ZHAO GAO:
And yet I have heard that the sage shifts his
course, goes along with changes, follows the
times. It is in the nature of things to change.
How can there be unchanging rules? When
spring waters stir and flow, ten thousand
things come to life. How can you be so slow
to see this?
(*Pause*)
At this moment, the fate of the empire hangs
on Huhai, and I am able to have my way with
him.

LI SI:
There were those who changed heirs, who
fought their brothers, who put their kinsmen
to death, and the results were turmoil, death,
a kingdom turned into a wilderness. Don't
talk to me of plots!

ZHAO GAO:
Listen! If you do, you will keep possession of
your fief and title, for generation after generation. But if you permit this chance to slip
away, then the disaster that will extend to
your sons and grandsons is enough to make
the blood run cold. The skilful man turns disaster into blessing. How will you proceed?

LI SI (*casting his eyes to heaven,
weeping and sighing*):
Alas! That I alone should face such troubled

times! Since I must live, what fate can I hope
for?

With this, he too came on board.

And the conspiracy that Sima Qian refers to as the Sand
Hill Plot moved forward. The three destroyed the original
letter and concocted an imperial edict making Huhai heir
and a fake letter that was sent to Fusu in the name of the
emperor, saying: While I have been touring the empire and
making sacrifices, Fusu and Meng Tian have been cam-
paigning with several hundred thousand to no purpose.
Moreover, Fusu has criticized and slandered me on many
occasions. 'Fusu has not acted as a filial son. I present him
with a sword so he may settle the matter for himself.' As for
Meng Tian, 'as a subject he has acted disloyally. I present
him with the opportunity to take his own life.'

Off went the letter carried by a trusted messenger, presumably not in an official carriage but on horseback for
speed, and anyway accompanied by a troop of fast horsemen. It was a 500-kilometre gallop to Meng Tian's HQ,
which at 100 kilometres a day would take them the best part
of a week.

On the northern frontier, at Meng Tian's dusty headquarters town in the eastern Ordos (where the Great Wall runs
to this day), Fusu wept on reading the fake letter, but
accepted it at face value. He was prevented from immediate
suicide only by Meng Tian, who pointed out there was perhaps something fishy going on. They had both been
appointed to guard the frontier with 300,000 troops; this
was a 'weighty responsibility'; yet here comes this letter,
delivered by a single messenger, out of the blue. They should
at least get confirmation.

Fusu thought this would show an unfilial lack of trust, and committed suicide anyway.

Meng Tian, however, said he needed to know the order was genuine. Of course, the messenger could not possibly allow this – it would delay things by two weeks – so he had the general and his entourage of officers arrested (it is this that implies the 'single messenger' had a substantial body of troops with him). Meng Tian and his officers were taken to a prison some 60 kilometres south-east of the Great Wall fortress of Jingbian (it means 'Warn the Border'). Only now could a message be sent back to the conspirators that all was well: Fusu dead, Meng Tian in gaol.

Meanwhile, on the road to Xianyang, the emperor's dead body was becoming a problem. The emperor had now been dead for over a week, and his carriage was beginning to smell, embalming en route apparently being out of the question. From his carriage, therefore, came an odd order: that all official carriages should take on board 30 kilos of dried fish, which gave off enough of a smell to disguise the stench of decay. The imperial procession was still 450 kilometres and one month from home. It was only when news arrived of Fusu's suicide that the conspirators could announce the emperor's death and the fake edict appointing Huhai as his heir.

So at last, in September 210 BC, the great procession arrived back in Xianyang and the business began of installing the Second Emperor and burying the First.

Well-formed plans swing into action. The foundations of the tomb are dug, of course. There are springs beneath the tomb and all around the surrounding area, which means that the base of the tomb needs a damp-proof course, a rather expensive one. Now, in Sima Qian's words, 'they poured in bronze to make the outer coffin', and the work-force completes the basics, in a famous passage that has fuelled imaginations ever since.

This is Burton Watson's translation:

[Replicas of] palaces, scenic towers and the 100 officials, as well as rare utensils and wonderful objects, were brought to fill up the tomb. Craftsmen were ordered to set up crossbows and arrows, rigged so that they would immediately shoot down anyone attempting to break in. Mercury was used to fashion [imitations of] the hundred rivers, the Yellow River and the Yangtze, and the seas, constructed in such a way that they seemed to flow. Above were representations of all the heavenly bodies, below the features of the earth. 'Man-fish' oil was used for lamps, which were calculated to burn for a long time without going out.[1]

This paragraph, often quoted without comment as if it were proven and literal truth, owes a good deal to hype. Sima Qian gives no sources. It is folk memory, much embroidered by the passage of a century. An underground palace, treasures, cocked crossbows, rivers of mercury, the constellations glittering in the ceiling, lamps glowing: this is Hollywood material, just right for the opening of an Indiana Jones movie.

Much of this work – the completion of the underground

[1] The words within square brackets are not in the Chinese, but are implied. Watson's has been the standard version, much quoted. Here is another: 'They filled the grave chamber with models of palaces, towers and the Hundred Offices in addition to valuable vessels and precious stones and wonderful treasures. Crossbows with mechanical automatic releases offered protection from intruders. The country's various waterways, the Yangtze and the Yellow River as well as the ocean itself, were imitated in quicksilver, and a mechanical device produced flowing waves. Above the stars and the firmament were depicted, below a geographically realistic relief of the earth. Lamps filled with whale oil burned permanently.'

palace, the burial within it, the digging of secondary pits – would have gone ahead at speed. No record, however, mentions the funeral itself. The only details given by Sima Qian were the gruesome ones. Huhai, now the 21-year-old Second Emperor, but firmly under the thumb of the dreadful Zhao Gao, ordered that all concubines who had not born a son should 'accompany the dead man', presumably so that they could fulfil their duty in the next life. How many received this strange honour? Sima Qian just says 'many'. We know the emperor had 20 sons, so a dozen or two seems a minimum, assuming that concubinage was not yet the sub-world of thousands it became centuries later.

Now comes the job of roofing the tomb and the Army. The roof would require a forest of timbers – about 18,000 5-metre sections of pine. Felled in the forests of Sichuan, Henan and Hubei 200–300 kilometres to the south, the trees would have been rough-cut with iron axes after the emperor's death had been announced, and hauled north-wards on cumbersome ox-wagons. The possible scope of this operation? Four beams to a wagon, 4,500 wagon-loads, the first ones arriving after a month, the rest rolling in over the following six months.

After the underground palace was sealed comes another of Huhai's grim decisions. 'Someone pointed out that the artisans and craftsmen who had built the tomb knew what was buried there' – so, to prevent word leaking out, 'the inner gate was closed off and the outer gate lowered, so that all the artisans and craftsmen were shut in the tomb and were unable to get out.'

This is another of those popular melodramatic details that turn up in every account. But I don't believe it. Horses were buried alive, and possibly a few people condemned for some crime. But teams of artisans and craftsmen, whose only fault was to have knowledge of the tomb's contents and their own work? It sounds more like the legends that arose around several other emperors: Attila the Hun, Genghis Khan, his son Ogedei, indeed any emperor (according to Marco Polo, who claimed that all living things on the route of the imperial funeral cortège were slain). Such assertions do not stand much scrutiny. Even a young maniac like the Second Emperor needed artists, if only to complete work on the unfinished Epang Palace. What would the deaths do to the morale of the survivors? What of the cocked crossbows? Well, we shall not know the truth until the day when the underground palace is opened.

There will be more digging to do – dozens of other pits for sacrificial animals, bronze carriages, suits of stone armour, officials, horses – but they can wait until the mound is either well under way or complete. So now, at last, comes the most formidable task of all: shifting the earth that covers the tomb and building the surrounding walls.

Today, the pyramid is between 50 and 75 metres high, depending on which side is measured. Remember from chapter 8, 'Digging the Tomb', that the official history of the Han dynasty claims the original height was 'more than 50 *zhang* (115 metres)', a figure often justified by reference to 'erosion' that has reduced it to its present dimensions. As far as I know, there is no evidence for such a massive reduction. Earth has gathered in some places at the base of the pyramid, but nothing that would suggest that the mound's height has been cut by 60 per cent or its floor area by a third. Today, you can hardly see its original shape – with a step halfway up – because of the trees, but on a photograph taken in 1914 the treeless, stepped shape is quite clear. If there had been severe erosion, that outline would have long since vanished. On other tombs (such as that of the Han emperor Wu Di), erosion has apparently had little effect. These thoughts make sense of Duan Qingbo's

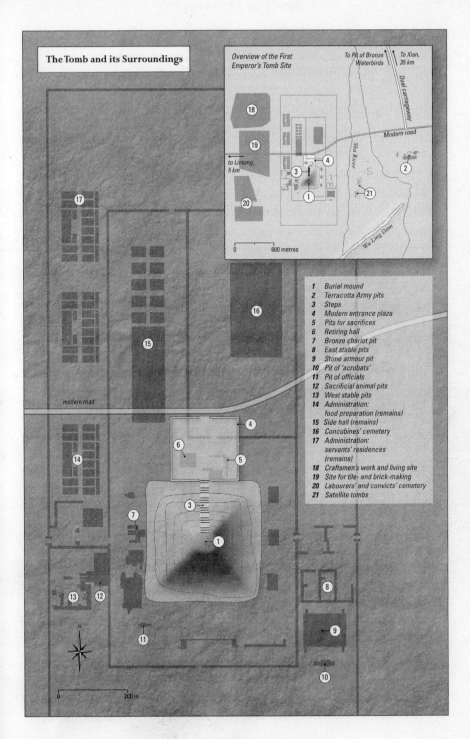

The Tomb and its Surroundings

Overview of the First Emperor's Tomb Site

To Pit of Bronze Waterbirds

To Xian, 35 km

Dual carriageway

Modern road

Sha River

to Lintong, 5 km

Wu Ling Dam

0   600 metres

1 Burial mound
2 Terracotta Army pits
3 Steps
4 Modern entrance plaza
5 Pits for sacrifices
6 Retiring hall
7 Bronze chariot pit
8 East stable pits
9 Stone armour pit
10 Pit of 'acrobats'
11 Pit of officials
12 Sacrificial animal pits
13 West stable pits
14 Administration:
    food preparation (remains)
15 Side hall (remains)
16 Concubines' cemetery
17 Administration:
    servants' residences
    (remains)
18 Craftsmen's work and living site
19 Site for tile- and brick-making
20 Labourers' and convicts' cemetery
21 Satellite tombs

modern road

N

0   200 m

insistence in speaking to me that the standard sources are wrong, that 115 metres was just the *planned* height, that today's tomb probably looks much as it did 2,000 years ago. (This interpretation also makes sense of his belief that the underground palace is 80 × 50 metres, far smaller than the estimate quoted by Yuan Zhongyi).

This means the volume of the tomb is, and always was, about 1.8 million cubic metres. That's about 2.7 million tonnes of earth to be dug up and carried in from outlying areas – perhaps one in particular: a research paper quoted by Yuan Zhongyi states that in mineral content and colour much of the mound's soil matches that found in a pond about 2.5 kilometres away to the north-east, implying that the soil 'came from two sources: one was the earth dug from the original tomb, the other was the nearby reservoir'. Unless the workers are to file through gates, thus limiting their numbers, the tomb must be covered before the walls go up. We can get an idea of the numbers involved, because we know that the tomb was not completed by the time the dynasty died four years later. Indeed, it may have stopped earlier, only one year after the Second Emperor's accession, because by then civil war had spread to Lintong.

Meanwhile, there would be a lot more going on. For a start, the architects had planned for two sets of surrounding walls, with a separate enclosure for the emperor's concubines. The walls would be about 8 metres wide and some 10 metres high. That's 6 kilometres of rammed-earth wall, or almost half a million cubic metres (another 750,000 tonnes, over three times the amount removed from the palace foundations) of earth to dig, and pound, and finish, not forgetting ten gates, each with three storeys. And the guard-towers at each corner of each rectangle. And the tiled roofs that covered the walkways along the top of the walls, for the whole complex would be patrolled by guards who needed to be protected from the rain and sun. To the 2.7 million tonnes of earth for the mound must be added the 750,000 tonnes that form the walls: a total of 3.5 million tonnes to be shifted in four years, maximum.

In round figures, 175 million earth-carrying journeys in 1,500 days comes to 120,000 back-and-forth journeys per day. Assume each man makes three journeys per day. That's 40,000 workers, minimum.

The walls, though, were merely the shells for the real business of the tomb, which would be to honour the emperor's memory with rituals. These would centre on the Room of Rest, or Retiring Hall, a huge complex measuring 57 × 62 metres – gateway, courtyard, tiled hall and a 'holy of holies' – which would be the centre for the cult devoted to the dead emperor. It was to contain the emperor's clothing, headgear and other accoutrements, which would be taken in procession every month to a temple nearby for sacrifices and veneration. Here, probably, the emperor's coffin would be placed, ready for when the time came, and here his body would lie before it was consigned to the coffin and then the tomb. Nearby would be the Side Halls, where members of the imperial family would don their mourning clothes and prepare for the monthly rites. Finally, there would be a building for the preparation of the sacrificial food – a complex of a dozen halls set between the inner and outer walls, which would be used for weighing, measuring, food preparation and cooking. Officials would have planned that these buildings would be used for daily, weekly and monthly ceremonies in the years to come.

All this demanded a second, smaller army of several thousand administrators: engineers, overseers, geomancers, priests and cooks, all of whom would need their own houses, most of whom would probably have their own families. So imagine a line of houses standing on raised platforms between the inner and outer walls: normal single-storey houses, with wooden beams and curly-tiled roofs with round, decorated tile-ends.

The 40,000 labourers have to be housed and fed somewhere among the surrounding villages that wrung a living from the soil. Were they all criminals without families, working in concentration-camp conditions? Did some have families with them (Zhao Gao's mother, remember, had been a criminal, yet had borne several children while imprisoned)? No one knows. Then there were the craftsmen who made the bricks and tiles: they needed their workplaces and their families and their housing – a whole sub-community that lay to the west, outside the outer wall, well removed from the ritual sites. And who took care of security? Long-term criminals had to be supervised, new ones punished, possible mutinies crushed, which meant contingents of soldiers, and a barracks somewhere. And of course, there were many deaths, from disease, overwork, malnutrition, old age, so there had to be cemeteries, also outside the outer wall.

Off to one side, 1.5 kilometres from the heaving mass of labourers building the main tomb and its walls, were the pits of the Terracotta Army – pits in the plural, for there were enough terracotta figures to stretch the original concept. Perhaps Pit No. 1 had been prepared long since. But now it was clear that work would go on for years, there was a chance to heighten the realism of the Army by adding four specialized units to back up the 6,000 warriors of Pit No. 1. In Pit No. 2, there would be 64 wooden chariots and their 256 horses (no grooms), a mixed force of 25 chariots, 100 horses, more cavalry and infantry, 108 more cavalrymen and 332 archers – 1,300 figures in all. There's something odd about the shape of this pit, as if it started as a rectangle but then the designers changed their minds and added an extension. Pit No. 3 was tiny by comparison, with 68 well-spaced figures and a four-horse chariot facing an exit ramp. Archaeologists suggest this was the command centre, the Army's headquarters from which the action would be directed in some battle of spirits, with a chariot standing by to carry a messenger into the field. Pit No. 4 is an enigma, unfinished, awaiting contingents that never came.

Adding the three additional pits to the first makes another 100,000 cubic metres, or 150,000 tonnes, of earth to be removed. By now the Qin quantity surveyors can take such figures in their stride, for it is less than a twentieth of the earth the workers have been shifting on to the tomb itself. If a quarter of the workforce (10,000) were seconded to the pits, they would finish the job in nine months.

Now we have to factor in another immense operation: the roofing. Recall the 4,500 wagon-loads of half-tonne beams lumbering in at the rate of half a dozen a day. To the beams must be added 3,300 3-metre supports which are to stand against the walls and help take the weight of the beams and the overburden of earth. That's another 1,000 tonnes of timber, another 250 wagon-loads.

How would the beams be handled? Not with a great deal of respect, for they remained rounded, with their bark removed, but not squared off to fit close. They could have been, for Qin craftsmen used adzes to make planks (as the flooring on one of the small sacrificial pits shows). So quality was not of the essence. Perhaps speed was: better, apparently, to have a quick roof than a pretty one. The next challenge would be to get the beams in position, fast, which could have been done by laying a couple of planks along the top of each wall and rolling the beams into position.

Pit No. 4 was mysteriously left empty, unfinished, unroofed and unfilled. Did they run out of terracotta figures? Or time? Perhaps more figures were on order when revolution forced overseers to drive the workforce away from the spirit army into the real one, to be scattered by the forces that would soon destroy all their labour.

11

CONSUMED BY FIRE

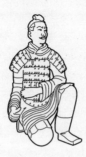

FOR FOUR YEARS THE TERRACOTTA ARMY STOOD IN PITCH-black silence, an eternal army ready for imaginary battle, until some time in 206 BC the real world intruded. As I imagine it standing deep within one of the corridors, distant sounds of digging give way to thumps of falling earth and the cries of intruders. Flaming torches send red light dancing between the shadowy statues. People begin to shove their way along the corridors. There's no room, and the intruders are in a hurry. Warriors teeter and crash like falling dominoes. Living hands seize still-bright weapons from clay hands. Someone trips, curses, drops a scattering of sparks.

Some such scene occurred, for there is evidence: an entry shaft, fallen warriors, scattered horses' tails, a fire. But before we get to the details, I should tell you how the intruders came to be here.

*

It was all the fault of the Second Emperor, the emperor who should never have been. His top adviser was, of course, Zhao Gao, the king-maker, the instigator of the Sand Hill Plot which had brought him to the throne. Huhai's hold on power was weak, and would fail completely if his guilty secret ever came out. How to strengthen it? By doing as his father did – by touring distant parts to show his people who was boss. That's what he did in the spring of 209 BC, visiting the same mountains as his father and adding to all his father's inscriptions. All he added, though, was a statement that the inscriptions were by the First Emperor, in the hope that venerating his father's name would claim his mantle. Not enough, really, as the young emperor whined to Zhao Gao. Life was a misery. 'A person lives in this world no longer than it takes a team of six thoroughbreds to gallop past a crack in a wall. I want to savour all the pleasures of eye and ear.' Besides, 'The chief ministers are unsubmissive, the various officials still have great power, and the other imperial princes are certain to contest my rule. What can I do?'

Zhao Gao proposed a Stalinist solution: unleash a reign of terror. You are surrounded by disloyal subjects, he said, eminent men who are, incidentally, jealous of me and my humble background. Make the laws sterner and penalties more severe! See that persons charged with guilt implicate others! Wipe out the chief ministers and sow dissension among your kin! 'By doing so you can strike terror into the empire as a whole, and at the same time do away with those who disapprove of your actions.

'"Excellent!" said the Second Emperor.'

The most immediate danger came from his own family, from those princes who ranked above him and below the true, but dead, heir, Fusu. Six princes were put to death, and three others, protesting their innocence, chose to fall on their own swords. Was the total nine or twelve? Sima Qian has both. He also mentions ten princesses killed by being torn apart by chariots. This could all be so, because so far 17 graves have been found with possessions showing that those buried there were nobles; 'and from their teeth', Professor Yuan added when he was briefing me, 'we can tell that most of them were in their twenties'. Of one group of seven skeletons, six had been dismembered, and two were women. The numbers do not quite add up yet, but there is surely more evidence still hidden to show that there was a terrible bloodletting as the Second Emperor did away with his rivals and critics. Fear spread from the imperial family to the population at large.

Zhao Gao, now lord high executioner, was free to turn on his old adversaries, the Meng brothers and their families. Meng Yi, accused of opposing Huhai's accession, was asked to commit suicide. He naturally denied the charge, and delivered one of his own in a long memo that ended, 'One who governs by the Way does not put to death the guiltless.' It did him no good. Zhao Gao ordered his execution. Meng Tian, still in prison after his arrest on the northern frontier, was confronted by an envoy also demanding his suicide. He too wrote a memo, which the envoy refused to pass on, saying he had his orders. Meng Tian despaired, and swallowed poison. Sima Qian gives him a tragic and highly imaginative death. 'What crime have I committed before Heaven that I should die an innocent death?' he asks. Then he realizes: in building the Great Wall he 'cut through the arteries of the earth. That must be my crime!' Not so, says Sima Qian, taking a swipe at his own emperor's ministers. He deserved to die for reasons that had nothing to do with the arteries of the earth. His crime was not standing up to the First

Emperor – 'He did not strive to bring about the well-being of the mass of the people.'

For his next project, the Second Emperor turned to the Epang Palace, which had hardly been begun when the First Emperor died. To complete it would be to strengthen his claim to his father's mantle. Unknown thousands were set to work. Then, because a show of strength is always of help to an insecure ruler, 50,000 crossbowmen were brought in from all over the empire to reinforce the capital's garrisons. Since they needed food, all farmers within 150 kilometres were forbidden to eat their own products. So cruelty and deprivation built on each other: complaints multiplied, suffering spread.

Later the same year (209 BC) came the first hint of revolt, an uprising with highly eccentric roots.

It started some 400–500 kilometres away to the south-east, in the old kingdom of Chu (mostly present-day Henan) defeated by the First Emperor fourteen years before, where 900 conscripts were being transported to their garrison. Heavy rain delayed them, and delay of any kind was an offence. The three commanders would exonerate themselves with excuses, but the two sergeants would be executed for dereliction. The two men, a former farmhand called Chen She and his sidekick Wu Guang, conferred. As things stood, they faced inevitable death, whereas if they revolted, though they would also face death if defeated, they would at least have a chance.[1]

---

[1] Sima Qian includes an aside about Chen She dreaming up a cover story. Fusu, the true heir to the throne, was dead, but ordinary people did not know this. The same went for a general who might or might not have perished in the First Emperor's conquests. What if he, Chen She, pretended to be Fusu and his sidekick pretended to be the general? This they do, but the subterfuge leads nowhere, so it becomes a footnote.

Having consulted a diviner, the two became convinced they needed a way to attract followers. Chen She got some silk, wrote on it in red letters 'Chen She shall be king', and secretly stuffed the banner into the belly of a newly caught fish which was about to become an item in the conscripts' supper. He also persuaded Wu Guang to hide in a clump of trees beside a nearby shrine, and told him what to do. That evening, a soldier duly found the banner and held it up. At the same time, Wu Guang, in his hiding place, lit a torch, partially concealed it in a basket and, with this ghostly light jigging about in the bushes, set up a fox-like wail that turned into words: 'Chen She shall be king!'

This rigmarole was enough to set the soldiers talking among themselves. Wu Guang, a popular figure, then stage-managed a fight with his commander, boasting he was going to run away until the commander started to beat him. At this, Wu Guang and Chen She seized swords and killed the commanders. Chen She then inspired the rest of the troops with a rousing speech: Missing the rendezvous means death! Even if you live, most of you will die fighting! 'If you would risk death, then risk it for the sake of fame and glory!'

The fires of revolt spread. Towns and counties fell in behind the growing army, until it had several hundred chariots, 1,000 horsemen and over 20,000 infantry, all united by the urge to restore their old state to independence. All across the region, locals embittered by Qin rule murdered officials and governors. Within weeks, Chen She was sending deputies off to seize cities and districts beyond Chu's borders and having himself declared king of a resurrected Chu. It was a remarkable thing, as the second-century BC Confucian scholar Jia Yi remarked in a famous study known as *The Faults of Qin*:[2]

[2] Quoted by Sima Qian at the end of his biography of the First Emperor, in *Records of the Grand Historian*.

Chen She, born in a humble hut with tiny windows and a wattle door, a day labourer in the fields and a garrison conscript, whose abilities could not match even the average ... led a band of some hundred poor, weary soldiers in revolt against Qin. They cut down trees to make their weapons and raised their flags on garden poles, and the whole world ... followed after them as shadows follow a form.

Quite quickly, it all went horribly wrong, as revolution bred armies and kings like weeds. One of Chen's commanders, now far away to the east, created a king of Chu, without knowing Chen She had done the same to himself. When he discovered what had happened he slew his own 'king', reported back to Chen She, and was himself executed for his error. Another of Chen's commanders, sent northward to seize what had once been Zhou, set himself up as king, then planned conquests on his own account, inspiring yet another bid for independence. Time went backwards. The empire was torn apart by Warring States – Chu, Wei, Zhao, Pei, Yan, Qi – each with its would-be king; each state was threatened by jumped-up feudal lords, every lord by self-declared generals. Fortunately for everyone, Chen was assassinated by his own charioteer. He had ruled, if you can call it ruling, for six months.

Back in Xianyang, the old state of Qin was also approaching collapse. In the winter of 209 BC an invasion force was approaching from the east, up the Wei valley, through the strategic Hangu Pass. Ban Gu says in his history of the Han dynasty: 'Construction of the Li Mountain grave site was not yet complete when millions of soldiers arrived, led by [rebel general] Zhou Zhang.' What was to be done? One of the Second Emperor's generals told him: 'The robbers have arrived. They are many and they are strong. It is already too late to call soldiers from other districts to help. But there are many forced labourers at the Mount Li grave complex. Grant them amnesty and supply them with arms.' Which is apparently what was done – a move that successfully blocked the rebel army, and also stopped work on the First Emperor's tomb.

The emperor became ever more removed from reality. First, when a messenger told him of the rebellion, he had the messenger executed. Thereafter no one dared tell him the truth: that the rebels were closing in, that his troops had lost a major battle, that a general had been captured, that a second rebel army of 30,000–40,000 men was approaching. Second, Zhao Gao played on his isolation, which became increasingly psychopathic. Always eager to increase his own influence, Zhao Gao advised the young emperor to remain aloof, hidden away in godlike isolation, ostensibly to save him from making youthful errors, while his ministers applied policies of increasing harshness.

Now, in another of his unpleasant intrigues, he turned on the ageing Li Si, whom he had arm-twisted into supporting the Sand Hill Plot to enthrone Huhai. Poor old Li Si was already a husk of his former self, having been refused the chance to remonstrate with the Second Emperor. Zhao Gao turned to guile. He complained to Li Si that rebellion was in the air, but that the emperor's attention was on the Epang Palace, dogs, horses and other useless activities. He suggested that Li Si was surely the one to reprimand the emperor.

Quite right, replied Li Si. But 'the ruler does not sit in the court. He stays deep within the palace, so I have no chance to see him when I wish.'

'Allow me to assist you,' said Zhao smoothly. 'I will see when he is at leisure and let you know.'

So when the emperor was dining, enjoying himself in the

company of women, Zhao Gao did just that. Li Si came calling three times, and three times the emperor refused him entry. He never comes at ordinary times, complained the emperor to Zhao Gao; 'then, as soon as I am enjoying myself in private, immediately he appears and wants to talk about affairs of state. Is it because I am so young that he treats me this way, or because he thinks I'm stupid?'

Zhao Gao made his move. Maybe Li Si is not to be trusted, he said. Remember this: he has a son, the governor of Sanchuan, who failed to quell the rebel Chen She, did he not? Surely this reeks of treachery.

Doubts having been planted, the emperor started to investigate Li Si's son. Li Si, still unable to gain access, wrote to the emperor warning him about Zhao Gao, a man of 'evil and unbridled ambitions and dangerous and treasonable ways', who has acquired immense wealth and is 'undermining Your Majesty's authority'.

A bad mistake. The emperor was incensed that Zhao Gao, the man he most relied upon, should be accused. 'Mr Zhao is a man of integrity and diligence. He understands other people's feelings and knows how to please me.'

No, replied Li Si. 'He has no understanding of principles, but is insatiable in his greed and never ceases his quest for gain.'

The emperor, of course, told Zhao Gao of this, who could smugly say: Obviously the old man wants me dead, so *he* can acquire wealth.

Next, Li Si dared join with two other top advisers to state the unacceptable truth: that bandits were arising without end because of the burdens of garrison duty, forced labour and heavy taxation. The emperor ranted at them like a child – I want 'a thousand chariots, to be attended by ten thousand, so I can live up to my name and title!' I've been on the throne two years, and all I get is bandits! It's all your fault! He ordered Zhao Gao to arrest the three of them. Two committed suicide, while Li Si was shackled and carted off to prison to await trial for treason. The old man railed against the injustice of the times: sad work . . . an unprincipled ruler . . . disorder imminent . . . an emperor who destroys his brothers, executes loyal ministers, enlarges palaces, increases taxes . . . won't listen . . . sleeping his way to insurrection . . . I'll live to see wild deer roam the palace.

All true, but all to no avail. All his family were arrested. He – who had devoted almost 40 years to Qin and was now 72 – was accused, and beaten on the soles of his feet 1,000 times until he confessed to plotting treason. He wrote an ironical memo listing his 'crimes' – upholding the law, honouring merit, annexing six states, elevating the Qin ruler to Son of Heaven, driving out barbarians, ensuring the loyalty of ministers, standardizing weights and measures and coinage, building fast roads, winning hearts and minds etc. etc. 'This is the kind of subject I have been, and my crimes have long been deserving of death!'

The emperor never even saw the letter, because Zhao kept it. More questions broke the old man utterly. By now his son had been killed by rebels. Zhao Gao controlled all the evidence, and could 'prove' his guilt. The Second Emperor condemned him to a terrible death by the 'five penalties' – branding on the forehead, amputation of the ears, nose, fingers and feet, flogging to death and exposure of the head and corpse in the market place; although some of the five seem to have been rescinded in Li Si's case, because he actually met his death by being cut in two at the waist.

Zhao Gao, almost supreme, was just one step away from total control, and in taking it he was helped by the emperor's increasing separation from reality. It started with a strange incident. In what seems a cross between a practical joke and a test of his own influence, Zhao Gao presented the emperor with a deer, but insisted it was a horse. Courtiers, totally cowed, backed him up. The emperor began to doubt his sanity. Was he losing his mind because of something he had done? Yes, said Zhao, it's because you are impure. So the emperor went off to a royal park to fast, and here he sank into superstition and psychopathy. He was worried by a dream in which his carriage horses were attacked by a white tiger (a symbol of malevolence from the river Jing, so a diviner said). When a passer-by happened to wander into the park, the emperor shot him. Zhao Gao reprimanded him: 'The Son of Heaven for no reason has wantonly shot an innocent man. Such conduct is forbidden by the Lord on High.' To avoid misfortune, he went on, it was necessary to carry out sacrifices. The emperor accepted, and retired to a palace in Xian, intending to drown four white horses in the malevolent river Jing.

As madness took hold, the end approached. Zhao Gao, fearful that he and his family would be blamed for the rebellions, planned a *coup d'état* with his brother and son-in-law, Yan Yue. Claiming the bandits were upon them, the son-in-law led a force to 'protect' the palace where the emperor was staying. The palace commander, protesting there were no rebels, was cut down, his guards over-whelmed, the emperor trapped. Yan Yue yelled at the emperor that it was his fault the rebels were upon them: 'You are arrogant and wilful and you punish and kill people without reason! The whole empire has turned against you!' There was only one way out: suicide. Desperately, the emperor tried to negotiate. Could he keep one province? Become a marquis? Become an ordinary person, with his wife and children? No, no, no, on all counts. There was nothing for it but to kill himself.

And, hard though it is to believe, he did.

Sima Qian does not record the court's reaction, but an

attempt by Zhao Gao to make himself emperor proved underwhelming, so he summoned a compliant grandson of the First Emperor, Zi Ying, who was not much younger than his dead uncle. Fear bred fear, and plots. Suspecting Zhao was planning to kill him, Zi Ying at once feigned sickness, locked himself away in a temple and started a counter-plot.

A few days later, as Zi Ying hoped, Zhao Gao came to demand that the coronation take place. Zi Ying (and his attendants, presumably) stabbed him, and quickly rounded up his family. After far too long, the empire was rid of a monster.

As it happened, Zhao Gao had not been far wrong: the rebels were at the gates, amid the birthpangs of a new dynasty. The peasant uprisings had led to the rebirth of the old kingdoms, and several new ones, nineteen in all. In the assault on Qin, two rival leaders had emerged, each with his own forces. One was Liu Bang, of peasant stock, future founder of the Han dynasty. The other was Xiang Yu, of special interest to us because he started off as leader and was responsible for the violence that destroyed Xianyang and the Terracotta Army.

Liu Bang came from Pei towards the coast of central China, where he had been a low-ranking official. According to the historian Ban Gu, he was a charismatic character, with a prominent nose, a beautiful beard and 72 black moles on his left thigh (72 being a number with many mystical connotations). His career as a revolutionary started through bad luck. He was escorting convicts to work on the First Emperor's tomb, but many of them escaped. Since he would be held responsible on arrival, he decided not to arrive. Instead, he freed the remaining prisoners, fled home and went on the run, gathering a gang of 100 or so. As rebellion spread,

Pei's local magistrate was ordered to capture Liu and his gang. Liu wrote on a piece of silk a message suggesting an uprising, and shot it over the walls. As a result, the townspeople rose up, killed the magistrate and placed Liu in charge. Having declared himself Lord of Pei, he led his army towards Qin.

Xiang Yu, from further to the south-east, also started off by murdering the local governor, then struck out northward with his army, joining up with Liu Bang before heading west into the Qin heartland. It was Xiang Yu – 'fiery, violent and very destructive', in the opinion of generals quoted by Ban Gu – who proved the more effective leader, but Liu Bang ('habitually generous') who was first into the Qin capital of Xianyang, an act that should by rights have allowed him to claim the succession.

When in late 207 BC the emperor surrendered – in a plain chariot, with his imperial seals packed up and ready for delivery – Liu Bang declared it would be inauspicious to kill him. He ordered a peaceful occupation, securing the treasures and records from harm so they could all be accounted for, and replacing all Qin's laws with two: death for murder and just punishment for robbery and injury. 'All I have come for is to deliver you, Elders, from harm,' he told Qin's surviving officials. He even refused to accept the cattle, sheep, wine and food that were offered, saying 'I do not wish to be a burden upon the people.'

Two months later Xiang Yu arrived, with a rather different agenda, and a reputation for brutality reinforced the previous summer, when he had massacred the whole population of one city. Jealous of Liu Bang's success and suspicious of his designs, he reversed Liu Bang's easy-going regime, killed the ex-emperor, massacred the people of Xianyang and burned the palaces. As Homer Dubs, Oxford Professor of Greek in the 1930s, says in his introduction to his translation of Ban Gu, 'That fire was the real "Burning of the Books," for in the imperial palaces there had been preserved the proscribed literature for the use of the imperial erudites and officials.'

A few months later, Xiang Yu turned the nineteen small states of the former empire into a confederacy, with himself at the top as king–protector. But this lacked legitimacy. Liu Bang had secured the victory; it was he who had taken Xianyang and received the emperor's submission; it was he who was the rightful heir to Qin. There followed a complicated civil war, the details of which we can ignore, except to say that it lasted for four years, with Liu Bang emerging victorious. In late 202 BC Xiang Yu was surrounded, forced his way through Liu Bang's lines, found himself down to 28 followers, and committed suicide. Liu Bang was free to accept the title of Emperor Gaozu, the first of the Han dynasty.

So Han replaced Qin, a dynasty that had shone low for many centuries, then exploded to fill its universe with a brief burst of energy before collapsing into madness and murder.

How did it come to this? Jia Yi in *The Faults of Qin* had no doubts of the answer. 'Because it failed to rule with humanity and righteousness.' The First Emperor had his faults, but the Second Emperor was a disaster, an example of how *not* to rule laid out in a fine passage describing what he should have done:

If the Second Emperor had acted in the manner of even a mediocre ruler, if he had employed loyal and worthy men and had joined with his officials in single-mindedly caring for the nation's ills, correcting the errors of the former emperor . . . If he had emptied the prisons, pardoned those condemned to execution, abolished slavery and other forms of humiliating punishment, allowed each person to return to his native village; if he had opened the granaries and disbursed funds to succour the orphaned and lonely and those in dire poverty; if he had lightened taxes and [forced] labour to relieve the distress of the common people, simplified the laws, and reduced penalties for the sake of prosperity; if he had allowed the people of the empire to make a new beginning . . . then the empire would have flocked to him.

*

So it was the appalling Xiang Yu who released the violence that broke the terracotta warriors. Sima Qian mentions the burning of the capital and the palaces. There are only fleeting references to the tomb, only one (doubtful) to the Terracotta Army. For practical purposes, all we have to go on is the evidence as it comes down to us. To reconstruct what happened requires more than good, old-fashioned archaeology. We have several crimes in one: breaking and entering, theft and arson. We think we know who did it. But how? Our particular concern will be the fire. How did it start? How come every beam collapsed, ensuring that, of all the 6,000 statues in Pit No. 1 and the 1,500 or so statues in other pits, not a single one survived intact? To answer these questions demands a forensic approach, drawing on scientific disciplines that would not normally count as part of archaeology.

To review the scanty written evidence:

From Sima Qian and Ban Gu we know that there was fighting in the area and that in 209 BC, the second year of the Second Emperor's reign, the on-site workforce became an army to fight off the rebels. They were successful, but they would surely not have returned to work on the grave because the war continued for another three years. In that case, work may have stopped dead that year, as the Archaeological Team for the Excavation suggest in a throwaway remark in brackets: '[209 BC, construction of the grave

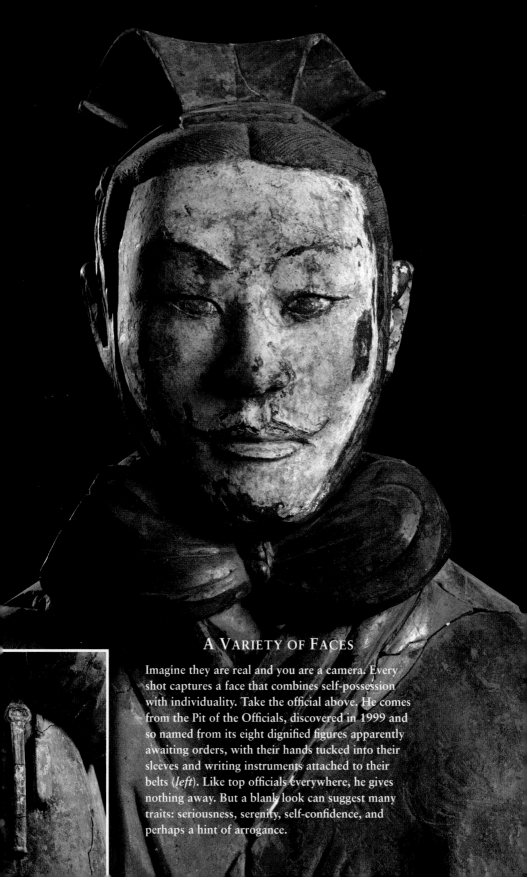

A VARIETY OF FACES

Imagine they are real and you are a camera. Every shot captures a face that combines self-possession with individuality. Take the official above. He comes from the Pit of the Officials, discovered in 1999 and so named from its eight dignified figures apparently awaiting orders, with their hands tucked into their sleeves and writing instruments attached to their belts (*left*). Like top officials everywhere, he gives nothing away. But a blank look can suggest many traits: seriousness, serenity, self-confidence, and perhaps a hint of arrogance.

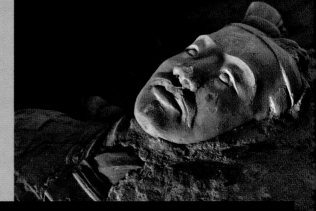

Right: A trick of lighting gives this soldier an expression of stoical patience.

Below: This rank-and-file soldier has a typical top-knot, but a personality all his own – a haughty bearing and a hint of a sneer that seems to express disdain for the enemy.

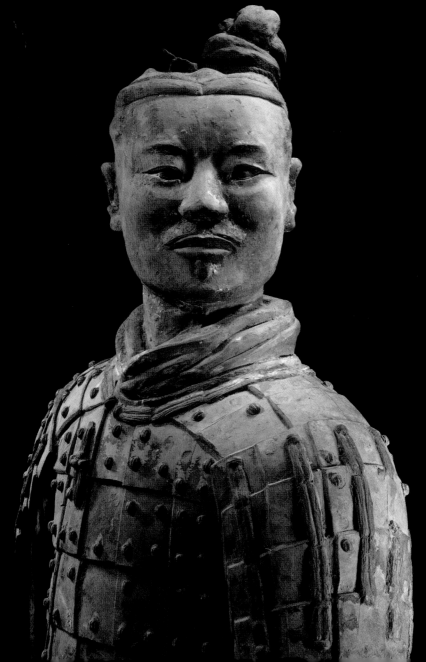

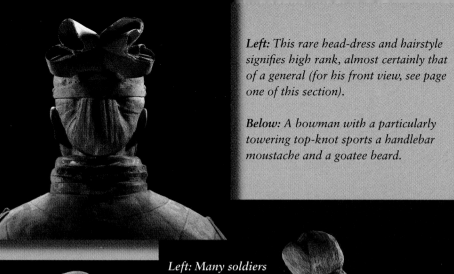

Left: This rare head-dress and hairstyle signifies high rank, almost certainly that of a general (for his front view, see page one of this section).

Below: A bowman with a particularly towering top-knot sports a handlebar moustache and a goatee beard.

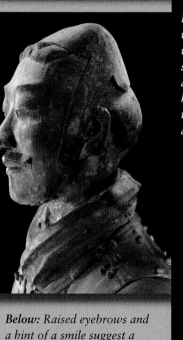

Left: Many soldiers wear caps of various shapes and sizes. This one with a prominent nose has a skull-cap that marks him as a horseman.

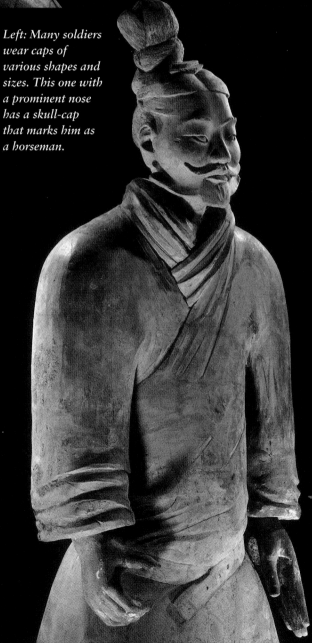

Below: Raised eyebrows and a hint of a smile suggest a restrained sense of humour.

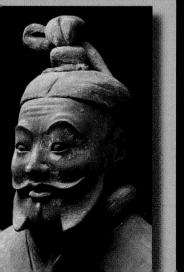

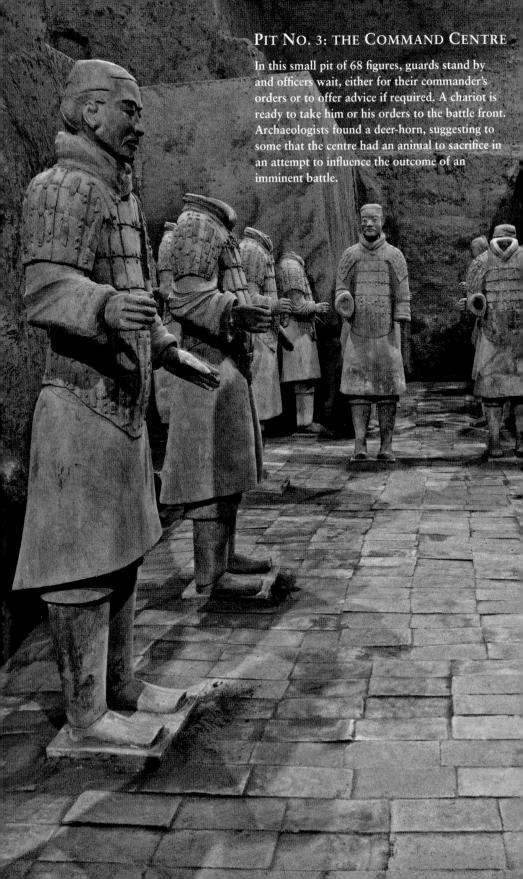

PIT NO. 3: THE COMMAND CENTRE

In this small pit of 68 figures, guards stand by
and officers wait, either for their commander's
orders or to offer advice if required. A chariot is
ready to take him or his orders to the battle front.
Archaeologists found a deer-horn, suggesting to
some that the centre had an animal to sacrifice in
an attempt to influence the outcome of an
imminent battle.

JEWELS IN THE CROWN:
TWO EXQUISITE BRONZE CARRIAGES

The two half-size bronze carriages (*below left*) – a lead chariot and the emperor's enclosed chariot – are unique in Chinese art. Discovered in 1979 (*below right*), they were found crushed into 3,000 pieces, and restored over the following nine years. The details of the lead chariot (*bottom*) are astounding: the reins, the miniature crossbow, the quiver, the moving wheels, the removable parasol.

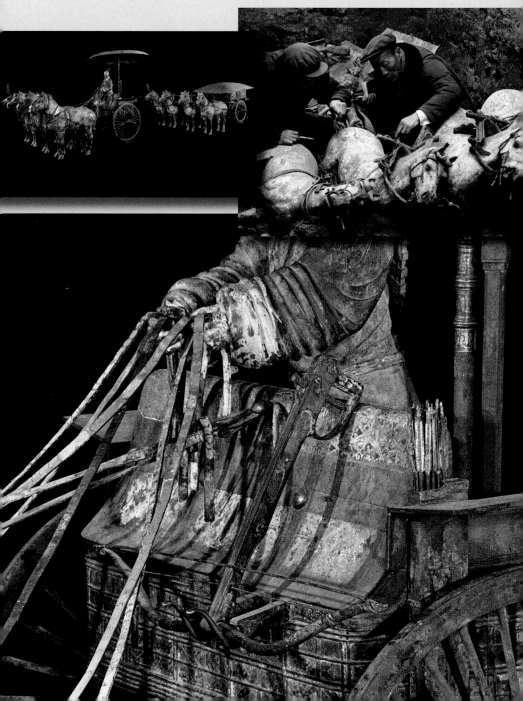

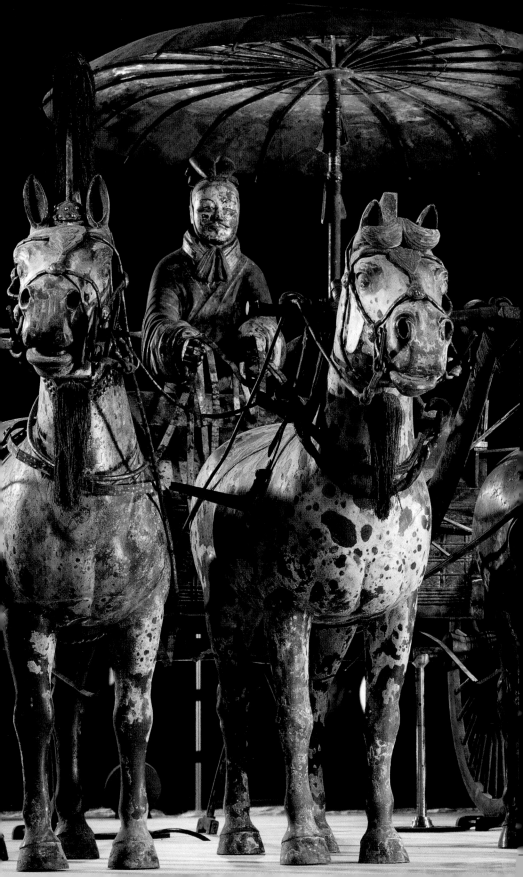

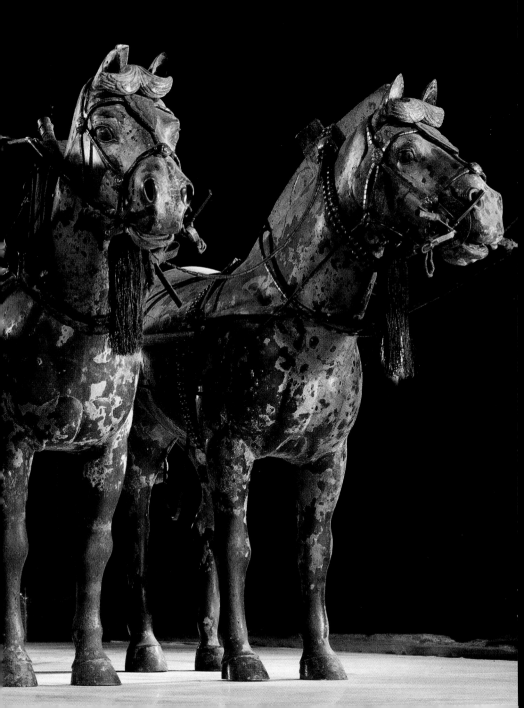

In close-up, the harnessing can be seen in all its intricacy. The horses were painted white, the colour of the west, suggesting that this was the direction in which the emperor would travel on an inspection tour.

A Real Watergarden, with Birds of Bronze

In 2001, archaeologists found 46 bronze birds – swans, cranes and geese – apparently grouped around a channel that must have been an underwater stream. They were attended by 15 terracotta figures, some sitting with their legs stretched out, some kneeling. When I was at the museum in 2007, one of the cranes, originally restored by Ma Yu, was in the laboratory for remedial work after a visit to Rome.

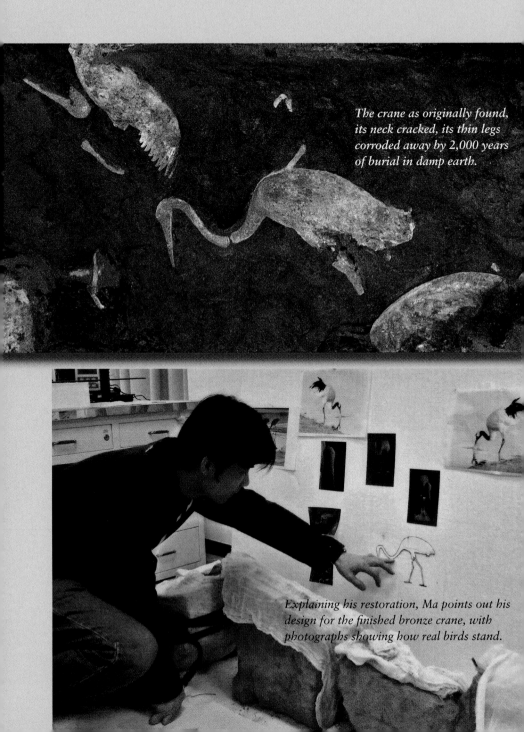

The crane as originally found, its neck cracked, its thin legs corroded away by 2,000 years of burial in damp earth.

Explaining his restoration, Ma points out his design for the finished bronze crane, with photographs showing how real birds stand.

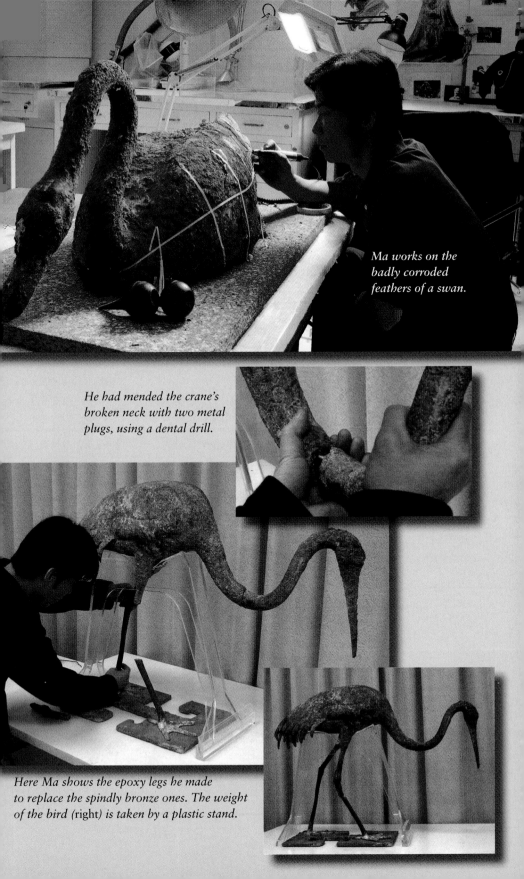

Ma works on the badly corroded feathers of a swan.

He had mended the crane's broken neck with two metal plugs, using a dental drill.

Here Ma shows the epoxy legs he made to replace the spindly bronze ones. The weight of the bird (right) is taken by a plastic stand.

STONE ARMOUR TO WARD OFF EVIL

Once, in one of the newly discovered pits, suits of armour made of limestone scales hung on walls like clothes in a wardrobe. When the pit burned and the roof fell, the copper ties corroded, leaving scales scattered by the thousand. Careful restoration has revealed how the scales fitted together. The suits were, of course, totally impractical, of use only in the world of spirits who would fear the limestone's symbolic power.

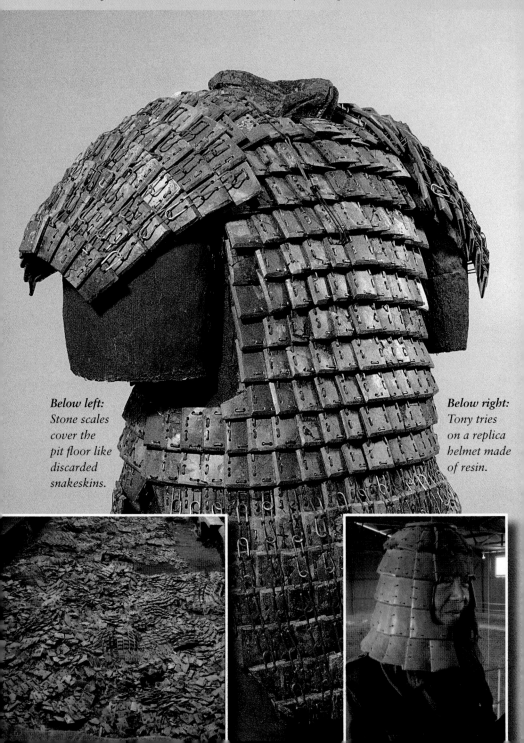

Below left:
*Stone scales
cover the
pit floor like
discarded
snakeskins.*

Below right:
*Tony tries
on a replica
helmet made
of resin.*

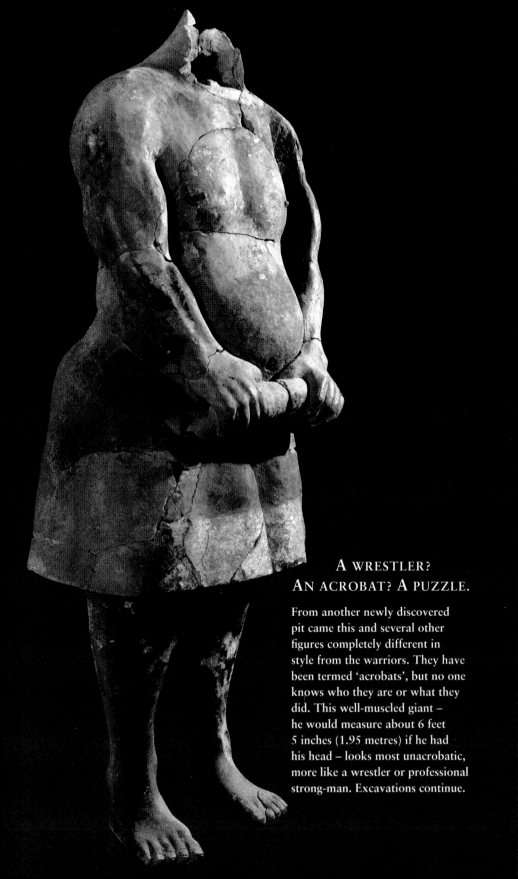

A WRESTLER?
AN ACROBAT? A PUZZLE.

From another newly discovered
pit came this and several other
figures completely different in
style from the warriors. They have
been termed 'acrobats', but no one
knows who they are or what they
did. This well-muscled giant –
he would measure about 6 feet
5 inches (1.95 metres) if he had
his head – looks most unacrobatic,
more like a wrestler or professional
strong-man. Excavations continue.

THE REPRODUCTIONS: AN ANCIENT SKILL REVIVED

Making replicas of the warriors is big business. The major player is Wang Lianyuan, who runs a factory a few kilometres north of the museum, making full-size figures by the hundred and smaller ones by the thousand every year. The methods – mass-production using moulds – are similar to those used by the First Emperor's artists. The numbers that he and his 20 workers produce suggest that the First Emperor could have had many more terracotta warriors than the estimated 8,000 found so far.

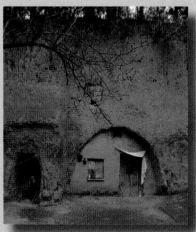

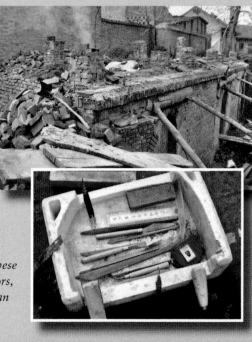

Wang's workers bake their figures in his rough-and-ready brick kilns.

A cave-house in the deep soil shows how Qin technicians would have made their kilns.

Sculptors don't need many tools (right). These are all that Wang needs to finish his warriors, or make new figures from which moulds can be taken for mass production.

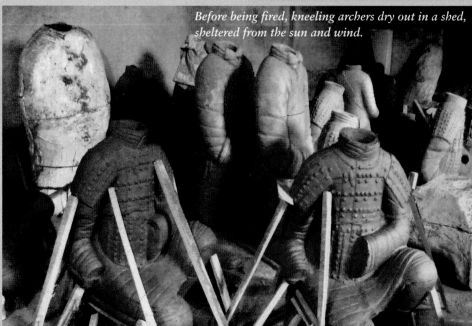

Before being fired, kneeling archers dry out in a shed, sheltered from the sun and wind.

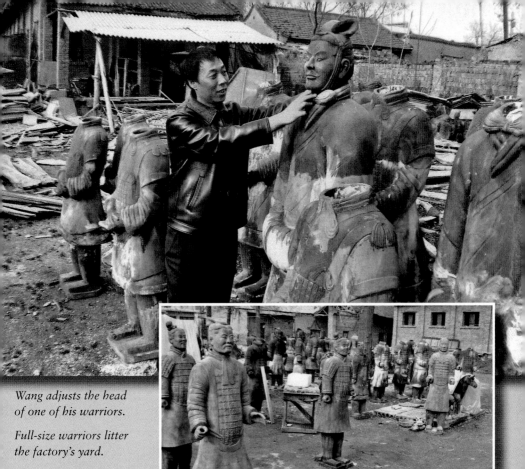

Wang adjusts the head of one of his warriors.

Full-size warriors litter the factory's yard.

Below: A full range of reproductions at the Xian Art Ceramics and Lacquer Factory.

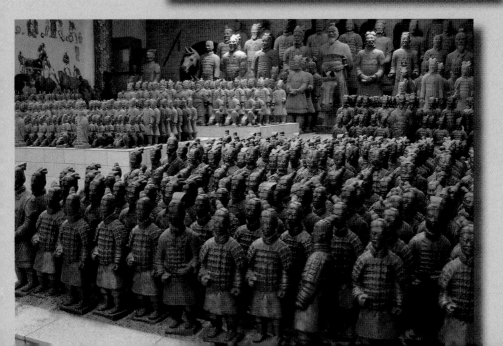

THE MYSTERY OF THE TOMB

This cut-away diagram shows the tomb's underground palace, based on the scanty evidence now available. Stepped 30-metre walls with two entrances east and west contain – what? The only answer so far is in Sima Qian's account: a coffin, rivers of mercury, treasures untold. The diagram includes the inner and outer walls of the site, but omits the other buildings. Nor does it show a roof, which would have been needed to hold the earth that topped the pyramid.

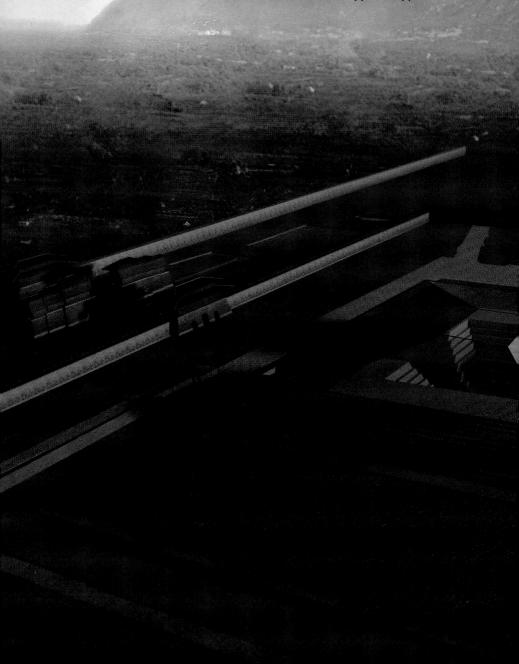

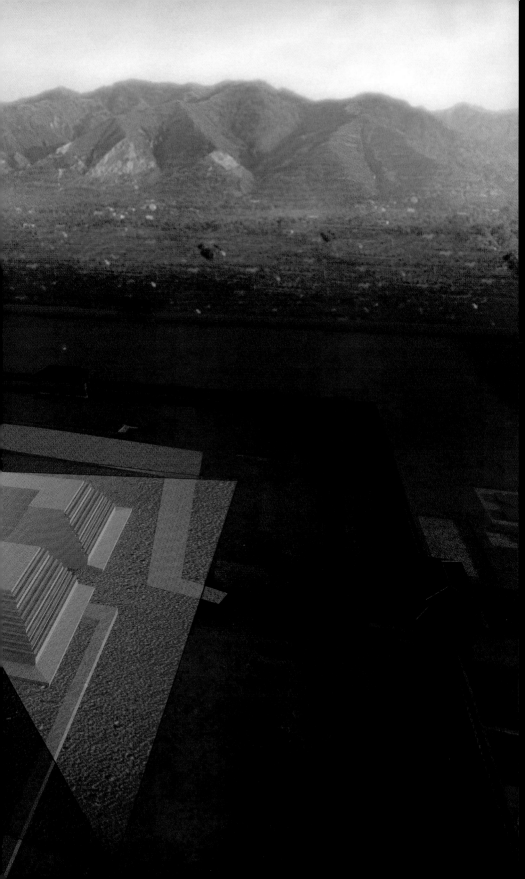

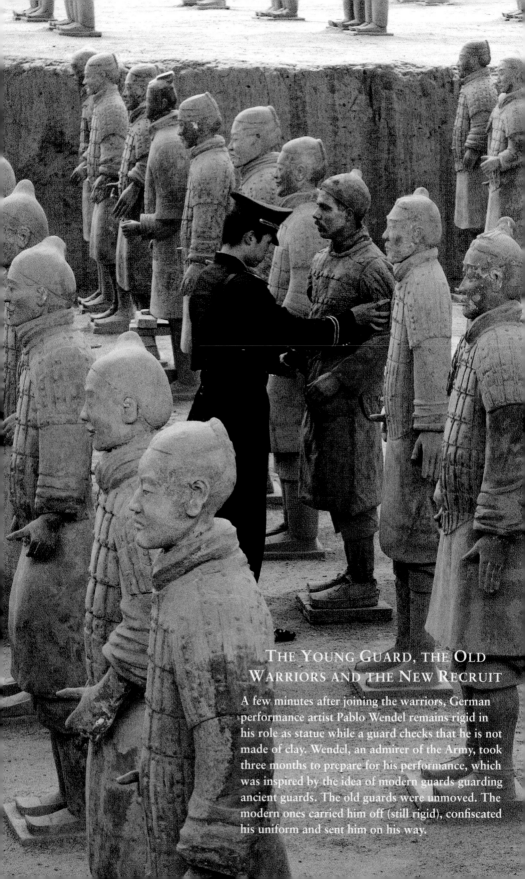

THE YOUNG GUARD, THE OLD WARRIORS AND THE NEW RECRUIT

A few minutes after joining the warriors, German performance artist Pablo Wendel remains rigid in his role as statue while a guard checks that he is not made of clay. Wendel, an admirer of the Army, took three months to prepare for his performance, which was inspired by the idea of modern guards guarding ancient guards. The old guards were unmoved. The modern ones carried him off (still rigid), confiscated his uniform and sent him on his way.

complex was interrupted]'. A suggestion only – there is no historical evidence. And then, three years later, according to chronicles quoted by Ban Gu, 'the soldiers entrusted with the grave complex dug it up' and 'the above ground grave complex was destroyed by the pillaging of Xiang Yu, the underground complex was trampled down by the herds grazing above'.[3] It's confusing. Which grave complex was dug up? Were these soldiers part of the original workforce or new arrivals? The 'above ground complex' could mean just the buildings, but in that case does 'below ground' mean the tomb, the Terracotta Army, the subsidiary pits – some or all of them?

Remember that both the historians were writing well after the events they describe, Sima Qian a century and Ban Gu 250 years later. The events themselves occurred during years of war and civil war. They were reporting memories passed down through generations (at best: Ban Gu often relied on Sima Qian). It's not surprising they are a little vague.

Let's imagine. Xiang Yu's people had known of the Terracotta Army since 209 BC, when they had been driven off by its hastily recruited labourers. There would have been prisoners, there would have been talk. So in early 206 BC, with the palaces of Xianyang still blazing, Xiang Yu arrives at Lintong, eager for more booty and more vengeance. He knows about the tomb, and also its dangers and difficulties: the risk of mercury poisoning, the loaded crossbows, the depth of soil. He knows, too, of the Terracotta Army, knows that it contains things that would be very useful: not the clay soldiers, of course, but the many thousands of real weapons they hold – the crossbows, bows, swords, lances, dagger-axes, arrows – almost all made of bronze. True, iron would

[3] These quotes are included in the Archaeological Team's survey in Blänsdorf et al., *Qin Shihuang*.

have been better, as several of the Warring States had discovered; but with more fighting to be done, bronze weapons, especially the crossbows with their superb bronze triggers, would be just fine.

In the film tourists see at the museum, it's the vengeance that is dramatized in a scene of pure vandalism. Soldiers break in en masse, as if through a door, and simply torch the place. The beams catch fire instantly. Obviously the whole pit is going to be a wreck in no time, and the inferno is going to be enough to incinerate the ceiling and create the layer of hard-baked earth discovered by the Yang brothers when they broke in through the roof in 1974.

Well, it couldn't have been like that.

Pit No. 1 was well covered, and would take weeks to open up. Xiang Yu did not have weeks. Qin had fallen, new kingdoms had emerged, but no one ruled in Qin and it looked as if there would be a showdown between Xiang Yu and Liu Bang. There was no time to strip off the 3 metres of earth and the thick beams that held it up. The best way in was to dig straight down. Is that what they did? Almost certainly, because that was precisely what was done in Pit No. 2, where a hole like a small mine-shaft seems to be a point of forced entry. It is a professional job, dropping vertically for several metres right at the edge of the pit to bypass the ceiling, then taking a right-angle turn at just the right depth to make an entry on to the floor. It's a metre or so square, big enough to hand out weapons and any other items of treasure. Clearly, no one was interested in the warriors.

So the thieves had good information. If they entered Pit No. 2, it stands to reason they entered the Army pit, even if no traces remain of the hole they dug. It would have taken them a few days (as the work done by the well-digging Yang brothers revealed), working with spades and a sling for co-workers to lift the loose earth clear.

This is not simply conjecture. It is a scenario inspired by the Army's senior archaeologist, Yuan Zhongyi.

'There is no evidence of *organized* destruction,' he said, as we sipped tea in his simple, impeccable apartment: lacquered tea-table, black leather sofa and chair, big cherrywood book cabinet and light-grey tiles. 'I imagine small groups going to different parts of the same area. But the warriors are close-packed, so it was hard to get through. They were in a rush. We found remains of warriors which seem to have fallen in a zig-zag pattern. This suggests they were pushed over as people forced their way through. One horse was standing apart from its tail, which lay a few metres away, as if someone had thrown it. One of the generals had a broken sword – the top bit, which had gold and jade decorations, had gone, leaving the bottom bit of the blade in its scabbard. And in the hole in Pit Number Two, we found the gold decorations for a horse.'

Then, somehow, the fire started.

'All the time, I wonder who committed this crime,' said Yuan. 'When we first saw the warriors in Pit Number One, we asked ourselves: who destroyed them? At first some of us said the fire could have been started by natural causes, by spontaneous combustion, from gas. But we could not find any materials that might cause a fire, like straw. Certainly, it could not have started with the warriors. So our second suggestion was that it was the result of a funeral ceremony, a sort of ritual immolation. The Qin burned everything to do with the emperor, perhaps. So I began checking the history books, and realized it must have been to do with Xiang Yu's uprising. But where would it start? That hole leading down into Pit Two – there are many ashes around the base. Perhaps what happened is that after robbing the place, the intruders started the fire to stop anyone else coming back for more.'

Here's an odd thing: there was no fire in Pit No. 3, the headquarters pit. You would think it would have been a natural target for anyone seeking revenge. Here were the top men conferring, and a chariot ready to take off with messages for the troops. Entry could have been gained by the same method used in the other two pits. But it didn't happen. My guess is that the grave-robbers knew from their informants that there was not enough here worth taking. And no one was interested in more destruction.

Breaking through at one end of Pit No. 1, the first soldier in smells rich earth, and sees—

—absolutely nothing, because it's pitch black. He stands, raises his arms, bumps his hands on hard, cold shapes. Behind him, above a colleague who is busy clearing more earth, a faint light filters down the hole. Pass me a torch, he calls. He doesn't mean a vegetable-oil lamp, but a cloth one steeped in pitch, with a big, bright flame. Its flickering light reveals the front lines of pink-faced archers, in their brightly coloured coats. Behind them, in cavernous corridors, the soldiers range backwards into darkness. And, as their informants had told them, they all hold a weapon or two. It's a treasure trove of militaria.

Others slither down the hole, more torches send shadows dancing away to left and right and down the corridors. But there's hardly room to stand up against the shoulder-to-shoulder statues. The intruders begin to shove their way through, grabbing weapons, passing them over clay shoulders towards the shaft-entrance and up to the open air.

There's chaos, men knocking over statues, trampling on them, grabbing weapons, passing them to each other and up the exit hole. Their work is badly hampered by the need for light. It is hard to grab weapons with one hand while holding a torch, so they improvise, passing torches between each other, maybe jamming a torch into the hollow bits of a broken statue. The destruction and the absence of weapons show that they penetrated only a few corridors, and no more than 40 metres. Most of the weapons were left behind. Something cut the break-in short.

The most likely cause was fire. It is easy to imagine a torch discarded or a piece of smouldering material lying under smashed pottery against a wooden pillar or on the floor of one of the wooden chariots. So two of the three elements for a blaze were present: fuel and a source of ignition. Flames lick up a pillar. Within seconds it is out of control.

To understand what might have happened next, I must introduce you to an extremely small, but growing specialism that links archaeologists and fire protection engineers. Traditionally, archaeologists have accepted the fact of fire in ancient structures without examining the cause, implying that fire is self-explanatory or the result of 'ritual destruction'. As a small group of experts in this arcane field say, 'Formal, ongoing collaborations with fire investigators and archaeologists are recent developments.'[4] So far, the Terracotta Army awaits that sort of collaboration, but as a start I asked for help from Joe Lally, an archaeologist with the US Department of the Interior's Bureau of Land Management in Albuquerque, New Mexico. He is interested in explaining fires in ancient buildings. He also understands about looters. 'We have a lot of looters here in New Mexico, and from my experience looters are usually better and faster at finding valuable items than professional archaeologists.' He tests scenarios with a computer program called CFAST, into which he fed mine, together with statistics about the

[4] David Icove et al., 'Scientific Investigations and Modeling of Prehistoric Structural Fires at Chevelon Pueblo', paper presented at International Symposium on Fire Investigation Science and Technology, Cincinnati, Jan. 2006.

Terracotta Army pit: the materials available, the entry-hole which would provide ventilation, the height and length of the corridors. This is his conclusion:

> With ventilation being on floor level and none within the upper portions of the compartment, there would be no exit for heat and smoke, which fill a compartment from the top down, no matter where the fire is burning. Heat would not be a problem. Heat loss to the walls (the heat being absorbed) would be more than ten times greater than heat loss through the looters' shaft. The corridors would fill with smoke at the rate of seven cubic metres a second. A medium growth fire would allow 3.8 minutes for a safe exit from anywhere within the structure. The exit time would be increased by creeping low beneath the upper, smoke-filled portions of the corridors.

It's the smoke that cuts the break-in short. That's why so many weapons remain behind in the pit, and why archaeologists today know so much about them.

The smoke spreads along corridors, and round the ends where the three lines of archers stand. There are yells and the intruders rush for the exit, toppling more warriors and horses. They have only a few minutes, and there is only room for one at a time up the exit shaft. Come to think of it, there could not be all that many down there – 30 or 40, assuming that each one takes ten seconds to enter the shaft – because they all made it out: Yuan and his co-workers found no charred skeletons down there.

But there is something odd about this fire. It takes hold, it flares, it catches a chariot, even the roof. But now it is a big beast, and it needs a flow of oxygen – the third vital element in any fire after fuel and an ignition source – to keep it going. There's not enough in the pit, and not enough coming in from outside to feed the flames. Perhaps some bright character orders the hole to be filled in, thinking to douse the fire and return at some later date.

In any event, the flames go out.

Yet we know fire destroyed the pit. No flames, yet a destructive fire – how is this to be explained?

E-mails back and forth threw up two possibilities. One is the phenomenon known as 'spontaneous combustion', familiar to anyone who has felt the inside of a pile of cut grass. Within hours, the core is warm, in a day or two it smokes, and a few days later, if you open it, you find ash. In nature, spontaneous blazes are quite common. I received this note from the US fire expert Jim Quintière. Having investigated several underground woody landfills, which can ignite spontaneously, he says:

> I believe the earthen-bamboo with moisture-promoting bacterial growth could first produce heat from the bacteria, then chemical heat due to oxidation of the bamboo. This can lead to spontaneous ignition. The nature of the subsequent fire is likely to be smouldering, but can also break out into flames. I have seen this happen. In one fire I know of, the fire moved across the land-fill beneath the ground in days. Later, when the land-fill was covered with asphalt to impede the oxygen flow, temperature soundings still indicated combustion.

A second model is a coal-seam fire, a subject that is worth a brief diversion. Usually these fires start in mines and spread underground along unmined beds of coal, but some are natural, started by bush fires or lightning. The US has hundreds of coal-seam fires, with at least 38 in coal-rich Pennsylvania alone: among them is a notorious fire 100 metres under the once-thriving town of Centralia that has been smouldering for half a century and may go on doing so for 250 years before its fuel is exhausted. China and India, coal-rich and coal-dependent, have thousands of these fires, which contribute about 1 per cent of the earth's carbon emissions. Scientists estimate that Australia's Burning Mountain, the oldest known coal fire, has been smouldering for 6,000 years. Coal-seam fires poison the earth, and the people, and the atmosphere, and there is absolutely nothing anyone can do about most of them.

Of course, the Terracotta Army's roof would hardly be a major seam fire. But it is a prime candidate for smouldering. So the scenario continues like this: the flames are dead, the pit dark again, smoke drifting along the corridors. But the fire has found a home in the roof, where the overlay of matting acts as tinder and the overburden of earth keeps a lid on the fire. Traces of oxygen seep down the shaft and from the surrounding earth, enough to keep the roof smouldering. Over months, the slow fire eats away at the beams. At some point, a few charred timbers fall, breaking a warrior or two. A section of earth from above follows.

And so it goes, for years, the beams being consumed until they fall, the warriors steadily smashed, the chariots and crossbows either burned or (occasionally) protected by fallen earth, the surface subsiding bit by bit, washed by the rains of the passing centuries until not a trace remains of what lies beneath. The foreign troops depart, locals see only the tomb-mound and forget about the warriors. Orchard and field succeed orchard and field, for 2,180 years, until the spades of the Yang brothers break through the shell of fire-baked earth.

III

THE EIGHTH
WONDER

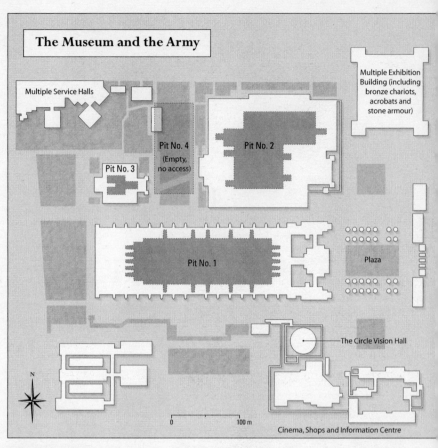

The Museum and the Army

Multiple Service Halls

Multiple Exhibition Building (including bronze chariots, acrobats and stone armour)

Pit No. 4 (Empty, no access)

Pit No. 3

Pit No. 2

Pit No. 1

Plaza

The Circle Vision Hall

N

0   100 m

Cinema, Shops and Information Centre

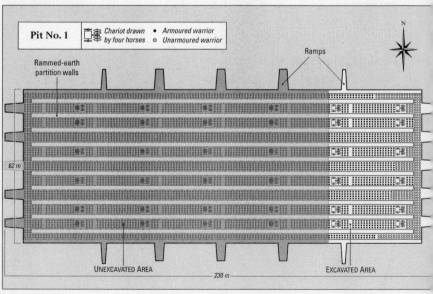

Pit No. 1

Chariot drawn by four horses   ● Armoured warrior   ○ Unarmoured warrior

Ramps

Rammed-earth partition walls

N

62 m

UNEXCAVATED AREA

230 m

EXCAVATED AREA

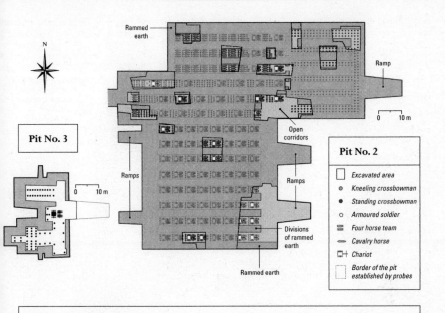

Pit No. 3

0   10 m

Pit No. 2

Rammed earth

Ramp

Open corridors

Ramps

Ramps

Divisions of rammed earth

Rammed earth

0   10 m

	Excavated area
⊙	Kneeling crossbowman
●	Standing crossbowman
○	Armoured soldier
☰	Four horse team
⌐	Cavalry horse
⊟+	Chariot
☐	Border of the pit established by probes

Pit No. 1 Ground Plan, East End

Chariot drawn by four horses	Armoured infantryman with pointed hair bun	◖ Officer	Soldier without identifiable headgear
◖ Armoured infantryman with round hair bun	Armoured infantryman with flat hair bun	O Charioteer	Unarmoured infantryman in military tunic
		⊙ Assistant charioteer	

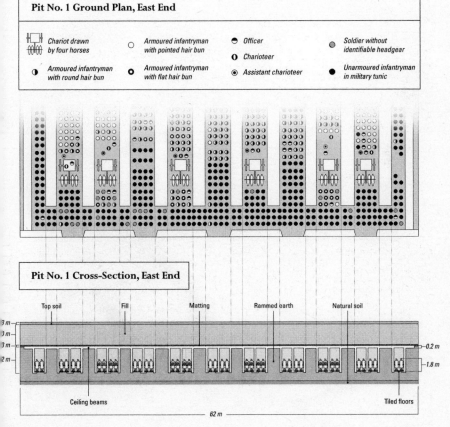

Pit No. 1 Cross-Section, East End

Top soil   Fill   Matting   Rammed earth   Natural soil

3 m
0 m
3 m
2 m

0.2 m

1.8 m

Ceiling beams   Tiled floors

62 m

N

12

SIX THOUSAND CHARACTERS
IN SEARCH OF A ROLE

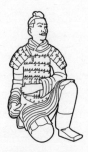

IT ALL SO NEARLY CAME TO NOTHING.

We are back in May 1974. The Yang brothers have abandoned their well under pressure from Zhao Kangmin, the local museum assistant, and his boss. Zhao is busy at work restoring the first warrior. Obviously, it's a wonderful find – the broken bits of statuary, the bronze arrowheads, the crossbow trigger, the bricks – and will complement the three kneeling servants which have been found over the years. But no one has a clue that the Yang brothers have actually broken through into the far south-east corner of the greatest archaeological discovery of the century. It could have remained hidden. Zhao, remember, was nervous about reporting the finds, nervous that he might be swept up again by the madness of the Cultural Revolution, whose teenage Red Guards had forced him to criticize himself for being involved with old things and therefore encouraging the revival of feudalism.

In fact, the excesses of the Cultural Revolution were five years in the past. The thuggish gangs of students waving their little red books of Mao's thoughts had had their day. Students by the million were back from 're-education' – hard manual labour – in the countryside. Universities and schools had reopened. The army was stable again, mainly in the face of a challenge being mounted by the Soviet Union along China's far western and north-eastern borders. China had re-engaged with the world.

Still, at the top, tensions multiplied. Mao, 80, was in physical decline, having been diagnosed with a form of motor neurone disease which would gradually make it impossible for him to walk, or even to swallow. He was not told, and was depressed by cataracts that made him almost blind until they were removed the following year. Despite all this, or perhaps because of it, he was ever more jealous of potential rivals. In 1971 his designated heir and main rival Lin Biao, knowing his days were numbered, had fled the country in such haste there was no time to finish fuelling his plane. It crashed in Mongolia, killing him. When Mao learned that Lin's son had plotted his assassination, he again purged the army. The affair, which seemed to discredit any remnants of revolutionary fervour, profoundly disillusioned Mao's supporters. Two main factions emerged. The country was being managed by Premier Zhou Enlai, but Mao's wife Jiang Qing and her three cronies, the Gang of Four as Mao called them, tried to preserve Mao's radicalism, whipping up a campaign to discredit Zhou. In late 1973 Mao allowed the balance to swing back towards Zhou and his protégé, the tiny, energetic future leader Deng Xiaoping, who had been purged and was now back in favour. So the top echelon of government was divided between the Gang of Four on one side and Zhou plus Deng on the other. This unresolved power struggle in Beijing was known to very few, certainly not to a lowly museum official like Zhao Kangmin. Yet that context would prove crucial to the fate of the warrior he was busy restoring, of the undiscovered Army, and of the whole tomb complex.

For the power struggle had an odd historical resonance. In much the same way as Sima Qian criticized his own emperor, Wu, by describing the excesses of the First Emperor, so the two sides of the ideological battle under Mao criticized each other by reference to the ancient dispute between Legalists and Confucians. Suddenly, and bizarrely for foreign observers, the politics of the Qin empire leapt into the present. The Confucians were Zhou Enlai and his supporters, who became targets for the 'Legalist' – and ardently Maoist – Gang of Four. Confucius and his followers were reactionaries and representatives of the slave-owning class; the First Emperor was chief representative of the up-and-coming, progressive landlord class. Traditional views were turned topsy-turvy. Confucius, previously revered for nobility and wisdom, was reviled; the First Emperor, tyrant and mass murderer, became the admired founder of the nation.

In fact the roots of this attitude went deep. Although in his later years Mao became power-obsessed as an individual, in the early days, before his personality became a cult, he was power-obsessed on behalf of the Party. He was a dyed-in-the-wool Legalist, a Machiavellian Prince, a Lord-Shang-style 'sage ruler', who defined the law according to revolutionary needs. He saw himself and his followers as 'truly great men' or 'the truly great man' (for Chinese does not easily distinguish between singular and plural), as he wrote in a famous poem, *Snow*, in 1936:

This land so rich in beauty
Has made countless heroes bow in homage.
But alas! Qin Shihuang and Han Wudi
Were lacking in literary grace,
And Tang Taizong and Song Taizu
Had little poetry in their souls;
That proud son of Heaven,
Genghis Khan,
Knew only shooting eagles, bow outstretched.
All are past and gone!
For truly great men [or 'the truly great man']
Look to this age alone.

He, of course, was one of the great men himself, greater as
a poet and as conqueror than all those long-dead rulers, particularly the First Emperor, Qin Shihuang. Like him, Mao
reformed Chinese script, introducing the simplified characters
now in use in mainland China. Like him, he was eager to
destroy the past in order to control the future. And like him,
he was utterly ruthless, even more so. At the Second Plenum of
the Eighth Party Congress on 8 May 1958, Mao scoffed:

The First Emperor – how great was he really? He buried[1]
only four hundred and sixty Confucian scholars. We have
buried forty-six *thousand* Confucian scholars ... You
democrats scold us for being like the First Emperor. You are
wrong. We are a hundred times worse than him. To the
charge of being like the First Emperor, of being a dictator, we
plead guilty. But we need to add to your accusations – they
are not enough![2]

[1] The problematic word *keng* (坑) again, which mixes the old meaning
'buried, killed' with the additional modern one, 'buried alive'. But he is not
suggesting 46,000 were buried *alive*. See p. 89.
[2] Trans. Polly Kwong.

In another of his poems, Mao responded to the eminent scholar Guo Moruo, who had criticized the First Emperor for practising slavery:

> Please don't slander the First Emperor, Sir,
> For the burning of the books should be thought through
> again.
> Our ancestral dragon, though dead, lives on in spirit,
> While Confucius, though renowned, was really rubbish.

Mao despised Confucian orthodoxy for its wishy-washy benevolence, the way it worked against the building of a strong state that would dominate the Chinese and neighbouring peoples. He would be a new First Emperor, ruling all China's traditional domains through the same kind of totalitarian institutions. Marxist ideology provided what he wanted, for it backed the monopoly of power by an educated elite (under his direction). It justified suppressing the self-determination of peoples whose destinies (he thought) lay in China's hands – Tibetans, Uighurs, Mongols. Lost territories should be regained, former tributaries whipped into line. Military success had freed China; now it would restore the empire, and extend its reach. That was why he intervened in Korea, invaded Tibet, bombarded Quemoy, demanded the return of Taiwan, attacked India over Tibet, confronted the Soviet Union almost to the point of war, and aided Vietnam.

The new approach was typified in a popular biography of the First Emperor by Hung Shih-Ti (Hong Shidi).[3] Hong emphasizes the Marxist view that history is controlled not by great men but by grand historical forces, which some great men just happen to represent. 'It was not because he

[3] Included in Li Yuning, *The First Emperor of China*.

had any inborn and extraordinary ability, but mainly because he was the chief representative of the rising landlord class ... the masses of people had an urgent need for the unification of China.' As Li Yuning, the editor of a book in which Hong's biography is included, writes:

> Now [in 1975] [the First Emperor] is seen as a farsighted ruler who destroyed the forces which had kept China divided, unified the nation, and established the first centralized state in Chinese history. In particular he is praised for following the Legalist policy of 'emphasizing the present while slighting the past' [a Maoist slogan] and scorning the Confucians. His achievements in creating a unified centralized government, it is now argued, justified his use of violence, in particular the 'burning of the books and burying Confucian scholars alive'.

Nothing could have put the case more clearly: now equals then, the First Emperor equals Mao, violence is OK if the cause is great, unification equals revolution and excuses all excess.[4]

All of this explains why Jiang Qing and the other three Gang-members accused Lin Biao and his successor Zhou Enlai of being treacherous Confucians, why they unleashed a campaign known as 'Criticize Lin [Biao], Criticize Confucius', why Lin and his treason were equated with Confucius's alleged attempt to roll back the tide of history by upholding slavery. In brief, as Yue Nan says in a detailed analysis,[5] the First Emperor was seen as 'a vigorous

---

[4] This simplifies a complex campaign which saw the publication of many articles in which every leading Qin character had a part to play in the present, including the loyal minister Li Si and the treacherous ministers Lü Buwei and Zhao Gao.

[5] Yue Nan, *Xi Bu Mai Fu* / 西部埋伏 (*Hidden Underground in the West*).

revolutionary, a true tiger', while Confucius and his followers were 'corrupt and clownish anti-revolutionaries'. Anything that could be used to support this view would come in handy.

Into this ideological maelstrom fell a very small stone of information about some pieces of clay discovered in far-off Shaanxi. That the news reached the ears of high-ups in Beijing was pure chance. It happened that a journalist named Lin Anwen, from the official news agency, Xinhua, was in Lintong on holiday and heard of the discovery. He came to see Zhao, who briefed him. On returning to Beijing, he saw the potential appeal of the finds – and, no doubt, the possibility of doing himself some good – and wrote them up, not for general consumption but in *Internal Affairs*, a journal for official eyes only. Its tediously long headline ran: 'A group of pottery figures unearthed near the First Emperor's mausoleum in Lintong County'. After Lin's report, another writer, Wang Yongan, added a paragraph to underline its political message: 'The discovery of the warriors has a great importance in helping us to evaluate the First Emperor in studying the struggle between Legalism and Confucianism, and the political, economic and military circumstances of the Qin dynasty . . . they are very precious, as they are modelled after Qin Dynasty soldiers and were never recorded in the historical records.' He then continued with, in effect, a call for action:

Because of the harvest, work has stopped. Some leaders in Lintong County placed their own self-interests first and so never reported the finds. The mausoleum is a national cultural relic, under the protection of the central government, but it has not protected it well. The commune just dug up the mausoleum and the cultivated land around it. Metals (i.e. the bronze arrowheads and crossbow triggers) were just treated as rubbish and the bits of pottery were cast aside.

When the Gang of Four read this, they at once saw its potential. One phone call from Mao's wife, Jiang Qing, to the head of media relations, Yao Wenyuan, was enough to get action. Yao called Vice-Premier Li Xiannian, once purged, now finance minister and deputy prime minister, and a future state president. On 13 June, Vice-Premier Li called the heads of Cultural Affairs and the National Bureau of Cultural Relics: 'Comrade Jiang Qing is very concerned about this discovery! Please consult with the Shaanxi Provincial Government and get them to move as soon as possible!'

In Xian, the provincial leader stuttered – No, he had no idea ... There had been no news from Lintong ... The farmers didn't know what they had found – and promised action.

So at last the news was out, and an archaeologist from Beijing went out to check the site with Zhao. He turned out to be quite polite, Zhao recalls. 'He said, "Your county and you made a big contribution to the country."' A few days later, about two months after the Yangs' discovery, five officials, including Zhao, turned up with 20 farmers to plan the work of excavation, which started the following month.

'It took us twenty days just to find out how wide the pit was,' said Zhao. We were sitting in the reception area of the museum he had designed himself, where he is still an honoured presence. 'From the well made by the farmers we dug in all directions. There was nothing to the south, but a wall to the north. So we discovered it was right on the edge in the pit's south-east corner.' (You can still see the place when you go into the pit today). 'We were working slowly, drilling by hand. We were just tracing the walls to find the edges, drilling down as far as we could, to the bricks. We had no idea what to expect. As we opened up squares of the pit, we realized the size of the discovery. We got an idea of the spaces between the warriors, we knew the size of the pit, and so we worked out how many warriors there should be.'

'You realized the warriors were Qin?'

'They had to be, because the bricks were Qin and the soldiers were on the bricks. So they had to be placed there on the order of the First Emperor. I was the first person to call them Qin warriors.' He paused to make sure I got the point. 'I was the first man to give them that name. Because before that there were figures, but no warriors. *Qin warriors.*' He nodded, as if to himself, lost in memory. 'Then [Communist Party Central Committee member] Gu Mu came. He was in charge of the building over Pit No. 1. He also told me I made a big contribution. I said, "It was the farmers." He said, "No, they found them but they didn't know what they found. You were the first who realized."'

Given the Army's international fame today, it seems odd that no one appreciated the scale of this discovery at the time. But bear in mind that this was just a single find, even if a large one. Whatever its size, some sort of protection obviously had to be provided for the site, as fast as possible. The man made responsible for this was a local architect, Li Naifu, now a senior member of the Xian Architecture and Technology University, a collection of concrete-and-glass rectangles hard to separate from the other 45 colleges and universities scattered across this extremely well-educated city. With eyes made heavy by years of teaching and poring over plans, Li recalled the strange assumptions made in those early days.

'In the beginning we thought we would only need a

building that would protect the site, the soldiers and the experts. We gave no thought to tourists at all.' Nor to foreign interest either, for Mao was still alive, just, and China was still largely shut away behind a bamboo curtain. 'We didn't think about a reception area, or administrators. We never considered we might need a car park, offices, toilets even. Besides, we hardly had any money. They just gave us four million yuan [£266,000].

'As you know, the pit is sixty metres wide. So we knew we had to build something about seventy metres wide, seventy-two actually. At that time, for that money, all we could think of was a simple arch. This was the simplest, most economic solution. At the time we thought it was quite ambitious, because there were not many arches with a seventy-two-metre span in the country. We didn't have to consider the whole site, because there was nothing but the single pit, and only fields all around. So up it went, just like an enormous greenhouse.' (Though the arch always conjured up a different image in my mind – a Victorian railway station, with the soldiers lining up to catch the spirit train to the battle front.)

It was finished in 1976, after not much more than a year of work. By then, two more pits, Nos. 2 and 3, had been discovered, alongside the 'greenhouse'. Excavation work began in Pit No. 1 in May 1978 and went on for the next four years. A team of 50 pressed on with the intricate business of removing the seven layers of earth, sand, gravel and sludge – for water had leaked in even before the roof collapsed. The layers lay in waves over the twelve walls and eleven corridors. Recording every shard of every shattered warrior, often over 200 of them, the teams began rebuilding statues, matching up their bits and sticking them together with special glue that does not dry hard, so that pieces can be unglued when necessary. It helped that all the pieces for any one of the warriors had to be close by, but it still took up to a year for a warrior to be completed.

Work having started at the Yangs' well and continued both northward and westward, decisions had to be made. How far to dig? How many to unearth and restore? After four years, work slowed. With just over one-fifth of the pit opened, the excavators had unearthed just over 1,000 warriors, 8 two-wheeled chariots, 32 horses, several hundred weapons and many thousands of arrowheads. Another section was left partially open, a final one still earthed in.

Excavation work, still under way in Pit No. 1, was started in the second and third pits, and was still going on when the museum opened for business on 1 October 1979 – to total chaos. There was a small car park and a ticket office ('Do you know the price of a ticket? Ten yuan [0.7p]!') but then people had to walk over grass, which soon turned to mud, to a building with no toilets, no entrance lobby for people to wait in, and no café. And from the start 30,000 or more people came every day, rising to 50,000 on main holidays, like May Day. 'There were so many people no one could see anything but people. Thousands just came, because it was all new, saw the crowds, and went away without seeing the soldiers!'

'We had to start again,' Li went on. 'So we applied for more money to do more building. This time we had a little more, 5.81 million yuan [£387,000].' Work started in 1986. 'Of course, now we realized the museum would be a landmark. We needed to do something special. It's easy to design a building, but hard to design a *great* building. We thought of the warriors as gold. To display gold you need a special sort of background, so the idea was to give them a setting that seemed like silk. Good design would emphasize the value, which would attract more people, so we would enhance the value twice over.'

Building went on for eight years in all, with Pit No. 3

opening in 1989 and the larger one, Pit No. 2, in 1994. This time, Li had the time and backing to plan proper buildings, their blockish look inspired by Qin architecture, with pepper-pot towers and black-tiled roofs – not that the Qin built in stone. This time, there were toilets, fire-proofing, a visitors' area, security for the warriors. 'We still made mistakes, though. We took care of the visitors, but we forgot that excavators would need to keep working when they came. So they have no separate paths to remove the soil. That has caused a great deal of inconvenience.'

There is far more to the site than three buildings over three pits: a Multiple Exhibition Building to show the best of the finds, service halls, restaurants, an information centre, bookstalls, the cinema, reproductions of the warriors, places to sell tourist kitsch: all the boring but vital extras that make a modern museum and excavation site. Along the way, Pit No. 1 acquired a proper entrance area.

At the museum's heart, though, is the great arch of Pit No. 1, in its day a miracle of efficiency, economy and speed, but a construction which, let's face it, becomes year by year more old-fashioned railway station than modern museum. There is no heating and no air-conditioning. Visitors freeze in winter and melt in high summer. And, as the experts know all too well, the warriors suffer, their remaining colours flaking off, their clay surfaces slowly gathering patinas of microscopic moulds.

The site has evolved, like a garden, in response to new and unpredictable needs. Yes, Li agreed, it is a medley of architectural styles, because styles changed.

'So it's like a survey of Chinese architecture in the late twentieth century,' I said.

'Yes, it is,' Li agreed thoughtfully. 'But I feel I have helped to create something for the future, and for the warriors. I'm proud of that.'

There is greatness here, but it does not lie in the buildings. It lies in the totality of the site, starting below, with the car park. There's not much inspiration in a car park, even when dominated by an immense statue of the First Emperor ('That's nothing to do with our team! That was the local government!'). But there is inspiration in the setting, with Mount Li and its neighbouring peaks and ridges rippling along the site's southern edge. There is inspiration, too, in the winding, uphill approach, that feeling of approaching something majestic. Li nodded when I remarked on it: 'Yes, the whole idea was that the approach would be a zigzag to give you a chance to think about what you are about to see.'[6]

The real genius lies in something that no one mentions. After your long, slow climb, you walk through a grove of firs – this is going to be wonderful in years to come, because there are 6,000 trees planted across the whole site, one tree per warrior in Pit No. 1, which I guess could stretch to 8,000, a *wan* of trees, as time goes by. Then there is the ticket barrier. And then, at last, the plaza. You are struck, perhaps, by the space, or the well-kept flower-beds, or the buildings. These are details, but the reason you focus on them is because of something you don't notice: they are well framed, not by anything physical, but by the colour. The plaza, the staircase, the buildings are all light grey stone-work that has a hint of other colours, like the overtones that lend depth to orchestral strings. It is this that turns an unresolved mix of styles and purposes into a unity.

[6] Not much inspiration, though, in the laboured English of the huge posters proclaiming the glories of Qin: 'Working together with many international fame design and build team featuring Qin culture.' Who writes this sort of thing? Who passes it as fit to print? Please, guys, forget your dictionaries and have your English checked by native English-speakers.

*

Li had mentioned security. Like all famous objects, the warriors occasionally draw the wrong sort of attention. Millions of yuan have been spent on them, millions of people come to see them, and it follows, in some minds, that they have a monetary value, and are therefore worth stealing. But the Chinese were honest and respectful of authority. When it was opened in 1979, the museum had no security system, and for a while it didn't matter.

Times change. In 1985, an unemployed 21-year-old named Wang Yengdi was set up by a friend who worked in the museum and his accomplice. The three hatched a plot to make them all wealthy. Wang would steal a head, for which he would receive 70,000 yuan (about £4,500), and which would then be sold in Hong Kong (so the court was told later) for a million yuan. The museum friend briefed him. Wang was to remain behind on the site after it closed, and after dark he was to go to a particular shed being used for restoration work. The door would be open. Inside, he would find the head of a general. Everything went according to plan. The head was instantly missed. Wang's friend was interrogated, and fingered Wang and the fence. In the friend's apartment police found the missing head, *and two other heads that no one knew were missing.* For the first time, the administrators realized that something would have to be done about security. Now comes the nasty bit. The two accomplices received life sentences, but Wang was executed by firing squad.

In went a security system, which proved its worth in a tale of love and idiocy. Once upon a time – in fact, 1993 – there was a poor Tibetan named Huan. He was 21, and desperately in love. His problem was that the girl's parents would only agree to a marriage if he came up with 3,000 yuan (£200). Such a sum was way beyond him. He heard he could get a job in Xian, and while looking for work he took a trip to the Terracotta Army. One of the tour guides, exaggerating the previous story, said, 'These statues are priceless. With ten warriors you could buy the whole United States! A few years ago a young man stole a general's head and could have got a million yuan for it in Hong Kong.' Huan's mind filled with dreams of cash and marriage. On 5 January 1994 he was back in the grounds of the museum, where he managed to undo the catch on a high window in Pit No. 1. He then hid outside in a pile of straw until after dark, when he climbed in, went to the back section of the pit where there were many unfinished statues, picked up a warrior's head, and tried to leave the same way. It is hard to climb while holding a pottery head, and anyway he had not taken any notice of the security cameras. Within three minutes, the doors were sealed and the guards were on him. Since he had not actually stolen the head, he got off lightly with a sentence of life imprisonment.

Since then there have been no serious problems, only an unserious one. In 2006 a 26-year-old German arts student, Pablo Wendel, from Stuttgart's Academy of Art, was on a short scholarship at the National Fine Arts Academy in Hangzhou. He was studying performance art, and had already had half a dozen installations back in Germany. He was low-key, even shy, but committed to original and disturbing acts, actions, occurrences, performances – I'm not sure there is a correct word for what he did (and does). In Hangzhou, he took a mud-bath in a canal and then walked the streets, observing reactions – amazement, amusement, pity, and finally rejection, by a taxi driver, who refused him a ride. On finishing his three months' study, he went travelling. He was drawn to the Terracotta Army, partly because the warriors look like performance artists. Haven't we all seen those 'statues' who intrigue holiday-makers by confusing flesh with stone and metal? He was also fascinated by the idea of armed guards guarding the First Emperor's guards. He conceived a strange tribute to the warriors: he would join them. This was not going to be a stunt. Confronting officialdom in China is no light matter, and he was prepared to end up behind bars.

Preparations took three months. He grew a moustache, dyed a long, stiff shirt, made a *papier mâché* hat, turned bits of a tyre into boots and organized a film crew to record the event. Mixing with crowds in Pit No. 1, he slipped over the side near the back, where a rail and a one-metre drop are the only barriers to a square secondary pit which holds about 50 reserve warriors. He had spotted a gap in the line, and was in place within seconds, frozen. A guard watching the CCTV screens saw a movement, stared, and could see nothing out of place. Many hundreds of people had, of course, and were busy taking pictures. But that was no help to the half-dozen guards, who began to search through the ranks for the intruder. 'I was looking for him, but I couldn't see him, because he was just like the real thing,' the security chief Jiang Bo said later. Wendel himself began suddenly to feel very frightened as the tension rose: the prowling guards, the camera-clicking crowd, his own discreet film-crew, himself locked rigid, trying not to blink. After a few minutes, they had him. They asked him politely to leave. No response. Wendel speaks no Chinese, but in the circumstances it hardly mattered. As he told me, 'For the duration of the performance, I was a sculpture, so of course I could not speak or move.' Jiang Bo raised his voice. Still no response. After another few minutes, six guards took Wendel by the elbows and levered him out of line. He remained in character, and toppled over. In the end, six of them carted him off rigid – 'like a fallen tree', in Wendel's words – for questioning, in faltering English. (You can see pictures on the Web.) By now the guards knew he meant no harm – indeed, the opposite – and could scarcely hold back their smiles as they confiscated his clothing. Wendel could hardly believe his luck. He left with as stern a warning as Jiang Bo could muster to a man who was obviously passionate about his art and his subject. Six hours later, he was free, on a train back to Hangzhou, in borrowed clothes, travelling into a storm of publicity that blew his story around the world, and in the process showed Chinese officialdom as surprisingly polite and cheerful. At least on this occasion. To a foreigner.

Passionate interest in China quickly whipped up equal passions overseas. Official backing from Beijing turned the Terracotta Army into big business for foreign tourism and also a must-see destination for visiting dignitaries. There have been dozens, scores, hundreds of such visits, more every year, very few adding much of value to the warriors or saying anything of significance about them. That's not the point. Honoured visitors are led there to show their respect, to pay homage to these symbols of a united and powerful China. There are only two who matter, the first because he's a star on a level with the warriors, the second because he really did add something stellar to the museum.

The first in star quality was not the Queen, or Putin, or Reagan (1984: guides like to tell Americans how Reagan, on his departure, turned back to the Army and said 'Dismiss!'), or even Nixon (1985). Star No. 1 was, and still is, Bill Clinton, who came with Chelsea and Hillary on an extremely rushed viewing during the 1998 state visit. On 25 June the three were granted an experience given to very few except scientists: a chance to get in among the warriors on the pit-floor. It did not make enough of an impression to figure in either of the Clinton memoirs, but it immediately seared itself into the collective memory of the locals, who recall the visit in the form of a completely untrue anecdote:

Clinton is coming. The museum chiefs are quivering with excitement. How to do something original, interesting, significant? Someone has an idea: the President should meet the old farmer, Yang Zhefa, who discovered the warriors (forget the complexities outlined in chapter 1; this is mythology). But they have to say something to each other. It has to be quick and simple, like this:

> CLINTON:
> Hi.
>
> YANG:
> How are you?
>
> CLINTON:
> I'm fine.
>
> YANG:
> Me too.

They grab Yang and brief him: 'Clinton's coming, with Hillary and Chelsea. He's going to shake your hand. All you have to say is "How are you? Me too." No, not in Chinese, in *English*.' They tell him the words, they make him repeat them, time and again, 'How are you? Me too. How are you? Me too.'

Clinton comes, with Hillary and Chelsea. He is introduced to Yang. The two shake hands.

Clinton says 'Hi.'

Yang, overcome with nerves, tries to say 'How are you?' and falters. Instead he says, '*Who* are you?'

Clinton, modest as ever, replies, 'I'm Hillary's husband.'

Yang, of course, says, 'Me too.'

It started as a joke. It became a behind-the-scenes anecdote. Now it's told by guides, with my-friend-who-was-Clinton's-interpreter as a source. English-speaking tourists tell other English-speaking tourists with swear-to-God certainty, which is how I heard it. If it goes on like this, it will get into a book, and become a truth.

The other star leader is the former French president Jacques Chirac, who owes his stardom to his knowledge of, and genuine passion for, Asian history. This fed into his presidency as a belief that the Chinese dragon was wide awake and that it was in France's interest to get on well with him. The interest goes back to Chirac's teenage years, when he was a frequent visitor to Paris's Guimet Museum, which has the largest collection of Asian art outside Asia. He is an old friend of one of China's greatest archaeologists, Han Wei, former head of Shaanxi's Institute of Archaeology and thus the Terracotta Army's ex-commander. During his tenure as president Chirac made four trips to China, where he won hearts and minds by revealing an intimate knowledge of the Sui and Tang dynasties.

Anecdotes about his erudition abound. In 2000, when he was the guest of President Jiang Zemin, he asked one of his companions if he knew how many emperors there were in the Sui dynasty. Yes, came the reply, two – Emperors Wen and Yang. 'No,' said Chirac, 'there were three.' It's a historical footnote: the third was a five-year-old named Gong, who was placed on the throne in 617 AD by the incoming Tang dynasty, and removed the following year. To Chinese politicians, this level of interest by a foreign diplomat is even more unlikely than Jiang Zemin being an expert on Joan of Arc. Chirac also revealed an interest in an eighth-century Tang poet, Li Bo ('wanderer . . . great drinker . . . supreme example of irresponsibility', says the *Penguin Book of Chinese Verse*), about whom he wants to make a film after his retirement, hoping to persuade Gong Li to play the role of an imperial concubine. So when he comes out with *bons mots*, official China laps them up. For example: People who haven't visited the pyramids have not really visited Egypt; people who haven't seen the Terracotta Army have not really visited China.

But most of this came later. On his first official visit to China in 1978, he was still Mayor of Paris. In acknowledgement of his expertise and his friendship with Han Wei, he was granted access to the Terracotta Army, even though it had not yet officially opened. It was here, having seen the Army's open pit and its other army of workers, that he commented, 'There are seven wonders in the world, and we may say that the discovery of these terracotta warriors and horses is the eighth.'

The Eighth Wonder. The perfect tag. The Chinese seized on it, and have pumped it out in articles and handouts ever since, encouraging it to float free of its context so that it sounds like an ancient saying or simply a historical fact. The Army 'is recognized as', 'is known as', 'is commonly called' the Eighth Wonder – never mind that two dozen other places, including the Great Wall, also lay claim to the same cliché; and never mind also that of the seven ancient wonders, only one (the Great Pyramids of Giza) survives. That's why Xi-la-ke (希拉克), as he is in Chinese, is a star. That's why his photo has a place of honour at the museum.

Lintong is a city reborn since 1974. Unpaved streets, simple brick houses and orchards have given way to boulevards, high-rises and a university campus. No one is in any doubt about why the wealth flowed in. A street placard proclaims: 'Thank the Communist Party for your changed status, but thank the First Emperor for making us rich!'

In the middle of Lintong is a reminder of this great truth. One of the world's biggest statues cuts apart the eastbound main road. It is the First Emperor on the warpath, driving 5,000 tonnes of pink granite. His horses form the bows of a triangle, bursting from the rock while he towers above them, impassive and remote as a mountaintop. Around him, forming the body of the triangle, are lesser mortals. Meng Tian, the general of the northern frontier and scourge of the barbarians, stares over his left shoulder, while charioteers and outriders surge about below. The statue is as gigantic as the emperor's ego, a monument to him, to his original achievement and to his significance for the town today.

I wanted to know where this immense object, the Unification Statue, came from. The sculptor, Wang Tianren, was out of town, so with Wang (yes, there are many Wangs) and Tony, I went to find out from his son, who follows in his father's massive footsteps. We wove into Xian's south-west suburbs through rain that reduced visibility to a few hundred metres. It was like driving along the bottom of the Yellow River.

'You know,' said Wang the Driver, 'I was at art school with Wang.' Wang Zhan, he meant, the sculptor son of Wang Tianren. I don't know which was the greater surprise, that Wang the Driver had once been an art student, or the coincidence of the two Wangs being fellow students. 'That was before the college moved into town, when it was in caves. Yes, dug into a hillside, like the house of the farmer who lived near the tomb of the First Emperor's grandfather.' As we moved slowly through the murk, he told his story, a lesson in how to get on in today's China. Having trained in design, he joined a Japanese film company in south China, which taught him Japanese and English. The pay was good, but he was far from home, 'and, you know, I was the only child for my parents, so I came back home. It is hard to make a living in art, so I bought this car and became a driver.'

By now we were, in Tony's phrase, in the back of beyond, and would have been lost without mobile phones, with which Wang the Sculptor was summoned to meet Wang the Driver at a roundabout. In convoy, we proceeded murkily, past vague apartment blocks, along a canal, through a maze of narrow side-streets, reversing clear of piles of cement and three-wheelers until we came at last to iron gates, and I understood why Wang the Sculptor needed the back of beyond. He wanted the space provided by this ex-farm, its cavernous sheds and its field to carve and cast and display his huge creations – landscape statuary, as he called it, including a twice-life-size bull, two 3-metre hands reaching out of the ground and a 5-metre Lenin look-alike which turned out to be the Canadian surgeon Norman Bethune, who was with Mao during the anti-Japanese war in the 1930s and is a hero in China.

Wang the Sculptor parked and got out, revealing himself to be ideally built for his chosen occupation. Beneath a head shaved into stubble was a small but solid body, with shoulders like a weightlifter, which, as he explained as he led the way inside, was because he used to be a swimmer. His studio, a converted barn, was a litter of screens, paintings, tables, copies of Han statues, a wagon-wheel, and black leather sofas and chairs. In a screened-off kitchen area, several people were skewering kebabs for a party that evening. Wang the Sculptor sat me down, poured tea from a pot of his own design, had a short, intense conversation with the other Wang about schooldays, vanished briefly to check on the kebabs, then zipped back to tell me about his father's statue. He was a man in a constant hurry. None of my photographs of him are in focus, which is entirely down to the fact that he was always a blur. It was like talking to a ricocheting bullet. His hair-stubble was created not by a razor but by air-friction, such as burns away the heat shield of a space capsule on re-entry.

The idea for the statue came from the Xian and Lintong councils, who wanted something grand to commemorate the First Emperor, something that combined historical significance and grandeur, a landmark that suited its position and a statement for centuries to come. This was in 1990. His father was eminent, a teacher in Shaanxi Art University, president of the Xian Institute of Sculpture and also a representative in the People's Congress, so he was a natural choice.

The first step had been to choose a shape, which depended on the site. The best place, where Lintong's incoming roads split apart, gave him the triangular outline. Then there was the choice of style. The statue was to commemorate Qin, so it had to be a rough-and-ready contrast with the sophistication of later dynasties. Then came the design – he led the way into a corridor to point out a table-top plaster model – then approval, then work. It was as simple to describe and as massive as any of the First Emperor's grand projects. Construction involved ordering 1,000 blocks – 'about a thousand, I never counted' – of granite, each weighing 5 tonnes. Then an army of masons started three years of work to turn the plaster model into an expression of raw power and Qin machismo.

'That's why we left the granite rough,' he said. By now we were moving fast through a studio full of gigantic heads. 'That's why you can see the lines between the blocks.'

'This was a project on an industrial scale!'

He shrugged. He and his father were used to operating like this.

'How many masons?'

'Three hundred, four hundred.'

'Good heavens. From all over China?'

'Not at all. We can find that many masons from just around here.'

And the cost? We were out in the garden now, circling the bull the size of a small house. About three million yuan (£200,000), and . . . Wang's words faded. He was on his way back inside, disappearing in the drizzle like the Cheshire Cat. It seemed to me astonishing value. If any western city wishes to create something like this, it should fly in a plane-load of Shaanxi's masons.

The story of how the warriors were brought into the light of day and the eyes of the world poses a deep question: what do the warriors mean? You may say that to ask about mean-ing is meaningless, that they simply are, full stop; and that once discovered everything else followed as inevitably as night and day.

Not so, as the details of their emergence reveal. They were lost to memory because the times changed. If the Qin dynasty had endured, so would all its rites, which would have been recorded for all time. Though known about in a sense, because so many finds leaked to the surface, they remained lost because no one wanted to know about them. They were found only when the political context was right. Originally, they fulfilled the purposes of a huge ego deter-mined to impose his will on the world; they emerged two millennia later to fulfil precisely the same purpose: to serve another huge ego, equally determined to impose his will on the world.

But there is another meaning, suggested not by history or by the immense and self-seeking characters behind their creation and emergence, but by the warriors themselves, which makes them even more appealing to China today. Thirty years ago they were propaganda justifying oppression. Now they have escaped from their roots – and from the context of their re-emergence – to serve the present (which is what Mao himself intended, ironically) as propaganda for the new, emergent China. It is not the emperor or present-day ruler who matters now, but the warriors themselves. They are seen as an expression of communal talents, a people's army, made and hidden by the masses, to use a Marxist term. They symbolize everything positive that China wishes for itself: a unified state, a creative people, a *compliant* people, and a government that works for the people. In the words of Don Fowler, an anthropologist in the University of Nevada, they are 'visible symbols of the strength and genius of the People throughout three millennia of oppression that ended in 1949' and thus 'serve to convince the governed that those in power rule legitimately'.[7] Whatever the course of China's future, the Army will be there, standing up for whatever the government defines as right.

[7] Fowler, 'Uses of the Past'.

13

NEW MARVELS IN BRONZE AND STONE

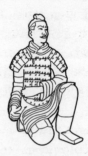

THIS IS A STORY TO WHICH MORE CHAPTERS ARE BEING ADDED year by year, with ever-increasing variety, and no sign yet that the end is in view. Let me give you an idea of the scope of the discoveries, some of which I used as evidence for descriptions of the creation of the tomb:

- Thirty-one skeletons of birds in clay coffins, attended by terracotta wardens, perhaps to recreate the First Emperor's pleasure garden (were they intended to breed spirit children, I wonder?).
- Between three and four hundred pits, 100 of which have been opened, each found to contain the skeleton of a horse, some buried alive, or the figure of a kneeling groom, like the one in Zhao Kangmin's museum, or both.

- A second stables-pit holding some 300 horse skeletons and kneeling terracotta grooms.
- Seventeen tombs that contain, together with objects of gold, silver, jade and lacquer, the remains of humans – all put to death either because they were victims of the Second Emperor or because they asked to follow their lord and master into the next world. Their limbs had been cut off.
- A graveyard of 100 more skeletons of convict workers who either died or were sentenced to death, buried in a crouching position, with accompanying clay tablets giving names, origins and fates. Of the nineteen inscriptions, which show the dead men came from Shandong, ten bear the phrase 'sentenced to labour'. These are the earliest tomb inscriptions found in China to date, and also proof that convict labour was used on the tomb.
- Remains of ramparts and gates and buildings galore, all producing huge collections of bronze bells, weights, lamps, porcelain bowls and tiles.
- An enormous stone workshop, measuring 1.5×0.5 kilometres, from which came iron tools, half-finished stone pipes, and limestone blocks.
- Terracotta figures totally different from any others. Clothed only in short skirts, they are highly individual, one being as slim as a male model while another has the paunch and buttocks of a weightlifter (see second plate section). Several have their arms raised, which suggests their official role – acrobats. All different, they may have been made individually, not with moulds.
- A pit made as a water-garden, complete with stream, for a collection of bronze birds, on which more in the next chapter.

This is a Pompeii of remains that will take decades to catalogue, let alone analyse. Meanwhile, there are two finds acknowledged to be world-class treasures and at least one Army pit that poses another mystery.

In 1978, even before the museum was opened, some experimental drillings at the western base of the tomb-mound turned up some small metal bits of horse harness, some bronze and one piece of gold. Two years later, after more detailed work probing down through almost 8 metres of soil, archaeologists found an irregular series of four pits, one of which had five 10-metre-long sections. And in the end section, in the remains of a wood-lined container, crushed beneath the fallen earth, lay what have become the crown jewels of the museum: two four-horse, two-wheeled carriages, in bronze, half life-size, complete with their horses and drivers. Over the centuries, the weight of earth had flattened the chariots and the lower limbs of the sturdily built horses like a car-crusher.

Careful excavation uncovered both the brilliance of the work and the extent of the problem. The horses were largely intact, but the carriages, their canopies and reins as thin as tinfoil, had been smashed into fragments, producing a giant, three-dimensional jigsaw of some 3,000 pieces. It would clearly be impossible to restore them while they were down their pit, so a base was slid under the whole 6 × 2 metre block, which was then lifted as a single 8-tonne unit and trucked to a workshop. Horses and carriages were separated, bent bits restored to their original shape; glue was devised to stick the pieces together, resin used to fill in small holes and cracks; plates, pins and metal wire were attached as reinforcement. Not much was lost (though the tassels on the heads of the lead horses, the two on the front right, had to be replaced because the originals were made of bronze wires just one-hundredth of a millimetre thick). After eight years' work by a team of 30, both carriages were restored to full working order. They are on display, beautifully lit, in the Multiple Exhibition Building (see second plate section).

They are breathtaking objects, perfect down to every rein and harness and free-spinning axle-flag, so minutely accurate that when talking about them it is hard to remember they are not the real things but two tonnes of metal. Several metals, in fact. They are mostly bronze (a 50–50 mixture of copper and tin), plus some lead, but different bits of the chariots have varying amounts of lead in them to alter their hardness. There is a thesis to be written simply on the bridles, alternating segments of inlaid gold and silver bosses, 42 of each. Of many intriguing details, here are two. Inside each horse's mouth, and therefore invisible to human eyes, each bit has a sharpened point that can be pulled on to the tongue in case the horse bolts. ('In case it bolts', indeed! You see how easy it is to forget that these are half-size bronzes, not going anywhere.) The second detail addresses this question: in a team of four, with loose leather harnesses that would allow the two outer horses to drift inwards and obstruct the central pair, what keeps them at the right distance? Answer: a sort of goad or spur attached to the outside flank of each of the central pair. The two outer horses have to keep their distance to avoid being pricked.

The first chariot, an open one variously known as a 'high', 'war', or 'inspection' chariot, has the driver standing on a platform holding six reins, with the inside reins of the two central horses attached to the chariot. It has a canopy that, rather like a modern beach parasol, has a pointed end for sticking in the ground while at rest, and a lockable joint that allows it to be set in any direction. In real life, the driver could drive or rest protected by his canopy from the rain and sun, and sleep under it at night. He was ready for anything, this driver. He had a long sword on his back and a crossbow beside him, along with a box of 54 arrows and a shield. These look like very special weapons, as much symbolic as practical. The crossbow has a nicely decorated trigger, and the shield (which would be wooden in real life) is beautifully curlicued and painted; the canopy's shaft is inlaid with gold and silver cloud motifs.

The second chariot is the emperor's, and it is an even more brilliant creation. It has a front section for a charioteer – who drives sitting back on his heels, poor chap – and a second, enclosed, section for the emperor. It (or rather the original on which this model is based) is big enough to lie down in. The roof, laid on a network of struts, is a dome of silk or leather waterproofed with grease. It overhangs all around to shelter the driver, shade the sides and carry rain well clear of the wheels. In the windows there is mosquito netting – all this being rendered in bronze, of course – and, on the side windows, a little sliding panel so the emperor can see out, get air in and issue orders without being seen. The walls and the outward-opening back door are decorated with detailed patterns. There is even a case, for personal possessions perhaps, or for bamboo-strip documents.

Clearly, the chariots were waiting for the soul of the emperor to emerge from his tomb and order a tour of inspection, such as he had undertaken four times during his life. Those who buried the chariots were clearly expecting the horses to wait a while before they saw action, because – weirdly – large quantities of hay were buried with them. Once again we see the paradoxical mixture of incompatible beliefs, the assumption that bronze horses would become spirits and need real hay.

The emperor's tours had been to the east. These chariots were facing west and were painted white, the colour of the west. Now, remember that there had been attempts on the emperor's life and he travelled in one of several identical carriages. There are four other sections to this pit, as yet unopened. His officials, if they had really been determined to model an alternative universe as real as his own, would have had another four carriages ready for him to choose from. One day, we shall know if they did their job or not.

Once again, the farmers pointed the way. By 1997, all the locals had known for years that any anomaly – a dip, a bump, a difference of earth – might indicate another pit; so when a farmer planting trees dug into a layer of red earth just outside the remains of the tomb's inner wall, the archaeologists took over. After probing this way and that, they realized they had another huge find: a pit of 100 by 130 metres, divided into thirteen sections by rammed-earth walls. Another 65,000 cubic metres, almost half the size of the Terracotta Army's pit, another 100,000 tonnes of earth to be dug out, another three months' work by the 40,000 labourers. And for what?

At first the assumption was that this was a tomb – the first to be found within the inner and outer walls – perhaps for crowds of concubines off to join their master in the next world. The following year, they had the beginning of a different answer. At a depth of about 5 metres they came upon a layer of little square slivers of stone, as if Qin craftsmen had manufactured a collection of symbolic fish-scales. As the earth was lifted clear grain by grain, however, it became clear that the scales had once been joined together. There was nothing fishy about these scales. They were suits of armour such as no one had ever seen before.

Beyond the mausoleum we turned south, towards the hills, right past an immense sewing-machine factory blaring music, then along what was once the outer wall of the mausoleum complex and was now a rough track. In a maze of paths and fields, the tomb-mound (east) and the mountains (south) were my anchors. The pomegranate orchards, as yet without buds, bore a disturbing crop of tattered plastic bags, obviously random rubbish blown from local tips.

Past the tomb-mound, we turned through low trees and a rickety iron gate, guarded by a black dog barking and straining at his chain, and parked by a line of blue corrugated iron sheds. Beneath us was our destination, the pit of the stone armour, a place for experts only. Our expert, Mr Niu – late thirties, black jacket, round face and hair as flat as a skullcap: the same Niu Xinlong who took me to the tomb of the First Emperor's grandfather – was expecting us. He led us inside, into the end shed, which was as simple as it looked from outside: an oven in high summer and a fridge in winter. A rough-cut wooden staircase led down into the pit. We followed him down, into shadows, past earth scarred with fire-scorched blotches and boards holding up crumbly bits. It's often surprising, the contrast between utter, down-to-earth basics on the surface and the treasures that lie beneath.

'This was very much like Pit Number One,' said Niu. Having worked here for almost 20 years, since his teens, he was an enthusiast eager to impress me with the significance of the finds. 'They dug this enormous pit, then put in rammed-earth walls, lined them with wood and put a roof over the top.' Easily said, but that meant another kilometre of walls, another 7,500 tonnes of earth, and another 3,000-plus beams to be added to the tomb's construction – and we hadn't got to the purpose yet.

At the bottom was a platform of planks on a beam framework, about 3 metres across and 10 metres long, except that the planks did not go all the way to the end. They were loose, so they could be moved about a few centimetres above what we had come to see: a litter of little stone flakes, which had once formed jackets of armour. Now the jackets were shredded into hundreds of bits scattered over the floor like shells on a tide-washed beach. They are incredibly delicate, having been baked by the fire that destroyed the pit and then partially dissolved by mineral-rich earth. Someone had been doing careful work down here, sticking tiny numbered labels on each flake to ensure they could be re-ordered correctly after being lifted (see second plate section).

My imagination does strange things at moments like this. Once, in Ulaanbaatar's university, I was with a Mongolian palaeontologist, Perlee, who had discovered and named a type of little herbivorous dinosaur. He opened a cupboard, took out a cardboard box, lifted out the skull of his precious find and handed it to me. It was delicate as a cobweb, fragile as porcelain, a jewel of a fossil. I thought: What if my brain seizes up and I drop it? And now: What if I slipped, lost my balance, fell in slow motion with flailing arms and crashed down like King Kong across those tiny brittle squares? I squatted for safety, as if suffering from vertigo on a cliff-top, and took a careful picture, to capture the patterns of tiny holes, the way the scales here and there still kept the shape of the armour. Some were still fixed with the copper wire, so delicate after two millennia underground that it would crumble when raised.

'How many of these suits are there, do you think?'

'We believe about two hundred. But we have not yet opened all the other chambers. We think there may be twenty-four chambers altogether.'

'But who wore them?'

'No one. They are too heavy to wear—' 22 kilos, actually '—and no use anyway. They are stone! They break if you hit them. We think they were hung on the walls, like baked meat.'

Back upstairs, two charioteer-warriors, their arms supported by wooden frames, flanked a suit of armour and a helmet on a simple wooden table. The warriors were real, the armour and the helmet copies in resin, to see how the plaques could hang together. The restored suit, though, was not the only style. 'We can identify different ranks,' Mr Niu went on. 'In one style, the pieces are very small, very delicate, like fish scales. We have found only two suits like that, so we guess they are for generals. These suits need one thousand and sixty pieces. The suits of lower officers have about six hundred, and those of ordinary soldiers just over three hundred.'

So the First Emperor's craftsmen had made over 100,000 of these fiddly little scales, and wired them into snugly fitting tops that were utterly impractical and, once in position, would never be seen again by human eyes, until the invaders came down and started the fire that burned the pit.

Unlike the mould-based techniques that produced the warriors, there could have been no short cuts here. Each flake was a work of art, smooth as oil (I felt one later, upstairs), a mere 8 millimetres thick, crafted for a particular spot in its suit, rectangular, square, trapezoid or rounded, with bevelled edges if they overlapped, so that when stitched together the garment moved as easily as the skin of an armoured dinosaur. My Mongolian palaeontologist would have loved them. Sizes varied, so that shoulder flaps descended in size as they followed the upper arm muscle downwards. On the flap below the waist, side flakes were trimmed into diagonals to skirt the hip.

There is one astonishing set of large flakes, not from the pit I was in, averaging 14 × 7 centimetres, notepad-sized plates. The first few were mysteries. Only when many more emerged did it become apparent that they were for a horse, or horses (no one knows yet how many), about 300 plates per horse. This was an amazing discovery, because the earliest horse-armour known up until then dates from about 430 years later (early third century AD, when an infamous warlord named Cao Cao unified north China, but failed to unite the rest). Here was evidence that the First Emperor owed his success to horses armoured in leather, though it has not survived the passage of time any more than the armour of the real soldiers has. Interestingly, it was not modelled in terracotta: none of the Army's horses are protected. Perhaps this was a new invention, reserved for only a few top generals.

In any event, all of this armour is totally impractical, as Mr Niu said. If you wore it, you would hardly dare move. Swing a sword-arm and you would sound like a wind-chime gone haywire – though not for long, because bits would crack and fall. In a fight, it would be as much use as porcelain. So what on earth was it for?

Perhaps knowing where it came from might help. Later, I went to see someone who knows, Yang Zhongtang at Xian's branch of the China Geological Survey. It would be nice to be able to describe him, but it had been a long day and I had a severe stomach problem. By the time I arrived, I could hardly take in the unremarkable office block or his office, let alone the personal appearance of my host. I remember him saying he had become intrigued by the armour and determined to discover the kind of stone it was made of and where it came from. 'When you feel them, they are so smooth, so perfectly made, so thin.' Other than that my mind is a blur. But I have my tape, his paper,[1] and his conclusions. He and his colleagues took 21 flakes, cut them – yes, you have to torture your subjects to make them reveal their secrets – analysed the mineral content, chose eleven

[1] Yang Zhongtang et al., 'Tracing the Source of Material of Stony Armours'.

minerals, and compared the results with rocks taken from all over the province. They discovered they were dealing with a rather special form of limestone which comes from northern Shaanxi, from hills outside a village called Manding, near Fuping, about 50 kilometres north of Xian. 'It is a source of very fine limestone,' he concluded, 'made five hundred million years ago by tiny shells deposited on the bottom of a shallow lake. This we think is the quarry that produced the limestone for the stone armour.'

One mystery solved, and another created. On my tape I hear his sigh. 'In this factory, we found some other limestone which is more thickly textured, unsuitable for the stone armour. What was it used for? We have no idea. For statues, perhaps? We have not found anything yet.'

As Ann Paludan, Britain's leading expert in Chinese sculpture, says, 'stone was a late-comer'. The Qin seemed to have very little interest in working in stone, although there are some intriguing hints to the contrary – that Li Bing quelled water spirits when he built his mighty system of water controls at Du Jiang Yan; that there had been a stone god-figure on a bridge over the Wei. There was a persistent folk tale that the First Emperor had a statue made of one of his guards, a huge man called Wengzhong, to scare the enemy. Events proved this to be effective: unification followed. From then on, statues of commanders on tombs were referred to as *wengzhong*. It is to such a statue that a sixth-century emperor referred when he wrote, 'One can find all the best qualities of scholar and soldier in a general wearing stone armour.' And we know that the following dynasty believed in the protective powers of stone, because one of them was buried in a jade suit every bit as intricate as these limestone ones. No extensive interest in stone *statuary*, perhaps – an interest that arose only a century later, at the beginning of the Han dynasty; but there was something in the air about stone and its supposed powers. Perhaps, like the discovery of horse-armour, there are surprises still to come.

But what was it all *for*? I'm sorry to say I have found only the most tentative answers. Obviously, it symbolized *something*, but that does not take us very far. If anyone would know it is the former president of the Army museum, Yuan Zhongyi, but the best he can come up with is a quote from a later emperor about the eleventh-century Song emperor Renzong, who had a stele 'carved with an inscription saying that this hard stone can suppress hundreds of ghosts'.

It may help to look at the elements that the stone armour shares with the warriors. Like them, it is life-size, and hyper-realistic, even better than the 'leather' armour worn by the warriors, because it actually moves, and because you cannot bevel the edges of leather scales to make them glide against each other more easily. And for whom was it intended? Were unarmoured terracotta warriors expected to leap through the earth and don stone armour in some spirit battle against demon foes? Or were the suits talismans, their very existence enough to scare off the enemy, like garlic waved at a vampire? Something like that, probably, because stone was indeed an important guardian – witness the seven stone stelae set up by the First Emperor on his tours.

It hardly seems likely that the First Emperor would invent out of the blue the idea that limestone would make a good talisman, send off experts to find the best source and train sub-armies of stonemasons, all so that he could have stone armour in his mausoleum. More likely, surely, that he grew up with the idea, and developed it.

On that assumption, there is good sense to be made of this. The First Emperor wanted the best for his spirit army. He had warriors, weapons, chariots, all life-size, all realistic. Let us suppose they fight their battles in the spirit world, and need replacement armour. Their own is of leather, which, after all, is not as eternal as it should be. They need something longer-lasting. Nothing lasts longer than stone. What better material for armour than something everlasting? Now the question arises of which stone to choose. You can't make granite or sandstone into fiddly little armour flakes. Jade would have been the obvious choice. Rare, beautiful and one of the hardest of stones, it had been central to art and belief for at least 3,000 years. By the time of the First Emperor it was sacred, its qualities making it a metaphor for virtue and spirituality. Senior officials loved to sport jade pendants. But there is a problem with jade: its hardness makes it extremely difficult to carve. Limestone is the perfect material.

One thing for certain: if this was some superstition held by the emperor, it would have been a lot more than that by the time he died. As Ann Paludan remarks, 'the quarrying, transporting and carving of hundreds of thousands of small panels . . . must not only have mobilized vast numbers of stonemasons and workers, but spread the idea among such people that stone could provide possible protection in the next world'. By then it must have been a universally accepted truth.

Mr Niu led the way across a living room – a couple of iron beds, an iron stove, a stovepipe through the corrugated iron roof – unlocked a door and took us into a dim room with a single window. It was lined with shelves stacked with what looked like the contents of a large garden shed. This was the store-room, where all the stuff dug from the pit was kept before anyone made sense of it: Qin drainpipes, cooking pots, bits of tiling, and bag upon grimy plastic bag of stone armour flakes.

'Look at this one,' said Niu. 'Broken before it was made part of a suit. That's the problem with limestone, it breaks very easily. It's still rough on one side, so it broke while it was being polished. And this one – broken while the maker was drilling the holes, so he threw it away. And this one, it has a slight bend, and is still unpolished.'

'So many different types. How many?'

'So many! They are like snowflakes, all different.'

Here in the store-room and down in the pit and on brilliantly lit display over in the museum was evidence of yet another highly sophisticated industry about which historical records are silent. This too would have remained unknown, its products consigned to near-oblivion by fire. Yet it was the fire that ensured discovery, baking the earth above into a red crust that gave away the pit's presence. How many other troves might await discovery?

Like a bunch of kids wandering home from school, we idled along the tomb's southern inner wall. Mr Niu was leading the way to another pit, in which a group of so-called 'officials' had been found, a pit with its own unique story. It was a warm spring afternoon, with Mount Li and its subsidiary peaks making a hazy barrier to the south and the tomb blocking the view northwards. A well-worn path ran along the remains of the wall, rising at one point to a mound of earth and stones that had once been the inner wall's South Gate. On either side were orchards of gnarled pomegranates fed by ditches that directed rainwater to their roots. Little store-houses dotted the fields. It was very pretty, except for the litter of plastic bags caught in the trees, which looked like the detritus left by a retreating flood.

'No, it is not just rubbish,' explained Tony. 'This is a very dry area. We learn from Israel. The plastic bags keep the fruit warm and preserve moisture, so it will be juicy and sweet, and also saves water for irrigation.'

Not *just* rubbish, so that I guess makes it acceptable.

The path dropped down from the wall and swung a few metres north, to another hut of corrugated iron, this time painted white. Inside it was not the rough-and-ready, hands-on workplace I expected – indeed, it was almost completely empty. All the work had been done; all the figures except for one charioteer had been taken for display. As a result, it was antiseptically neat, with boardwalks along the side of the pit, which was made up of a square and three rectangles – two in the pit, one a 45-metre access ramp – like the start of a game of giant dominoes.

Yes, this building was better than the stone-armour ones, said Niu. There was a reason. It was because of President Chirac. 'You know that Xi-la-ke is a big fan of China. When he came back in 2000, he had heard of the new excavations and wanted to dig something up. That's why they made it nicer.'

Chirac was right to be interested. These were phenomenal finds: four charioteers, a chariot (or rather its faint remnants), and eight dignified and very unmilitary men, with their hands tucked up their long sleeves. They were officials, whose job involved taking notes, as revealed by the writing implements hanging from their belts: writing tablet, brush, ink and knife for scraping the tablet clean. Other finds suggested exactly what their job was, and turned the scene into a tableau of life and death.

For at the far end of the pit were found the bones of many horses. We wandered along, staring down into the pit. It was like a fossil bed, all the bones jumbled as if they had been tipped in from a refuse truck. Mr Niu said there had been nine horses, but there may be 20 or more. Sacrificial offerings, I assumed.

'No, they were alive,' said Niu. 'How do we know? Because we found a wooden stick among the bones. It is the sort of stick used to hitch and control horses. So they must have been led down the ramp, tethered and then sealed in. They would have died days later from lack of oxygen.'

This added a new element to the First Emperor's paradoxical belief system. First, the lifelike soldiers. Next, bronze horses and real hay. Then the protective symbolism of the stone armour. Now, not only more terracotta figures, but live horses, despite the fact that they were destined to die. Apparently, this was a hang-over from the old idea that the emperor would need real flesh and blood with him in the tomb.

Perhaps it was something to do with the status of the sacrifices, suggested Mr Niu. Who can tell? Perhaps it had something to do with being closer to the tomb, those horses further away beyond the walls of the tomb-city being all terracotta, those inside the walls being sacrificed in the pit. This was becoming a drama, the purpose of which I couldn't see.

'But these are not complete skeletons. They're all mixed up.'

'It seems that after they died, there was a leak, a flood, which washed all the bones together.' An underground stream, perhaps, escaping from beneath the Wu Ling Dam.

It also softened the floor so that the line of officials and charioteers, once standing patiently along one side of the pit, fell flat on their faces in the mud.

'We also found four *yue*, a sort of axe that had developed into a ritual object.' These ceremonial axes, like the axe carried by the Beefeaters' second-in-command in the Tower of London, had been used as status symbols for 1,000 years. 'We know from official records that once the emperor had granted an official a *yue*, that man had the power over life and death. So we guess this must have been a law court.'

As Mr Niu elaborated, a picture began to emerge. 'Qin

was a centralized regime, with all important decisions being made in the capital. Then the decisions, the written tablets, would have to be taken to other cities. That's what they needed the horses for – to pull the official chariots.'

It was a vivid tableau, thanks to an odd circumstance. This is the only other pit, besides No. 3, which was not destroyed by fire. If my scenario of how the other fires started is correct – a break-in, a spark, a blaze, a long, slow, smouldering collapse – then in this pit there was no break-in. It sounds to me as if the rebel forces knew enough about the place from their local informants: It's only small, sirs, containing a few officials and some dead horses, and (crucially) no weapons. Definitely not worth the effort.

14

ON HANDLING TREASURES

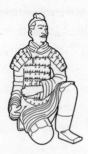

REMEMBER HAN FEI'S ADVICE TO THE RULER TO BE STILL AND observe from the place of darkness? Well, the First Emperor hides behind his Army, a spirit behind his spirits, and the closest we can get to him is to pay homage to his spirit Army's outward and visible manifestations. As we approach on our uphill climb, passing through the entry gates only when we have purified ourselves by paying, we become a little awed. Then, as we enter the Army's sanctum, Pit No. 1, we are treated like the Qin populace. We are kept back, on platforms and walkways, not allowed to get close to the emperor's guardians, who exist on a different plane from us. Getting close is a privilege only granted to near-equals of the First Emperor, and to courtiers, who now call themselves experts and officials.

I am stretching a point. This is, after all, a museum, and

museums must protect their exhibits. In early 2007 I visited an exhibition of early Chinese bronzes and terracotta statues in Rome, just before the show ended. Here, a few terracotta warriors and various Qin objects were presented as magical things, spotlit like jewels in a shop window, like film stars on opening nights, set apart not only by lighting but by screens of fine netting that protected them from being touched.

One glowing exhibit was a recent discovery. In summer 2000, farmers (of course) identified a possible pit some 3 kilometres north-east of the tomb, close to where the new motorway from Xian runs. By 2003, another treasure trove had been unearthed: 46 life-size bronze water-birds – 20 swans, 20 geese and 6 cranes, one of them on the point of seizing a fish, another swallowing a worm. They had been placed in a water-garden, on the wooden banks of a stream, for the pit floor showed the footprints both of Qin workers and of others who had broken in: nothing of value found, apparently, but much damage done. Nearby were fifteen terracotta statues dressed in caps and heavy coats, in odd positions. Seven of them kneel, one hand raised as if holding something; the others sit with legs stretched out, reaching forward as if to touch their toes, but with their fingers bent, one hand facing up, the other down. What they are doing is a mystery. The sitting figures look to me as if they are loading crossbows, pulling on the strings while pushing on the stock with their feet – getting ready to shoot geese, perhaps.

Displayed in the lobby of the Scuderie del Quirinale was one of the cranes, supported by a Perspex frame, its snaking neck and head poised to strike, its star quality emphasized by the spotlight, the protective netting, a plexiglass box – and a peculiar ban on photography, which was made impossible anyway by the netting and the plastic. It was as if the crane were a totem, its high priests nervous that we commoners and our rude cameras would suck out its power.

*

The sense of worshipful remoteness is the same in the museum, in the pits, and in the carefully dramatized presentation of selected figures – a crane included – in the Multiple Exhibition Building. Not being Clinton, it never occurred to me to ask if I could get on intimate terms with the warriors or anything else.

So what happened one afternoon was a shock. I wanted to talk with someone actually involved with hands-on restoration, mainly to appreciate the frustrations and joys of piecing the warriors together. I had acquired an army of my own – Tony the guide, Wang the driver, Jin from the museum – all of whom were keen to get behind the scenes. My informant was Ma Yu, who worked in the Conservation Department, in one of the grey concrete blocks at the back of the museum site. You know you are getting on a bit when conservation officers start to look really young. Ma, in a tracksuit and with a shock of Beatles-style black hair, seemed hardly more than a teenager. In fact, he was 36 and had been doing this job for fifteen years, having trained with Italian experts in Rome. He had worked on the stone armour and the warriors, and they no longer awed him. It crossed my mind he had become a little blasé, handling these priceless objects every day, even a little cynical about the fundamental purpose of his daily work. What was restoration, anyway? he wondered, drifting off into philosophy. We dig the warriors out of the ground, add glue and plaster to them, make them look authentic, but it's a pretence. A figure stuck together is not the original. Anyway, they are not repainted, so not properly restored. Was there a better way? I asked. He didn't know. Perhaps it was a mistake to restore them at all. Perhaps it would be better to expose them and leave them half uncovered. Or completely covered, like most of the warriors, where they are quite safe. I wasn't sure this was getting me anywhere, but he suddenly suggested I go and see what he was working on right now, which was saving a wooden pole.

He led us all into his laboratory next door, and showed the first item on view, a wooden halberd-handle, which was being saved by the injection of chemicals. Very interesting, no doubt, if you like that sort of thing. I felt my curiosity draining away.

'Are there perhaps any warriors here?'

Ma pointed over my shoulder. I turned, and—

It was like being electrocuted. There, lying on its back on a table, unprotected by anything, was the body of a kneeling crossbowman, right knee down, left knee raised. Instantly, I denied the evidence of my own senses.

'It's a copy, I suppose?'

'No,' he said. 'It's real.'

Oh. My. God, as my teenage daughter would have said. There are other kneeling archers, of course, all from Pit No. 2, which contains between 112 and 144 (no one knows how many exactly because so little has been excavated).[1] According to the accounts I had seen, seventeen were registered in the museum, and about ten others remained in the pit, half-buried. It is hard to keep track of what was uncovered and recovered when, and which statues were moved when and where, but I had assumed that all those excavated must have been restored by now. Yet here was one in the process of being cleaned, not by Ma as it happened, but by team-members who were working elsewhere.

'Can I touch it?'

He shrugged a why-not. So began an exploration as gentle

[1] Blänsdorf et al., *Final Report 2006: Testing and Optimising Conservation Technologies*.

as a seduction, not as sensuous as it might have been, given that this archer was missing his head. It was my first time with a warrior, so I felt a responsibility to remember every touch of the hard, smooth clay. While the others went a little wild with cameras over this first-ever chance to feel what they had so often seen only from afar, I went over the over-lapping leather plates of his armour, feeling the rivets and ties, still with traces of red on them, as if I were learning Braille. The right hand was missing, but the left was perfect, down to the well-trimmed fingernails. Fingers that once held the stock of a crossbow rested on a lump of light grey mud that the archer had been pressing against his waist for 2,213 years, give or take a few months. I counted the stipples across and down the non-slip soles of his boots (they seem to have been made with a little cylindrical tool, and there were about 800 in all). I ran my hand over the robe as it swung up over the remarkably solid left thigh. I spotted the maker's signature etched into one of the armour-plates so that his supervisor could hold him to account if need be: his name was Chao or Zhao (朝; same sign, two different pronunciations), and no one had any reason to accuse him of lack of quality. It was a shame the head was missing, but its absence did allow me to feel down inside the neck, where Chao or Zhao's fingers had left their mark as they squeezed the clay into its mould.

For many minutes I was absorbed, finally raising my head to re-engage with the world. I looked across the room, and in the far corner was another sight, another oh-my-god moment, another sharp intake of breath.

It was a bronze crane, its snaking neck and head in a strangely familiar pose, for it was the very same bird I had seen in Rome two months before. There, it had been made remote by netting and plexiglass. Here it was not only close up but touchable. Not only touchable, but liftable, because it was Ma's very own handiwork and now, seeing my response, he was eager to show it off. I felt like a child being offered a present, seething with excitement at what was on offer, and equally anxious that it would be snatched away.

Ma started to explain. 'When we found it, the leg was snapped off and a bit in the middle was missing. The neck was broken as well. So we had to analyse how it looked originally, so we could restore it correctly. We found pictures of cranes so that I could get the correct height and shape.' They were still there, pinned up on a notice board. 'Then I made new legs to fit the broken bits. I tried new bronze, but the old bronze was too weak to attach it. I tried glass, and in the end settled on epoxy.'

All this was down to Ma, who was emerging as a man of awe-inspiring self-assurance. He was a master craftsman, and he knew it. At one point he actually said, 'I am a genius at restoration.' If he didn't – and I only have Tony's translation to go on – he should have done, because it's true.

Originally, the crane had been fixed, standing firm on a bronze plinth, but now, with its epoxy lower limbs, it could not stand on its own; hence the need for the support. 'When I was restoring it, I gave it an iron support. The plastic one is for exhibitions.'

Then, to my surprise, without explanation, Ma reached out and started to wring the bird's neck, as if he were practising butchery. But the neck was broken already, and had been for over 2,000 years. He pulled, and it came apart in his hands, revealing two sturdy little metal studs sticking out of the stump. They looked dreadfully familiar.

'Oh, they're like the posts my dentist used to fix a new tooth,' I said.

'Yes, the tools I use are dental drills. First you drill a hole in both sections, then you insert the little support posts in the stump. It's a technique I learned when I was in Rome.'

He handed me the head and top part of the neck. Thoughts careered through my brain: Please God, let me not drop it, it's 2,000 years old, it's gorgeous, and oh-oh it's *heavy*. About 5 kilos, I guessed, which meant the whole bird weighed in at about 30 kilos. The surface, once a delicate patina of feathers, was roughened by corrosion, as if it were growing barnacles. Close up, it was a kaleidoscope of rusty greens and earthy browns and sky blues, with little flecks of white.

'Is the neck solid metal, or did you fill it in to make the join?'

'Most of it is solid, but not the head, which has to be lighter so it can be supported. We took an X-ray of the neck, which shows how much is solid. Inside there is a spine made of heavier bronze, to act as a support between the body and the head. It broke at the most vulnerable spot. I could see on the X-ray that if I could make a strong joint, it would support the head again.'

The bird was a fine example of sophisticated bronze casting, he explained as I fitted the neck together again with a satisfying little clunk. The neck and legs were made separately from the body. The neck's spine of denser bronze was made first, then the 'skin' of a different mix cast around it. The body was hollow—

'What – made in two halves like the head of a warrior?'

'No. It was made in a double mould, probably with clay round the outside and wax in the middle.'

'Oh, what we call the lost-wax method?'

'Yes, I think so, with the wax being melted out through a hole after the outer mould was removed. That's what I think. No one has done any work on this, except me. But there are many things we don't know. Look at these feathers. They overlap each other. We suppose they must have been pressed in during casting, and bent out afterwards.' He touched the wafer-thin flanges of bronze sticking out of the back of the body. 'And they are so delicate . . . oh.' The end of one of the feathers moved with his fingers. 'This one got damaged in Rome.'

What sacrilege was this? *The Romans damaged a feather?*

He sighed. 'It's what happens when these things get sent abroad. Many have been damaged. I reglued this, and this, and this.' He ran his fingers along feathers as if over a keyboard.

'You have to glue? Can't you reweld the bronze?'

'This is another theory of restoration. In the West, you reweld, but to do so adds new material, and it is no longer original. That would be re-creation, not restoration. It changes the texture. So I will repair what the Romans damaged with glue.'

'What about the colour?'

'The feathers would have been white, but we don't know if the colour was painted on or done by firing, with heat.'

'Would you ever scrape off the rust and repaint it?'

'Never!'

Of course, silly of me. That would be re-creation, not restoration. 'I'm glad to hear it,' I said. 'It's lovely as it is, the colours, the simple shape.'

'Come. I will show you the X-ray.'

He led me back across the room, with its arrays of desks and lights. By now I was wide awake to the possibility of lurking treasures, so I was drawn towards a desk with a clutter of devices on stands, a big magnifying glass, an arc-light and a vacuum-pump for removing dust. Beneath them lay a large piece of crumpled paper which had been gently pressed over a lump of something. While Ma opened a drawer across the room, I raised the paper.

Staring up at me was the head of the kneeling archer.

'Tony, Wang, Mr Jin. Look at this. I've never, I mean,

what a.' I was incoherent with astonishment. While showing his piece of wood earlier, Ma had not thought to mention the archer's body. During those intense minutes with the body, he had not mentioned the head or the crane. He was obviously as used to handling treasures as dealers in gold bars or diamonds, and could no longer imagine what it was like coming to them fresh. 'Oh my God' didn't come near.

I set about getting to know this archer with hands, and eyes, and camera. He looked stern, determined, with a slight aggressive frown that dispelled any hint of Zen-like calm. His head was turned a little to the left, with almond eyes looking even further left, the direction in which he would be firing his crossbow. A neat little moustache, divided into two, and an underlip beard made up the 'three-drop' style of facial hair. He still had the mud of centuries on his face, but through rub marks – his skin was as smooth and hard as metal – it seemed he had a blue face, which would have been quite a rarity. All other archers so far had skin-pink faces, except one whose face was green, which Catharina Blänsdorf guesses is 'make-up, maybe some kind of war-paint'. But no, this was the original blue-grey terracotta, all traces of lacquer and paint removed by mud. He had the look of an experienced warrior, about 35, I should think.

When I came to study him further, in photographs, he seemed somehow familiar. I realized why when, in one of the museum's publications, I saw him staring proudly out of a muddy background near the north-east corner of Pit No. 2, his original base. He had been ninth from the front in a corridor of 40 archers. He had not been pushed over, like his immediate neighbour, when the intruders came barging through, and had suffered less than most when the roof fell in. Though cracked across the shoulder, he had not lost his head. After 2,000 years, he was exposed with twelve others, most of them in pieces, by excavation. He had been given an official name, SH002, and an official address: T19G18, that is, Pit No. 2's nineteenth excavation hole, which is in Corridor 18. After 2,000 years underground, he had had quite an exciting life just recently, having been exposed in 1977, lost several colleagues to restorers, re-covered when the building was put up over Pit No. 2, half-uncovered again in 1999 – shortly before the portrait I had seen was taken – then finally lifted out for restoration in 2006. That was when he lost his head. Now one of seventeen registered by the museum as ex-members of the pit, he was due to be ready for display – head on and mudless, if also colourless – at the end of 2007.

'We could get a bed in here for you,' said Ma, breaking in upon my rather intense relationship with SH002. Well, liking him didn't mean sleeping with either his body or his head. It was time for lunch.

15

TO BE REVEALED

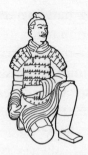

TO CALL THE ARMY 'THE EIGHTH WONDER' SUGGESTS A SENSE OF fulfilment, as if the caravan of discovery has reached a plateau. In fact, when you look closer, you might think that it is close to falling off the far side. Work on the Army and the tomb has slowed almost to a standstill. When I was there in early 2007, no one was digging anything out of the ground, or piecing together broken warriors, or probing to find more pits. In Pit No. 1, visitors freeze or sweat, roofs leak, earth walls dry and crack and moulder. Great discoveries are hidden away in cheap sheds. Like the film shown in the circular screen, with its fading colours and overused soundtrack, the site is showing signs of complacency and decay.

Do not be deceived. It is not complacency and decline you are seeing; it is more like a gathering of breath for the next big effort. The labour of the past 30 years has been a warm-up for what is to come. In 2007, work was about to begin on a new park that will take in the whole vast complex of the tomb and its surroundings – 57 square kilometres in all, 25 times the size of the tomb itself. Three thousand households were on a long-drawn-out move to the old village of Xiyang, much extended by new housing, just east of the museum, leaving as empty shells their old houses in the villages around the tomb. It has been a long, slow process, with many hiccups.

I spoke to one young building contractor who had done well: big-screen TV, minimalist glass table, water-cooler, huge reproduction view of the Yangtze gorges on the wall. 'Usually they offer a hundred thousand yuan [£6,500]. But my house was big so they offered me three hundred thousand yuan [about £20,000], but because I'm in the construction business I got the new one for a hundred and fifty thousand.' A fat profit, then? 'Not really. I lost it all gambling.' But what the hell, he could afford it.

Poorer people tried to profit in other ways. 'When they know there is compensation coming, they quickly build more houses,' as Tony said. But the change was inexorable, as always when dealing with authorities determined to have their way. In July, just as this book was going to press, the process was complete, freeing the archaeologists to begin a detailed survey of the whole area.

It is anyone's guess what will be revealed, beyond the 180 pits and several hundred graves already known. If the Han emperor Jing Di had 81 government departments to serve him in the afterlife, perhaps the First Emperor has as many, not in a tight-knit circle, but scattered randomly, their positions in death dictated by their original positions in the First Emperor's capital, Xianyang.

The problems that persuaded experts to keep the remaining warriors buried are being solved. Only a few years after restoration started, the museum noticed that decay sets in the instant a soldier is released from the earth: it's not a prison, more a protective womb. There is, for instance, a sort of mould that grows on clay when it is exposed to damp air, mixed with the breath of millions, rising ground moisture and thousands of cubic metres of wood-mulch. In fact, as two experts say, between May and September the temperature (averaging 18°C) and humidity (65 per cent) are 'ideal for the growth of micro-organisms'.[1] And it's not just one mould, as it turned out. No fewer than 48 different species of fungi have been found in and around the pits – even, at one place in Pit No. 2 in 1995, mushrooms.

Help was at hand. In 2000, the Belgian anti-fungal experts Janssen Pharmaceutica agreed to set up a laboratory with four Chinese companies to identify and eradicate 'the fungal problem'.[2] Opened in 2001, the laboratory grew into one of China's most advanced in the field of mycology. In 2006, after much experimentation with fungicides, the partners proclaimed in a press-release headline, 'Terracotta Army Museum now officially declared mould-free'. A new agreement that year extended research for another five years, and also enlarged the lab's remit to include silk, wood, bones – indeed, anything that has been or will be discovered at the site.

Mould-free clay is an essential base for the colours. Already an encyclopaedic amount of work has been done on

[1] Thomas Warscheid and Curt Rudolph, 'Microbiological examinations . . .' in Blänsdorf et al., *Qin Shihuang*, which also contains many technical articles on lacquer, colour identification and conservation, and is the source for the information in these paragraphs, together with personal communications from Catharina Blänsdorf.
[2] Xian–Janssen Pharmaceutica Ltd, a joint venture with four Chinese companies.

them and the base layer. At first, of course, with most of the colours gone, no one knew what they were or how they were applied. When the first studies in the 1980s revealed an uncoloured bottom layer, experts guessed it was a sort of glue known as gum arabic. Only in the mid-1990s, after experiments that analysed the atomic structure, did it become clear that the material was lacquer – at which point work could start to solve the problems created by 2,000 years of burial. Much of the lacquer peels off like a child's transfer, taking the colours with it, when the earth is removed. But then comes further trouble: if air humidity is below 84 per cent, which it is for most of the time, lacquer shrinks, rolls itself up and falls off.

There is a dilemma here, with no easy solution: the very attempt to preserve and restore leads to destruction. The preservation of lacquer demands high humidity; the control of moulds, the opposite. That is the prime reason for keeping all the other warriors covered up.

But all is not lost, thanks to the cooperation between the museum and Bavaria's Office for the Protection of Monuments. If a piece of clay is to be unearthed, it can be bagged in plastic, transferred to a humidified container which has built-in gloves, and operated on in isolation. The lacquer can then be fixed with chemicals which work magic by combining with the lacquer, holding it flat and allowing it to dry. One chemical, polyethylene glycol, worked pretty well, but didn't stick the lacquer on to the clay strongly enough. More experiments revealed that a substance known as HEMA (2-hydroxyethylmethacrylate), vital in the making of soft contact lenses, was almost perfect: coated with this chemical, a slab of lacquer-based colour flattens out, sticks and dries. The remaining lacquer and paint would, in brief, pretty much return to its original condition. Simplification of highly technical material inspires an odd thought: a warrior blinded by his re-emergence can have his eyes restored with the chemical equivalent of contact lenses.

More results emerge every year. Until 2006 no one knew what held the paints together, for ground-up minerals cannot be painted on without being suspended in some sort of liquid; and until that could be identified no one would understand how they were made, how to conserve them, how to restore them. Work on eleven minute flecks of paint by a team in Pisa came to a startling one-line conclusion: 'The binding medium used in the polychromes of the Terracotta Army is egg.'[3] So if someone really wants to do a good job on restoring – or perhaps I should say re-creating – a warrior as he was before the roof fell in on him, they will need whole farmyards of eggs. No doubt other details of this conclusion await examination: Chickens' eggs or ducks' eggs? Yolk or white? If both, in what proportions? Will it matter? Experiments will tell.

In years to come, the mausoleum will receive tourists on a scale dreamed of only in the upper echelons of government departments. Lintong, already transformed, will be transformed again, by places like the lavish Aegean Hot Springs Hotel, with its 26 steaming pools, in one of which live 'kissing fish' nibble at your flesh with soft lips ('we call it fish-massage', said Maggie the English-speaking manageress). And by other places, like the Flourishing International Hotel (yes, the name is in English), whose owner has a rags-to-riches story:

In the early 1990s, she was without a job, down and out. She climbed Mount Li and found a fortune-teller who told her, 'Don't worry; you will be a millionaire.'

[3] Ilaria Bonaduce and Maria Perla Colombini, 'The Binding Medium of the Terracotta Army Polychromies', in Blänsdorf, *Final Report 2006*.

'How can I be a millionaire?' she said. 'I do not even have enough money to buy food.'

'Have patience.'

So with patience and hope, she and her husband set up a little restaurant to cater to buses bringing tourists to see the Terracotta Army. One thing led to another, and now she has a big hotel – all, she says, thanks to the First Emperor.

The tourists will come, in their millions, because those corrugated iron sheds over the armour, the officials and the 'acrobats' will become museums in their own right. The unpaved cross-country tracks will be access roads and walk-ways taking in all the outlying areas, the craftsmen's homes and the tile-factory. Perhaps the walls will be restored, with paths to the side-buildings, the food-preparation room and the stables. There are no plans yet, for this is decades down the line, but one day Pit No. 1 will be as ultra-modern as the Han Yangling Museum a few kilometres away. Glass corridors and floors will bring visitors face to face with the warriors in air-conditioned comfort, complete with virtual-reality shows.

And one day, decades hence, the Army will appear complete, if not restored to its full colourful glory, and we shall know if the estimates for the numbers of warriors are correct: whether there really are 6,000 in Pit No. 1, whether the numbers 8 and 64, so significant in Daoist teachings, are reflected in the layout of the pits, whether – as hypothetical reconstructions suggest – there really are 64 soldiers behind every chariot in Pit No. 1, or 64 chariots in Pit No. 2 and 256 (which is 2^8) soldiers in the pit's southern square.

The big one, of course, is the tomb itself. The dangers and mysteries it conceals are the stuff of folklore now, but many years hence they will become the stuff of research and then, perhaps, of direct experience. Jin Kai, one of the Army's guides, echoed the general opinion: 'We believe that one day we will find the treasures inside, and they will be far more wonderful than the treasures outside.'

So they will be, if Sima Qian is anything to go by. We should discount the idea of automatic crossbows still being ready to shoot down intruders after 2,000 years, but drillings have revealed the presence of large-scale structures, even if the actual shape is a matter of dispute. The most intriguing snippet is his suggestion that the tomb contains representations of the constellations and the earth – presumably the empire – with mercury 'used to fashion [imitations of] the hundred rivers . . . and the seas, constructed in such a way that they seem to flow'. It sounds incredible, but often what is apparently folklore and legend turns out to have a basis in fact. In this case, the First Emperor's obsession with immortality suggests that Sima Qian's depiction – or something like it – should be taken seriously.

We can be sure what the First Emperor was aiming for: to make his physical remains immortal – or at least, to last as long as possible, so that his heavenly soul would then find its way skywards, while his earthly soul took command of the government departments – the officials, the entertainers, the water-garden, and of course his waiting warriors – to continue life as he knew it while alive.

How was this to be achieved? Well, we can be sure it has something to do with mercury. In 1982 researchers undertook a series of 560 drillings into the tomb and its surroundings to test for the presence (or absence) of mercury vapour. They could have saved themselves a lot of work by trusting Sima Qian. All the soundings round the edge of the tomb showed no more than background traces of mercury vapour: less than 70 parts per billion. But actually on the

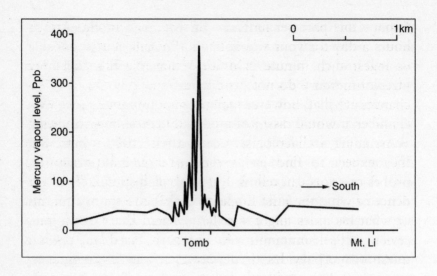

Mercury vapour in the tomb

tomb, 120 results (20 per cent), all crowded together around the middle, mainly on the south side, showed double the background reading, with a sharp peak of eight results at four times that level, one of which recorded over five times the background reading. In other words, an irregular patch of about 8,000 square metres is being created on the surface of the mound by something emitting a mild whiff of mercury, with something just to the east of the middle emitting a much stronger dose. Probably it all comes from the same source, since the vapour would diffuse sideways as well as vertically through the overburden of earth.

This sounds dangerous, if and when archaeologists gain entry. What might 350 parts per billion at the surface represent 50 metres below ground? No one knows. It could be 1,000 times stronger than the surface reading, or 10,000. But this is not as nasty as it sounds. Mercury vapour is usually measured in parts per *million*, not per billion. According to the standard guidelines, you could breathe

1ppm – one part per million – of mercury vapour for eight hours a day for your whole life without ill effects. Most of us ingest such minute quantities from our fillings. A few litres of mercury do not produce a lethal gas. Anyway, the chances are that, however high the vapour content inside the chamber, it would dissipate rapidly if the tomb were opened.

Assuming archaeologists proceed with care, what could they expect to find inside the underground palace? No probes or scans can tell us directly, but there is indirect evidence of what the First Emperor could have wished for and of what his aides might well have made. In an astonishing review of 'self-mummification', Joseph Needham poses a question and provides an intriguing answer. In the quest for incorruptibility, could one believe that anything ever really succeeded? Before 1972 the answer would have been no; if researchers had opened the tomb any time until then, they would have entered expecting to find a skeleton. But in that year an unprecedented discovery showed that the ancient Daoists knew how to achieve almost all that the First Emperor dreamed of.

In three tombs excavated in 1972–4 at Mawangdui, near Changsha, Hunan, were buried three members of a noble family: the Marquis of Dai, his wife and (probably) their son. The graves, dating from the early second century BC – only 30 years or so after the First Emperor's death – contained 3,000 objects, which on their own would have made the tombs a treasure trove. One tomb contained three maps drawn on silk, the oldest Chinese maps then known. The greatest surprise, however, was the tomb and body of the marquis's wife. Layers of white clay and charcoal protected an outer container of cypress planks, which held a nest of five lacquered coffins, one inside the other like a Russian doll, at the centre of which lay the marchioness, wrapped in 20 silk garments, and astonishingly well-preserved: her

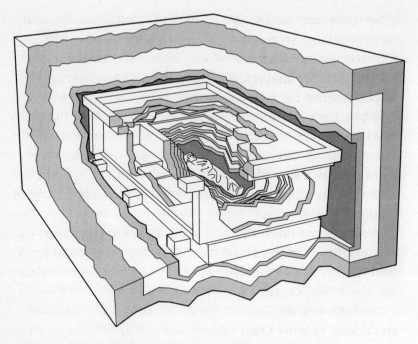

The multiple coffins of the Marchioness of Dai

joints still mobile, her organs and surrounding tissues still intact, the skin still flexible. When the skin was pressed, it returned to normal; an injection of preservatives raised swellings that subsided shortly afterwards. She could have been dead a week. She was in such good condition that an autopsy was performed, revealing that she had probably died of a heart attack. She had been preserved not by embalming, or mummification, or freezing, or tanning, but by the extreme circumstances of her burial: in an air-tight and water-tight nest of coffins, at a constant temperature of about 13°C, and partly immersed in a brownish liquid which turned out to be a bath of mercuric sulphide, otherwise known as cinnabar, the ore from which the First Emperor's workers made their red paint.

So now we know, as Needham concludes, that the incorruptibility stories of the Daoists were not all myth. It is fair to assume that the emperor's aides knew of these preservation techniques. He could therefore aim to preserve his body until his two souls were ready, one to rise to the heavens, the other to roam the earth and continue the great work of empire-building in the afterlife. We know the First Emperor used mercury and its products. We know there is something in the tomb producing mercury vapour. Does this mean that it's him in there, preserved in mercury or one of its derivatives?

Well, yes and no. If the emperor is in a nest of coffins, and the mercury is in there with him, how does mercury vapour find its way out and percolate to the surface? The readings on the tomb suggest a strong source outside the coffin. Either he's not the only one pickled in mercury or there is something in Sima Qian's account after all, mercury having been used to preserve not simply the emperor, but his empire, or at least a map of it on silk, like the one found in Mawangdui.

If other royal and aristocratic tombs are anything to go by, there will be a mass of burial goods around the coffin. Assuming that the government departments with their own accoutrements are buried in subsidiary pits, whether already found or awaiting discovery, the tomb-goods are likely to be the First Emperor's personal treasures, the best examples of craftsmanship from Qin and all the conquered regions, a *wan* of things, ten thousand of them: jewel-encrusted weapons, ritual cauldrons, bronze bells, ceramic figures and vessels, gorgeous lacquered plates, odd-shaped coins, hand-written scrolls of silk and bamboo, clothes and armour and masks and tiles and model buildings, and on and on to the limits of the imagination.

Whatever is in there will not be easily won. There was, for

instance, a roof, presumably of wood, which must have collapsed long ago. The chances are that the work of excavation will be long and difficult. Experience has shown what happens when hidden treasures are exposed: bones collapse, paint peels, clay grows mould, precious information vanishes, unless everything is well protected while still in an earthy bed.

No one yet has dreamed of building such protection. It could be done, discreetly, with an air-conditioned, air-locked wing over one of the underground palace's entrances. But surely such a site demands a vision to rival that of the First Emperor's. How about a domed roof over the whole site? It's possible, if China wished to build the world's biggest enclosed space, 500 metres across, which is what the tomb's diagonal is – 1.5 times the size of London's Millennium Dome.

What a triumph it would be to celebrate the centenary of the Revolution in 2049 with a tribute to the man who unified the nation 2,270 years before. And what an astonishing outcome for an emperor aiming to live for ever in the spirit world by burying himself and an Army in eternal darkness – to gain immortality of a different sort, in the light of day and the eyes of the world.

Appendix 1

DATES AND DYNASTIES

(Many early dates are traditional, and unreliable.)

Period	Dates
Ancient times	
Xia (legendary)	2207–1766 BC
Shang	1765–1122 BC
Zhou (western and eastern, including Warring States, 475–221)	c.1100–221 BC
China united (1)	
Qin	221–206 BC
(Interregnum)	206–202
Han (Western or Former Han)	202 BC–AD 6
(Interregnum)	6–25
Han (Eastern or Later Han)	25–220
Middle Ages	
Three Kingdoms	220–65
Western Jin (brief reunification)	265–316
Many kingdoms	317–580

Sui (reunification in 589)	581–618
Tang	618–907
Five Dynasties, Ten Kingdoms	907–60
Song (unified nation)	960–1127

In north:

Liao (Khitans)	907–1125
Jin (Jurchen)	1115–1234
Mongols	1234–

In west:

Xi Xia (Tanguts)	1032–1227

In south:

Southern Song	1127–1279

China united (2)

Yuan (Mongols, unification 1279)	1234–1368
Ming	1368–1644
Qing (Manchus)	1644–1911
Republic	1912–49
People's Republic of China	1949–

Appendix 2

QIN AND THE TERRACOTTA ARMY IN CONTEXT

Year BC

441   Qin conquers Shu.

356   Lord Shang initiates Legalist reforms in Qin and moves capital to Xianyang.

316   Qin conquers Ba.

*c.*300   Li Bing builds Du Jiang Yan irrigation system.

*c.*261   Lü Buwei befriends Prince Zichu, father of First Emperor.

259   Zheng (future First Emperor) born.

256   Qin deposes ruler of Zhou.

250   Zichu becomes king of Qin with Lü Buwei as his counsellor.

247   Zichu dies. Li Si arrives in Qin.

246   Zheng, aged 13, crowned king of Qin, with Lü Buwei as regent.

238   Lao Ai's rebellion.

237   Lü Buwei exiled. Li Si becomes Zheng's main adviser.

234   Han Fei comes to Qin. Li Si forces him to commit suicide.

230   Qin conquers Han . . .

228   . . . and Zhao.

227   Jing Ke attempts assassination of King Zheng.

225   Qin conquers Wei . . .

223   . . . Chu . . .

222   . . . Yan . . .

221   . . . and Qi. Unification of China. King Zheng becomes emperor as Qin Shi Huang Di, the First Emperor. New administration standardizes weights, measures, currency and script. Work starts on imperial tomb on Mount Li, and possibly on Terracotta Army figures.

219   First Emperor makes first imperial tour.

215   Expedition to search for elixir of immortality. General Meng Tian retakes the Ordos.

214   Meng Tian starts building Great Wall.

213   Burning of the Books, under Li Si's advice.

212   'Burial' (alive?) of *c*.460 scholars. Banishment of First Emperor's son and heir, Fusu, to northern frontier. Work begins on Epang Palace.

210   Death of First Emperor. Sand Hill Plot by Zhao Gao and Li Si: forced suicides of Meng Tian and Fusu; accession of Huhai, the Second Emperor. Burial of First Emperor. Work starts on completion of tomb. Terracotta Army pit finished and sealed.

209   Royal family purged. Peasant uprising led by Chen She starts.

208   Zhao Gao seizes power in Qin.

207   Zhao Gao forces Second Emperor to commit suicide. Ziying ascends throne. Zhao Gao is killed. Liu Bang beats Xiang Yu in bid to control central Qin. Ziying submits.

206   Ziying is killed. End of Qin dynasty. Civil war.

Xiang Yu's troops raid Terracotta Army, and start the fire that destroys it.

205 Xiang Yu defeats Liu Bang.

202 Liu Bang defeats Xiang Yu, who commits suicide. Liu Bang enthroned as Emperor Gaozu. Start of Han dynasty.

BIBLIOGRAPHY

These are only those works I consulted, and they are therefore biased towards western, mainly English-language, sources. For recent comprehensive bibliographies, see Ledderose, *Ten Thousand Things*, and Blänsdorf et al., *Qin Shihuang*, a staggering trilingual volume which, while dedicated mainly to the warriors' colours, also includes the best overall specialist surveys of the Army and the tomb-site by the Mausoleum's Archaeological Team, Yuan Zhongyi and Lothar Ledderose. Rather oddly, the Team report has the same title as Chen Simin's translation (see below), and covers the same ground, but it is in fact different.

The most detailed report in any language – particularly useful for its diagrams – is Yuan Zhongyi's 596-page volume in Chinese (2002), but it was finished too soon to include the discovery of the bronze water-birds.

The best general survey – and by far the most beautiful book on the subject – is *The Eternal Army*, edited by Roberto Ciarla, with Araldo de Luca's stunning photographs.

Archaeological Team of Han Mausoleums, *The Coloured Figurines in Yang Ling Mausoleum of Han in China*, China Shaanxi Travel and Tourism Press, Xian, 1992

Berke, Heinz, 'Chemistry in Ancient Times: The Development of Blue and Purple Pigments', *Angewandte Chemie*, vol. 41, no. 14, 2002

Blänsdorf, Catharina (ed. and main contributor), *Final Report 2006: Testing and Optimising Conservation Technologies for the Preservation of Cultural Heritage of Shaanxi Province, PR China*, vol. 1: *Technique and Materials of the Polychromy of the Sculptures from Qin Shihuang's Burial Complex*, Bayerisches Landesamt für Denkmalpflege, Munich [2006]

Blänsdorf, Catharina, Erwin Emmerling and Michael Petzet (eds), *Qin Shihuang: The Terracotta Army of the First Emperor* (in Chinese, German and English), Bayerisches Landesamt für Denkmalpflege, Munich, 2001

Bodde, Derk, *China's First Unifier: A Study of the Ch'in Dynasty as Seen in the Life of Li Ssu*, Brill, Leiden, 1938; Hong Kong University Press, Hong Kong, 1967

Bodde, Derk, *Statesman, Patriot and General in Ancient China* (trans. from Sima Qian's essays on Lü Buwei, Jing Ke and Meng Tian, with a commentary), American Oriental Society, New Haven, 1940

Bodde, Derk, 'The State and Empire of Ch'in', in Denis Twitchett and Michael Loewe, *The Cambridge History of China*, vol. 1: *The Ch'in and Han Empires, 221 BC–AD 220*, Cambridge University Press, Cambridge, 1986

Chen Simin (trans.), *The Pits of the Terracotta Warriors and Horses of the Qin Shihuang Mausoleum: The Excavation of Pit No. 1, 1974–84*, Wen Wu Chubanshe (Cultural Relics Publishing), Beijing, 1988

Ciarla, Roberto (ed.), *The Eternal Army: The Terracotta*

Soldiers of the First Emperor (photographs by Araldo de Luca), Vercelli: White Star, 2005

Erdberg, Eleanor von, 'Die Soldaten Shih Huang Ti's – Porträts?', in *Das Bildnis in der Kunst des Orients*, Franz Steiner, Stuttgart, 1990

Fowler, Don D., 'Uses of the Past: Archaeology in the Service of the State', *American Antiquity*, vol. 52, no. 2, 1987

Han Feizi, *Basic Writings* (trans. Burton Watson), Columbia University Press, New York, 2003

Hulsewé, Anthony, 'Laws as One of the Foundations of State Power in Early Imperial China', in S. R. Schram (ed.), *The Scope of State Power in China*, University of London, London, 1987

Hulsewé, Anthony, 'The Legalists and the Law of Ch'in', in W. L. Idema (ed.), *Leiden Studies in Sinology*, Brill, Leiden, 1981

Hulsewé, Anthony, *Remnants of Qin Law: An Annotated Translation* . . . , Brill, Leiden, 1985

Hung Shih-Ti [Hong Shidi] *see* Li Yuning

Kajick, Kevin, 'Fire in the Hole', *Smithsonian Magazine*, May 2005

Kern, Martin, *The Stele Inscriptions of Ch'in Shih-huang: Text and Ritual in Early Chinese Representation*, American Oriental Society, New Haven, 2000

Komlos, John, 'The Size of the Chinese Terracotta Warriors', *Antiquity*, vol. 77, June 2003

Lally, Joe, 'Prehistoric Arson Cases', *Fire and Arson Investigator*, Oct. 2006

Ledderose, Lothar, *Ten Thousand Things: Module and Mass Production in Chinese Art*, Princeton University, Princeton, 2000

Ledderose, Lothar, and Adele Schlombs (eds), *Jenseits der Grossen Mauer: Der Erste Kaiser von China und Seine*

Terrakotta-Armee, Bertelsmann, Munich, 1990

Lewis, Mark Edward, *Sanctioned Violence in Early China*, State University of New York Press, Albany, 1990

Lewis, Mark, *Writing and Authority in Early China*, New York State University Press, Albany, 1999

Liu, Z., A. Mehta, N. Tamura, D. Pickard, B. Rong, T. Zhou and P. Pianetta, 'Influence of Taoism on the Invention of the Purple Pigment Used on the Qin Terracotta Warriors', *Journal of Archaeological Science*, publ. online March 2007, available via www.sciencedirect.com

Li Yuning, *The First Emperor of China*, International Arts and Sciences Press, White Plains, NY, 1975 (includes Hung Shih-Ti [Hong Shidi], *Ch'in Shih-Huang*, People's Press, Shanghai, 1972)

Loewe, Michael, *Records of Han Administration*, Cambridge University Press, Cambridge, 1967

Loewe, Michael, and Edward L. Shaughnessy (eds), *The Cambridge History of Ancient China: From the Origins of Civilization to 221 BC*, Cambridge University Press, Cambridge, 1999

Lord Shang, *see* Sun Tzu

Lü Buwei, *The Annals of Lü Buwei*, Stanford University Press, Stanford, 2000

Needham, Joseph, *Science and Civilisation in China*, vol. 5, pt 2: *Chemistry and Chemical Technology* (esp. the last section, 'Terminal Incorruptibility'), Cambridge University Press, Cambridge, 1974

Olsen, John, 'The Practice of Archaeology in China Today', *Antiquity*, vol. 61, 1987

Paludan, Ann, *Chinese Sculpture: A Great Tradition*, Serinidia, Chicago, 2006

Rawson, Jessica, 'The Eternal Palaces of the Western Han:

A New View of the Universe', *Artibus Asiae*, vol. 59, nos. 1–2, 1999

Rawson, Jessica (ed.), *Mysteries of Ancient China: New Discoveries from the Earliest Dynasties*, British Museum Press, London, 1996

Rawson, Jessica, 'The Power of Images: The Model Universe of the First Emperor and its Legacy', *Historical Research*, vol. 75, no. 188, May 2002

Selby, Stephen, *Archery Traditions of China*, Hong Kong Museum of Coastal Defence, Hong Kong, 2003

Selby, Stephen, *Chinese Archery*, Hong Kong University Press, Hong Kong, 2000

Shang Yang, *see* Sun Tzu

Sima Qian, *Records of the Grand Historian: Qin Dynasty* (trans. Burton Watson), Columbia University Press, New York and Hong Kong, 1993

Sima Qian, 'Treatise on the Feng and Shan Sacrifices' (trans. Burton Watson), in *Records of the Grand Historian: Han Dynasty*, vol. 2: *The Age of Emperor Wu*, Columbia University Press, Hong Kong and New York, 1993

Sun Tzu, *The Art of War*, and Shang Yang, *The Book of Lord Shang*, Wordsworth, Ware (Herts), 1998

Twitchett, Denis, and Michael Loewe, *The Cambridge History of China*, vol. 1: *The Ch'in and Han Empires, 221 BC–AD 220*, Cambridge University Press, Cambridge, 1986

Wang Yu-ch'ing, 'Excavation of the Ch'in Dynasty Pit Containing Pottery Figures of Warriors and Horses at Lin-t'ung, Shensi Province', *Wen Wu* [Cultural Relics], 1978, no. 5; trans. Albert Dien in *Chinese Studies in Archaeology*, vol. 1, no. 1, Summer 1979 (in fact this is a first report on Pit No. 2)

Yang Zhongtang et al., 'Tracing the Source of Material of

Stony Armours Discovered Near the Qin Shihuang
Tomb', in *Essays Collected for the 15th Anniversary of
the Founding of the Shaanxi Provincial Cultural Relics
and Archaeological Projects Association*, No. 5
(undated)

Yuan Zhongyi (Yuan Chung-i), 'First Report on the
Exploratory Excavations of the Ch'in Pit of Pottery
Figures at Lin-t'ung Hsien', first publ. in *Wen Wu*
[Cultural Relics], 1975, no. 11; trans. Albert Dien in
Chinese Sociology and Anthropology, vol. 10, no. 2,
Winter 1977–8

Yuan Zhongyi, 'Hairstyles, Armour and Clothing of the
Terracotta Army', in Blänsdorf, Catharina, Erwin
Emmerling and Michael Petzet (eds), *Qin Shihuang: The
Terracotta Army of the First Emperor* (in Chinese,
German and English), Bayerisches Landesamt für
Denkmalpflege, Munich, 2001

Yuan Zhongyi, *Qin Shihuang Ling Kao Gu Fa Xian Yu
Yan Jiu / 秦始皇陵考古发现与研究* (*Qin Shihuang's
Mausoleum: Archaeological Discoveries and Research*),
Shaanxi People's Press, Xian, 2002

Yue Nan, *Xi Bu Mai Fu / 西部埋伏* (*Hidden Underground in
the West*), Zhejiang People's Publishing, 2002

Zhang Lin, *The Qin Dynasty Terra-Cotta Army of
Dreams*, Xian Press, Xian, 2005

INDEX